Pirates of the South China Coast
1790-1810

PIRATES

OF THE SOUTH CHINA COAST
1790-1810

Dian H. Murray

Stanford University Press
Stanford, California

Stanford University Press
Stanford, California
© 1987 by the Board of Trustees of the
Leland Stanford Junior University
Printed in the United States of America

Published with the assistance of the
Andrew W. Mellon Foundation

CIP data appear at the end of the book

TO MY SISTER JANE AND
FRIENDS AT LINFIELD COLLEGE

Acknowledgments

It is a pleasure to acknowledge those who have contributed to this study. As the chairman of my doctoral committee, Sherman Cochran went far beyond the call of duty in giving of his time, energy, and ideas so that the pirates might live. The other members of my committee, Knight Biggerstaff, Charles Peterson, and David Wyatt, also deserve thanks for their encouragement and support at each step of what has turned out to be a very long way.

Others who have labored over this manuscript, contributing to it their insights and inspiration, are Suzanne Barnett, Beatrice Bartlett, Richard Bodman, Ch'in Pao-ch'i, Paul Cohen, James Coyle, Chu Te-yuan, Merle Goldman, Gary Hamburg, Vince Jacobs, Philip Kuhn, Father Manuel Teixeira, and Wei Ch'ing-yüan. My debt of gratitude to them is immeasurable.

I am also grateful to the directors and staffs of the following institutions: National Palace Museum (Taipei), First Historical Archives (Peking), Academia Sinica (Nankang), Ch'ing History Institute at the People's University (Peking), India Office Library (London), British Museum and Library (London), Public Records Office (London), London School of Oriental and African Studies, Harvard-Yenching Library (Cambridge, Mass.), Fairbank Center for East Asian Research (also Cambridge), and the Olin Library, Cornell University (Ithaca, N.Y.).

Funding for this study was provided by the Fulbright-Hays Doctoral Dissertation Research Abroad Program and the Social Science Research Council at the doctoral level and by the Andrew Mellon Faculty Fellowship in the Humanities Program of Harvard University, the Committee for Scholarly Communication with the People's Republic of China, and the Institute for Liberal Studies at the University of Notre Dame at the postdoctoral level. I am indebted to Charles Walker,

Kenneth Williams, and the late John Housley of Linfield College and to Rev. Thomas E. Blantz, C.S.C., of the University of Notre Dame for the flexible teaching schedules that allowed me to take advantage of these many opportunities.

Technical assistance has come from many quarters. The efforts of Susan Charland, Huynh Tai Ngoc Anh (Anh Coyle), Susie Curtis, Ge Min, Nila Gerhold, Nancy Kegler, Cheryl Reed, Andy and Nancy Sy, Wang Miao, and David Wyatt who, in providing everything from typing and word-processing consultation to map-making and calligraphy, have eased my burden considerably. Without their endeavors, I would still be hard at work and probably lost at sea.

Finally, I want to thank the subjects of this book, the 70,000 pirates who, in letting me peer into their world, enlivened my own for more than a decade. I will miss them and, in return, pray that I have done justice to their story.

D.H.M.

Contents

Pirates of the South China Coast
1790-1810

Introduction

In 1760 piracy along the South China coast was limited to a few "struggling banditti" who sheltered in the offshore islands and carried out nocturnal depredations in shallow waters.[1] The arrival of an imperial junk usually sufficed to round them up or drive them off. Their ships were small, their gangs tiny, and their capacity for inflicting damage limited. Among Westerners, China's maritime trade had a reputation for peacefulness that caused some shipowners to order their cannon left ashore as "useless lumber."[2] The Chinese themselves regarded piracy as little more than a coastal nuisance or irritation. As late as 1793 the Ch'ien-lung Emperor observed: "In Kwangtung there are no urgent affairs. On several occasions Fu-k'ang-an has searched out and arrested the pirates so that they have gradually withdrawn and not a trace of them remains."[3]

Imperial optimism notwithstanding, by 1793 China's days of controllable piracy were nearly over; three years later the government would find itself at the mercy of large, well-organized fleets that dominated the coasts of Kwangtung, Chekiang, and Fukien provinces for more than a decade. Between 1795 and 1810 government officials were forced to deal with their most serious maritime threat since the suppression of Cheng Ch'eng-kung (Koxinga) and the conquest of Taiwan more than a century before.[4]

Nowhere was the confrontation more intense than in Kwangtung province, where by 1805 a confederation of between 50,000 and 70,000 pirates was coming into control of the coasting trade and fishing industry. Scarcely a junk dared leave port without first paying the pirates protection money against attack. From the coast, the pirates then moved into the waterways of the interior, where they extorted considerable sums in the form of semiannual payments from the vil-

2   *Introduction*

lages and towns, burning with impunity those that refused to pay. On
repeated occasions they severed communications between Canton and
Macao, causing domestic prices to skyrocket and the bottom to drop
out of the foreign market. Even Europeans were forced to negotiate
with them for their safety, and in 1809 a confident pirate leader
boasted to the Portuguese that in return for the loan of three or four
men-of-war, he would give them two or three provinces after he had
toppled the Ch'ing dynasty and conquered the mainland.[5] In bringing
Kwangtung to its knees, the pirates succeeded in transforming their
enterprise from a petty nuisance into a national and even international
threat.

When I began this project, it was my intention to deal with the practice of piracy throughout the late eighteenth and early nineteenth
centuries, to trace its escalation as a single phenomenon occurring
along the China coast from the Yangtze River to Vietnam. But it soon
became apparent that the "pirates" themselves were hardly a single
group. In fact, the Min-speakers of Chekiang, Fukien, and eastern
Kwangtung had little in common with the Cantonese speakers of
western and central Kwangtung, and their few attempts at cooperation ended in failure. Moreover, the dynamics and activities of the two
groups pulled them in different directions. Pirates from Chekiang
and Fukien operated in the waters around Taiwan and the Ryukyu
Islands; those from Kwangtung were more interested in Canton,
Macao, and Vietnam. These findings have convinced me that it is no
longer possible to think of maritime China as an undifferentiated watery realm stretching from the Yangtze River to Hainan Island.[6] Just
as there were tenuously connected economic, administrative, and cultural regions defining people's worlds on land, so, too, there were separate or at most slightly overlapping "water worlds" at sea.[7]

This book is set in what I call the Cantonese water world, a region
roughly coterminous with the coastal and seaward portions of central
and western Kwangtung that extended west from the Han River basin
of eastern Kwangtung across the international border a slight distance into Vietnam. Piracy was by no means new to this region, which
had been subjected to attacks for centuries, but in the period of this
study, 1790 to 1810, it escalated there dramatically. Why just then?
Was there a specific natural disaster or ecological phenomenon to
which its growth can be attributed?

Scholars of China are now beginning to ascribe outbreaks of popular movements and rebellion to ecological causes and to view them as
"survival strategies" in environments where resources were in short
and unpredictable supply. Whether a particular strategy was "preda-

tory" or "protective," it was conceived of as a sustained form of collective action that could, and often did, end in rebellion when ecological conditions worsened.[8]

Does the ecological model, which was devised to account for occurrences of rebellion on the continent, apply to maritime communities as well? Did piracy within the water world represent an ongoing survival strategy on the part of its practicers? Was there an ecological crisis in the form of famine, overpopulation, or alteration in the economic activities of coastal inhabitants that accounts for the surge in piracy during the late eighteenth and early nineteenth centuries?

The testing of this hypothesis involves an inquiry into local history of a new sort. It is regional history, to be sure, but in a region not studied as such before. For, as I have argued above, the Cantonese water world was a distinct part of maritime China, endowed with rhythms, dynamics, and lifestyles peculiarly its own. In turning our attention to the sea, this book takes a first step in endeavoring to discover and define this maritime realm.

Our quest cannot end in local history, however, for like pirates elsewhere in the world, those in China did not operate in a vacuum. Their actions had ramifications that drew them ultimately into national and international spheres where, like it or not, they could not escape contact with outsiders.

Social scientists have long been aware that the impact of outside forces was sometimes the crucial element in transforming collective violence from one level of intensity to another. The need to cooperate in the face of a common enemy, for example, often had the effect of forcing popular protesters to organize and pushing them to levels of activity to which they might otherwise not have resorted.[9]

But outside forces sometimes served to support, rather than suppress, popular movements. This was especially true of piracy. In the many parts of the world where it appeared, patronage by an outside force was often the key element in its rise. In repeated instances pirates who transformed themselves from "chance robbers" into large-scale operators were able to do so only through the backing of the state or significant portions of its elite.

Piracy reached its apogee in the Mediterranean during the sixteenth and seventeenth centuries, for example, when, under the guise of privateering, two equally backed groups, the Barbary Corsairs and the Knights of the Order of St. John acted as warriors in an extension of the Holy War between Catholic Spain and Muslim Turkey. It was, however, the otherwise impossible exchange of goods between Muslims and Christians that garnered for these corsairs backing in the highest political realms. So integral to the Mediterranean economy as a whole was their endeavor that the Sultan in Constantinople acquiesced in it by first appointing the Barbary ringleader Kheyr-ed-din the governor-general of Algiers (in 1518), and later making him high admiral of all the Ottoman fleets (in 1535).[10]

Wide-scale backing by the coastal elite similarly served to transform British channel rovers of the Elizabethan era. Throughout the sixteenth century British gentry along the southern coast turned quick profits by marketing the prizes of local marauders. Local conditions accorded well with royal aspirations to the extent that war with Spain was the prevailing international concern of Tudor sovereigns. But waging this war was a real problem because the monarchy was still dependent on voluntary forces for its military endeavors. By sanctioning the pirates' transformation into privateers, Elizabeth gained an inexpensive navy at a time when the national government was unable to support its own.[11]

Many other examples might be cited—Henry Morgan, whose disruption of Spanish shipping was encouraged by colonial governors in Tortuga and Jamaica; William Kidd, whose violation of the British Navigation Acts of 1696 was endorsed by the governor of Massachusetts—but we need not linger over them here.[12] The point is that in different places and in different periods official patronage was instrumental in transforming piracy from a petty operation to a large-scale enterprise.

Was this true of the dramatic upsurge of piracy in China? Did Chinese pirates, like many of their counterparts elsewhere, perform some useful economic, political, or social function that made East Asian governments willing to overlook their excesses?

There is still another possibility. Perhaps in the case of China this phenomenon cannot be attributed either to changing ecological circumstances or to outside patronage, but owed its rise to internal developments. Might the impetus for growth not be traced directly to the pirates themselves, to some element such as the emergence of skilled leaders, who through inspiring appeals and the effective mobilization of their followers successfully increased their scale of activity? Given the almost insurmountable difficulties in staging collective violence of any kind, was there something special about piracy that impelled leader and follower alike to lay their lives on the line?

This brings us to the very difficult question of human motivation. Always elusive even under ideal circumstances, the subject becomes the more so when those involved are from a segment of society that leaves behind few records of its own. Yet unless one understands what the aims of the pirates were, it is impossible to determine whether their endeavor succeeded or failed. Of even more relevance here is the relationship between piracy as one form of collective violence and rebellion as another. Were pirates rebels?

The question is a timely one, given the continuing interest on the part of Sinologists in peasant rebellion. While it is clear that the pirates who are the subjects of this study engaged in violence against the Ch'ing and were perceived by Chinese officials as enemies of the state, it is not at all clear that the term rebellion can be usefully applied to their activities. Was it an ideological confrontation with the "old order" or something else that induced the pirates to launch their enterprise?

With several approaches at hand to account for the escalation of piracy in late-eighteenth-century China, it is now time to test them against the realities of the South China Sea to discover, if we can, which best explains this remarkable development.

1

The Water World

The majority of the pirates encountered in this study started out as fishermen or as sailors on fishing craft. Most were Cantonese-speaking "water people," pejoratively referred to by the landsmen of Kwangtung as "Tanka" or "egg families."[1] Most were single men in the prime of life who hailed from the maritime regions of central and western Kwangtung. Most had fished regularly in Vietnam and became pirates in the Sino-Vietnamese border town of Chiang-p'ing (Vietnamese: Giang Binh), which by the late eighteenth century had emerged as the principal pirate headquarters of the entire South China coast.

My examination of the sources turned up 93 men of known occupation who voluntarily took up piracy between 1794 and 1803. More than half were either fishermen (44) or sailors (13; see Appendix A, Tables A.1 and A.2). A significant proportion had Vietnamese and, more specifically, Chiang-p'ing connections. Almost three-quarters (32) had habitually fished in Vietnam, and more than half (23) actually transacted business in Chiang-p'ing. The Vietnamese connection was just as strong in the group of 62 pirate volunteers of unknown occupational background. All but one had Vietnamese connections, and 59 had ties with Chiang-p'ing (Table A.3). The captives who voluntarily decided to become pirates were of similar background. Half of the 52 of known occupation were fishermen, and 21 of these 26 fishermen had fished in Vietnam. Only 6, however, had a Chiang-p'ing connection (Table A.5).

What was it that impelled these men to forsake their "legitimacy" and their homeland for a life of crime at Chiang-p'ing? What were the conditions that made that life workable?

Geographical and Economic Factors

No explanation of piracy along the Sino-Vietnamese coast can overlook the fact of an amenable geographical setting. From the perspective of a pirate, a coastline crossed by countless waterways in which to
hide, and protection afforded by a chain of islands on its periphery,
was geography made to order. This coastal region, moreover, was as
fully set off economically from continental China as it was geographi-
cally by the mountains that separated its plain from the interior.
Linked internally by its own dynamics, the Cantonese water world was
a region of seafarers who moved to the rhythms of tide and monsoon.

Westward from the Pearl River Delta, the maritime universe of the
fishermen-pirates extended nearly 2,000 miles along a narrow, broken
coast that jutted south 70 miles into the sea to form the Lei-chou Peninsula. Ten miles beyond lay the strategic island of Hainan. Sand-
wiched between mountains and water, the peninsula was sculpted by
countless streams cutting their way seaward from the barren heights
of terraced hills. Western Kwangtung, though devoid of a major river
system, was crossed by numerous short streams that ran directly into
the sea. Farther east, the Pearl River Delta comprised a 50-by-70-mile
triangular expanse bounded on the west by the Portuguese settlement
of Macao and on the east by what was, until 1842, the barren island of
Hong Kong. At its apex in the north was Canton, the cultural and
commercial hub of the region. The delta was created by the channels
through which the West, North, and East rivers reached the sea. It
supported 1,500 miles of naturally flowing rivers and streams to which
man, over the centuries, had added an additional 3,000 miles of inland waterways and canals.[2] This was the heartland of central Kwangtung, the largest extent of level ground in the province, and the site of
dense habitation. In the nineteenth century more than a third of the
province's population was squeezed into this small area.

Within this realm water-cut plains gave the illusion of inland seas
dotted with islands, and along the coast rivers dissecting the land were
often indistinguishable from seas surrounding islands.[3] The agrarian
activities of the coastal strip took place on tiny deltaic plains, whose
settlements tended to be situated along bodies of water, which like a
complex network of arteries and veins linked hamlet, village, and
town. In this region where roads were few, the junks, with their masts
and sails peeping out over the rice fields, seemed to be buoyed aloft
on seas of green.[4]

Offshore the open expanse of the South China Sea stretched from

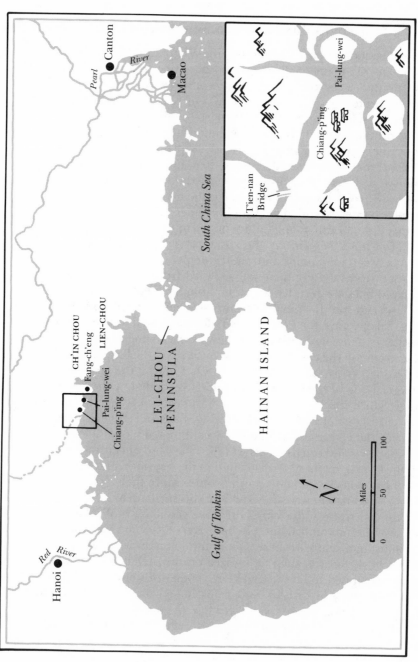

Map 1. The South China water world. The inset is taken from a map enclosed in the *Ch'in Chou chih*, comp. Tu I Kuan, 1834. Even without a scale that map is valuable as one of a very few that show where Chiang-p'ing and Pai-lung-wei ... ... lost in relation to each other as perceived by Chinese cartographers of the 19th

the border of Kwangtung and Fukien provinces around Hainan Island and the Lei-chou Peninsula to the Gulf of Tonkin on the eastern coast of Vietnam. This saltwater realm of shallow seas and inshore islands was referred to in Chinese sources as the "inner sea" (*nei-hai*) or "inner ocean" (*nei-yang*). Amid a landscape of canal and sea, the coastline twisted and turned, recessing often to form sheltered bays and hidden coves, and giving way occasionally to wide estuaries where fresh and salt water mixed. Along a littoral of mountains and water, islands and peninsulas, Kwangtung flowed imperceptibly into Vietnam.[5]

The most prominent geographical feature of the "inner seas" was the chain of islands that dotted the coast in all directions. Kwangtung alone was flanked by more than 700 of them. Some, such as the Ladrones, were important in navigation; others served as convenient anchorages for fishermen. But the majority were untilled pinpricks of territory surrounded by the sea.

Once the shallows deepened, the inshore islands gave way to offshore islands farther from the land, and the South China Sea (Nanhai) became the Southern Ocean (Nan-yang). In practical terms, the Chinese conceived of the Nan-yang as a "circle encompassing the mainland Southeast Asian countries bordering the South China Sea and the Gulf of Siam; i.e., Vietnam, Cambodia, . . . Siam, southern Burma, the Malay peninsula, Sumatra, western Java, and the northeast coast of Borneo."[6] This region of deep seas, offshore islands, and coral reefs constituted the "outer sea" (*wai-hai*) or "outer ocean" (*wai-yang*). The shallower waters of the Nan-yang were formed by the continental shelf that extended 150 miles offshore to include both Hainan Island and the Gulf of Tonkin. In these waters, which descended to depths of 200 meters, could be found the bulk of the region's maritime resources. Beyond the continental shelf the waters plunged to oceanic depths (4,000 meters) in the China Sea Basin.[7]

To an already superb geography, the economics of the water world added another prerequisite for piracy: waterways abounding with traffic on which to prey. Over the sea lanes a continuous progression of goods and people moved in and out of the port cities. The wealth of the region was legendary. Commerce was its lifeblood, and fortunes could be made by fitting out ships, purchasing cargoes, or servicing those engaged in such pursuits.

Part of the key to the region's economic success was the relative ease of maritime transportation, which put even the smallest ports within reach. Maritime transportation, even though premodern and unmechanized, provided a degree of access to markets that simply did not exist in many regions of the interior, for a single junk could often call at settlements ranging in size from coastal villages to regional cities. Nowhere was this more the case than among domestic coastal traders that made their way up and down the coast, stopping at every port, selling a few goods here and buying a few there, until complete cargoes had been exchanged several times.[8]

In the holds of two-masted "seagoing junks" (*hai-ch'uan*), bulky cargoes of staple items skimmed over the water. Lumber, charcoal, roofing tiles, jars, cooking oil, rice, soybeans, chickens, pigs, and ducks were among the goods most commonly transported. Shipments of liquor also made their way along the coast, as did local consignments of cotton and silk. People, too, frequently made their way up and down the coast on the private passenger junks (*k'e-ch'uan*) that were managed by women.[9]

More professional, far-ranging, and highly adapted to the water were the "junk traders" who conducted China's commerce with Japan, the Philippines, and the rest of Southeast Asia. The junk trade was at its height during the late eighteenth and early nineteenth centuries, when Chinese merchants monopolized the exchange of "Straits' produce" from Southeast Asia—rattan, seaweed, and pepper—and thwarted European attempts to supply these goods to China.[10] The cargoes of these oceangoing junks (*yang-ch'uan*) were a rich source of pirate prey, for these trading junks kept China supplied with raw materials and unprocessed foodstuffs such as rice, wood, salt, coconut oil, animal hides, brown sugar, copper, lead, indigo, cotton, sticklac, horns, and ivory, and carried out its exports of fans, textiles, preserves, and crockery.[11]

Further contributing to the commercial pandemonium of the water world were the activities of outsiders who, long before the sixteenth century, had found accommodation within its economic sphere. First to come were the Malay, Persian, and Arab traders. They were followed by the Japanese and later by Western Europeans, led in their first wave by the Portuguese, and in their second by the British.[12] The Portuguese, arriving in the sixteenth century, came to China on the dual mission of "converting the heathens" and trading, but the British, in the eighteenth century, were interested primarily in trade. Unlike the Portuguese, who had managed to procure a foothold on the East Asian mainland at Macao, the British were without a base of their own until 1842, and their merchantmen were thus forced to anchor during the offseason months in Macao at the pleasure of the Portuguese. At the end of the eighteenth century, the Western presence in China was further buttressed by periodic appearances of Swedish, Dutch, French, German, and American vessels.

For many of these traders the final destination was Canton, a regional metropolis and highly specialized center replete with warehouses, anchorages, and shipbuilding facilities. Besides serving as a port of call for the seagoing junks that carried the domestic trade of the South China coast and the oceangoing junks laden with produce from Southeast Asia, Canton played host to the small, private country ships licensed by the East India Company to conduct a triangular trade between India, the Indonesian archipelago, and China. The large square-riggers and Indiamen berthed offshore at Whampoa, 12 miles to the south. By 1697 Canton had become a flourishing center whose vessels crossed the "eastern" and "western" oceans to Japan, Manila, Indochina, Achin, Malacca, Siam, and Batavia, and plied the coast from Macao to Kiangnan.[13] In 1703 Captain Alexander Hamilton described the city as a frenetic port where on any given day no fewer than 5,000 junks could be seen lying at anchor awaiting service.[14]

In 1757 the linkage between the West and Canton was forged even more explicitly when the city was made the sole port through which European trade with China was allowed. Thereafter, its markets were deluged by such a range of merchandise that even Western handbooks could only hint at all the items for sale. Within the city itself, craft of every description clogged the canals and waterways.[15]

Another major focus of Chinese commerce in the Nan-yang was the island of Hainan. On its north shore Ch'iung-chou, the major trading center, guarded the mouth of the Limou River, and in the south Yai-chou flourished as the main port. Much of Hainan's commerce consisted of domestic trade with the continent. The island furnished a variety of tropical products—like betel nut, coconut, and sponges—not found on the coast, while the mainland furnished the rice that was the staple of the islanders' diet. But it was the more luxurious cargoes of salt, knives, cattle, cotton, and aromatic woods flowing continuously between the mainland and Hainan that attracted the pirates.[16]

Hainan was also an attractive target because of its heavy trade with Macao, Cochinchina, and especially Siam. Junks from Hainan were the smallest but most numerous of all Chinese craft engaged in this trade. By taking advantage of the island's westward location, between 20 and 45 junks would leave annually from Hainan and reach Bangkok in January, well ahead of all other Chinese craft, which did not make their appearance until late February or March. Thus by the eighteenth century Hainan had become a point of transshipment for the Sino-Siamese junk trade and was widely known as a place where the Siamese could obtain metal tools, raw silks, and porcelains from China and where the Chinese could obtain products from Southeast

Asia.[17] Moreover, the island drew still other international traffic to its shores simply because the shipping lanes of the world converged on it. Ocean junks en route from Southeast Asia were forced to pass through either the narrow, dangerous channel to the north or the deeper more amenable headlands of the Hainan–Paracel corridor to the south.[18]

The favorite route of Chinese mariners to the Nan-yang ran along the western and southwestern margins of the China Sea, through the Hainan–Paracel gateway to Vietnam, then back along the coast to Poulo Condore (K'un-lun Island), whence one proceeded directly across the sea to Malaysia, Siam, and Sumatra.[19] Whenever possible, Chinese mariners preferred to keep within the Hainan–Paracel corridor (and hence above the continental shelf) and avoid the dangerous waters beyond. Even with favorable winds and correct compass settings, this corridor took six or seven days to cross.[20] A second route, known as Palawan's Passage, ran along the eastern waters of the Nan-yang near the Philippines, before bending north and west across the open water to Canton.

Ships plying these routes often used Hainan for refuge and provisioning before setting out for the coastal strip. Sometimes they even had to remain there awaiting the onset of favorable winds because the passage to Canton was impossible without them.[21] Most desired were the southerlies and westerlies that blew between September and January.

The Boat People

Although probably no other region of China possessed more wealth-generating capacity than the water world, not all who resided there shared equally in its resources. The intense commercialization of such heavily populated areas as the Pearl River Delta led, over time, to the rise of landlordism as increasing numbers of unsuccessful owner-farmers were forced into tenancy. The result was a highly stratified society in which, during the late eighteenth century, the rich operated side by side with growing numbers of people struggling desperately to make ends meet. As landlords prospered and society polarized, the atmosphere of the water world became increasingly volatile. More and more of the "have-nots" resorted to preying off the rich, and bandit gangs proliferated.[22]

Ethnic rivalry contributed its share to this violence-prone atmosphere. As a region at the edge of an empire, the water world had absorbed periodic infusions of immigrants since prehistoric times, and by the eighteenth century these groups resided side by side in constant tension. Their settlement patterns were every bit as fragmented and complex as the geography itself.

Since the third century B.C., when Chinese armies and settlers from the north first came to the region and displaced the indigenous Yüeh peoples, slow, steady migrations of Chinese had made their way to the water world. Over the centuries, however, distinctions had endured based on who had come when. Those who traced their arrival from the T'ang and Sung dynasties referred to themselves as natives, or "Punti" (the Cantonese pronunciation of Pen-ti). They were the rice growers, who claimed the flattest, most fertile fields of the delta and coast. Among these groups, traditions of family and clan were strong. Within Kwangtung they resided in close-knit familial units; entire villages were often inhabited by a single family that traced its descent from a common ancestor. Proud of their origins and proud of their region, the Punti regarded themselves as "pure" Chinese whose dialect (Cantonese) most closely resembled the original language of China.[23] Besides dominating the countryside, the Punti also settled in the cities and towns, where they controlled much of the region's commerce.

As "natives," the Punti or Cantonese distinguished themselves most markedly from their fiercest rivals, the Hakka (Mandarin: K'e-chia), or "guest families," who migrated from Fukien and Kiangsi in the thirteenth century. The Hakka settled in the hilly regions of the delta and in the mountainous territory north of Canton. As occupants of the less fertile, less desirable farmland, they tended to be truck farmers more than rice growers, and to specialize in the production of groundnuts, sweet potatoes, and green vegetables. By 1669, pressed continually for territory and space, the Hakka had begun moving in large numbers from the mainland to the islands, where they opened up virgin territory and turned unused salt flats into paddy.[24]

Further complicating the ethnolinguistic map of the water world were the occasional settlements of the Hoklo, who migrated into Kwangtung from southern Fukien. Since the heaviest concentration of these Fukienese-speakers was in the Han River Delta of eastern Kwangtung, they do not figure prominently in this study. Nevertheless, throughout the centuries small groups of Hoklo from eastern Kwangtung pushed their way west to settle on the Lei-chou Peninsula and Hainan Island. Others established themselves on the smaller inshore islands, where they were active in salt smuggling until the end of the Ming dynasty (1368–1644).[25]

In competing with one another for territory and resources, the Punti, Hakka, and Hoklo added to the tensions already manifest

within the water world's society. These tensions were further exacer-
bated by a population grown so dense that by the late eighteenth century it was beyond the carrying capacity of even this fertile and inten-
sively cultivated region. As the struggle to survive heightened, those
unable "to get their bread on shore" were "obliged to live upon the
water."[26] Thus the fishermen-pirates who frequently emerged from
the ranks of those seeking refuge among the water world's floating
cities tended to be people who had already lost the first round in the
struggle to survive. Most were the poorest of the poor who, after having
been pushed off the land, lived permanently on board ship.

Along the shore large assemblies of junks, moored in long regular
"streets," provided visual evidence of the land's inability to support all
who sought their livelihood on its surface. Within these anchorages
each junk had its permanent berth, and it was possible to live an entire
lifetime without ever setting foot on land. Floating markets, in which
business was transacted on board ship, facilitated life afloat. Along
traffic-clogged water courses marine peddlers, hawking everything
from household goods to haircuts, could be seen poling their way
from craft to craft. Fishmongers, eager to beat their competitors to
the daily catch, often conducted their business from junks as well.[27]

Approximately 80,000 boat-dwellers are thought to have resided
near Canton alone during the mid-nineteenth century.[28] As fishermen, they occupied an important niche in the food chain of the water
world, where fresh, salted, or preserved fish instead of meat or soybeans constituted the major protein source in the daily diet. Dietary
conventions, therefore, fostered interaction among the four major
ethnic and social groups of the water world: Punti rice farmers who
cultivated the plains, Hakka vegetable growers who farmed the hills,
Tanka protein-producers who fished the seas, and the artisans and
merchants who served them.[29]

From this perspective, the South China coast must be seen not as a
simple strip of land demarcating land and sea, but rather as a large
and somewhat indeterminant region embracing a variety of settlement patterns. Just as there was an "inner Asian frontier" around the
Great Wall in the north where the sedentary agriculture of the plain
gradually gave way to the pastoral nomadism of the steppe,[30] so here,
in the south, there was a maritime frontier where sedentary settlement patterns gradually yielded to those of maritime nomadism.

Despite their niche in the South China food chain and the importance of their produce in the water world's economy, fishermen, more
than any other occupational group, tended to become pirates. The

reasons for this are not difficult to understand. At best fishing was a small-scale enterprise that offered even the most industrious few chances of getting ahead. To a fisherman, "big" meant at most a couple of junks and 20 people. More commonly, fishing was a family endeavor, with all the functions handled by one or another family member. Fishing junks were typically owned by their operators, family heads or fathers, who tended to be their captains as well.

Among the boat people, families tended to consist of parents and children, though at times a married son and his wife and children might also live on board. In marked contrast to the onshore society, the boat people possessed no large lineage organizations. Because their lives were organized around the nuclear family or a limited collateral extension of it, extended lineages had little raison d'etre. Boat people seldom kept track of their progenitors beyond a generation or two, and with the exception of a few gravesites, they possessed no collectively owned ancestral halls or property.[31] For these reasons, they had little sense of permanence or cause to form strong sentimental attachments to a given place. This, more than anything else, put them out of touch with the prevalent value system of the continent, which placed a premium on long-term residence and close ties to native place. The boat people's penchant for mobility, however, was more a perception than a reality because in practice fishermen tended to conduct their operations out of specific coastal villages and to "migrate" in well-defined seasonal rounds for long periods of time.

On another level, the lack of large lineage organizations with substantial income-generating capacities made it almost impossible for fishermen to amass enough capital to launch themselves into more lucrative careers. Even had they possessed the means to underwrite the long and costly education that might have gained them positions in the bureaucracy, they were often barred from the civil service examinations.[32] Although the majority of boat people were Cantonese who adhered to the dominant forms of social organization, from the point of view of their counterparts onshore, their marine lifestyle made them socially, if not physically, remote.[33] Scorned by the onshore society, the Tanka were a pariah group, relegated throughout much of the Ch'ing to the status of "mean people" for whom the door to an official career was formally closed.

As a community without gentry, the Tanka lacked the literati connections that would have pulled them into the administrative hierarchies. This, plus their perceived mobility, put them beyond the reach of government authorities, who during certain periods did not even attempt to collect taxes from them.[34] The result was a subculture that lay largely outside of government control.

During Ming and Ch'ing times, when natural disasters and local government breakdown occurred frequently enough to make life precarious and unpredictable, voluntary organizations, ranging from clan, crop-watching, and defense associations to secret brotherhoods, guilds, and popular religious sects sprang up throughout much of China. They functioned to promote group security and economic well-being.[35] Kwangtung was particularly rich in its assortment of such voluntary groups.[36] Among the well-established, familial and lineage organization ran strong, while the uprooted and those in marginal or illegal professions (such as yamen runners, professional gamblers, pimps, and criminals) found protection and fraternity in secret societies.*

The Tanka had their own set of voluntary associations. Firecracker societies and organizations for the building of junks were found all along the coast. Members of these organizations willingly aided one another in fashioning hulls, rigging, masts, and sails, and in creating debts that they could call due when it was their turn to build a junk.[37] Tanka community life was also marked by religious celebrations and shared worship of T'ien-hou, the Sea-goddess; Hung Hsing, the reincarnated Dragon King who ruled over the South Sea; Tam-kung, a local saint with influence over the weather; and Kuan-yin, the Buddhist Goddess of Mercy.[38] Although these associations functioned for the most part as protective, peaceful forces on the side of law and order, they had the potential to be mobilized for activities deemed predatory by the state.

Participation in these organizations was tempting to people continually strapped for money, and what characterized fishermen more than anything else was their poverty. Their occupation was a highly commercial one, subject to the whims of the marketplace. Lumber and other materials for junks could be obtained only through purchase. Gear and tackle had to be replaced frequently, and bait procured on a daily basis. At times, extra hands had to be hired to manage the lines.

*Yamen were the administrative headquarters of local government in Ch'ing China. The menial tasks of each yamen were carried out by a number of runners, who acted as messengers, guards, policemen, and the like. Some of these runners were legally classified as "mean people," to whom the privilege of sitting for the civil service examination was denied. Because of their undesirable occupations and low legal and social status, runners were scorned by gentry and commoner alike. Ch'u T'ung-tsu, *Local Government in China Under the Ch'ing* (Cambridge, Mass., 1970), pp. 61–62.

As producers of a cash crop, fishermen depended on complex systems of credit and loans.[39] They were able to cover their daily expenses by running up accounts at the local general store. As the marketing centers of coastal villages, these stores sold everything from rice, beans, oil, tobacco, and incense to fishing line and tackle. Their proprietors, small businessmen with little capital of their own, were prepared to extend credit to clients whom they had known all their lives.[40] But they could not accommodate the fishermen's larger credit needs. The loans that were essential to the fishermen's survival were, in almost every instance, procured through complex arrangements with a specific fishmonger or "laan" (*lan*). These were people who, under ideal circumstances, loaned fishermen money, purchased their catches, interceded with local officials on their behalf, and looked after their interests onshore. In practice, however, the *lan* often took advantage of their clients, who then became indebted to them on a long-term basis. Unable to discharge their financial obligations, fishermen were often compelled to supplement their incomes through sideline activities such as small-scale trade. Yet even then the result was a livelihood so miserable that, for many, a successful piratical foray was the sole hope for a better life.[41]

For fishermen pushed to the brink of survival and shut out from the more prestigious careers ashore, piracy as a temporary survival strategy made sense. Like their other sideline activities, piracy could be pursued on a part-time basis. It also accorded well with the fishing, which for most was a seasonal pursuit that lasted only 120 to 150 days.[42] During the summer, when fishing was both poor and dangerous, it was easy for financially pressed fishermen to take advantage of the southerlies and sail north to plunder and rob along the coast. Then, with the changing winds and the approach of fall, these part-time "pirates" would return home and resume their fishing. With almost predictable regularity, piracy along the South China coast increased dramatically during the third and fourth lunar months.[43]

The connection between boat people and piracy did not escape the notice of Chinese officials. As early as 1384 one observer had remarked on the tendency of the boatmen and fishermen in Kwangtung to collaborate for the purposes of piracy,[44] and by the late eighteenth century officials commonly identified piracy as an enterprise of poverty-stricken fishermen scrambling to make ends meet.[45]

2

The Petty Pirates
of Vietnam

During the late eighteenth century, piracy in the South China Sea
was practiced much as it had always been—as the part-time, sporadic,
and small-scale enterprise of impoverished water-world inhabitants.
Foremost among those using piracy as a means of making ends meet
were the fishermen, who often had little choice other than supple-
menting meager incomes with a venture or two when the opportunity
arose.

Chiang-p'ing, the Headquarters
of Sino-Vietnamese Piracy

At this time there was one place above all others to which Chinese
went as fishermen and from which they emerged as pirates: the border town of Chiang-p'ing. Located in An Quang province at the side
of a small watercourse on the Van Ninh Chau peninsula, Chiang-p'ing
was technically a part of Vietnam until 1885, but it functioned primarily as a market to which Chinese engaged in all phases of the fishing industry flocked.[1]

During the late eighteenth century Chiang-p'ing was heavily populated by Chinese in various stages of assimilation. Its Celestial Dynasty
Street was a polyglot community of merchants, traders, and fishermen from different Chinese provinces who lived intermingled with
the Vietnamese.[2] Some, from Chinese families who had been in residence for several generations, had forsworn their queues, let their
hair grow, and assumed an outward guise that little distinguished
them from the Vietnamese around them. Others, more recently ar-

rived, had kept their queues but married Vietnamese women and settled into the community. In addition, traveling merchants came to town on short shopping sprees. Noticeably absent from the Chiang-p'ing environment were any manifestations of permanence or community roots.[3]

Chiang-p'ing's rise as a pirate headquarters can be attributed to several factors. The first had to do with its location. In terms of the major shipping routes of the day, the town was ideally situated. Most of the Kwangtung-bound forays launched from Chiang-p'ing took the Pai-lung-wei (White Dragon Tail) passage to the sea. (Pai-lung-wei was the peninsula located just east of Chiang-p'ing that marked the administrative divide between maritime China and Vietnam; see inset, Map 1, p. 8). From there it was easy to sail to China by going around the southern tip of Hainan Island and then swinging north to the mainland, but this was a dangerous route that passed through deep and turbulent waters. Hence, the preferred passage was along the northern coast to Lien-chou, through the narrow strait between Hainan and the mainland, and on into the waters of the Lei-chou Peninsula.[4]

Yet despite its outlet to the sea, Chiang-p'ing was easy to defend, for its location on the river limited the size of craft that could approach it. Moreover access to it was as difficult by land as it was easy by sea, for Chiang-p'ing was almost cut off from the continent by nearly impenetrable terrain. Situated 50 *li* (about 15 miles) from Tung-hsing at the edge of China, it was three days away from Fang-ch'eng township in Ch'in Chou, Kwangtung. En route, one had to pass through several military posts, including Szu-le, described as the gate for entering and leaving the Middle Kingdom.[5]

Accessible to fishermen but remote by any other standards, Chiang-p'ing was a rough-and-ready frontier town from which pirates could operate with little fear of detection. Moreover, far from strong administrative centers in both Vietnam and China, it was scarcely reached by the arm of the law. Because the Vietnamese who were administratively responsible for the area had been preoccupied with continental strife throughout their history, they had had little time for maritime matters and had turned their attention to the sea with great reluctance. As a result, An Quang province was barely organized. In 1491 it had only three formal districts (*huyen*), and there is little to suggest that much additional ordering took place thereafter.[6] For all practical purposes Chiang-p'ing, in the late eighteenth century, was a town without governance.

On the other side of the border, Chinese control of the region was not much stronger than that of the Vietnamese. Local gentry attempted to settle disputes among violence-prone settlements, but if no agreement was reached, communication broke down and rival lineages took to arms. Bloody battles between Punti and Hakka were legendary as well. The result was that Kwangtung's four lower prefectures, Kao-chou, Lei-chou, Lien-chou, and Ch'iung-chou (Hainan), were a political no-man's-land. By sea, regulation was even more difficult, for the myriad islands, coves, and bays reduced to mockery laws formalizing the routes and controlling the shores. To Ch'ing officials more at home on land than sea, trying to regulate the movement of people and junks through the water was an ongoing battle. Seeking to govern the water in the same way they governed the land, Ch'ing officials applied the same concepts of local defense to shore and sea alike. Instead of dividing the coast into long administrative units with mobile defense forces that could sweep through the water world in all directions, they established a hierarchical construct of bureaucratic authority that resulted in confusing and overlapping military jurisdictions.

The Political Geography of the Water World

Further contributing to the power vacuum in the water world was the perception of the border, shared by officials on both sides, as a delimiter of precise political units. As a result, the water world, unified in so many ways by patterns of livelihood and local affinities, was split into rigid administrative jurisdictions. Although most officials, Chinese and Vietnamese alike, would have been hard pressed to locate the Sino-Vietnamese border by either land or sea, they saw it in clear psychological and administrative terms as the place where their governance ceased. For them, the administrative divide was at Pai-lung-wei, where maritime patrols and the pursuit of offenders stopped lest they sail uninvited into their neighbor's waters.[7]

Problems of governance were compounded because the officials' perception of the border was not shared by the residents of the water world. Fish did not recognize political boundaries, and the key to survival for most inhabitants lay in the freedom to range back and forth across the border without hindrance. Attempted regulation was of little avail in stemming the intercourse that flowed across the water's surface. By artificially dissecting a natural and cohesive realm, the border functioned primarily to delay official transactions across it.[8]

Chinese officials, long preoccupied with their continental empire and more specifically with the northwest, had an equally vague sense of the sea as a separate world in its own right, different from the land in its movements, rhythms, and dynamics. Although they implicitly recognized the zones of the water world—coastal strip, inshore waters (*nan-hai*), and deep sea (*nan-yang*)—they did not conceive of them as an integrated whole.

It is not surprising, then, that the vocabulary they used to describe their maritime environment is at best imprecise and unclear. Whereas in the West the terms sea and ocean are roughly differentiated to the extent that a sea is thought of as being bounded in some way, for the Chinese *hai* (sea) and *yang* (ocean) were completely interchangeable.[9] Although a few cartographers did make a vague distinction between *hai* as the shallow waters lying immediately off the coast and *yang* as the deep waters farther out, it is impossible to find a Chinese map showing where one gave way to the other. Most Chinese maps label all expanses of water as one or the other. The only important distinction for the Chinese was between the "inner" (*nei*) sea or ocean and the "outer" (*wai*) sea or ocean.[10] In this study, the waters referred to as the "inshore seas of the Nan-hai" usually appear on Chinese maps as either *nei-hai* or *nei-yang*; and those referred to as the "deep seas of the Nan-yang" usually appear as *wai-hai* or *wai-yang*.

For the fishermen and merchants who lived in the water world, the bounds that differentiated "inner" from "outer" seas were ecological ones: the depth of the water, the distance from shore, the kind of fish to be found, and so forth. By contrast, for government administrators and literati, the distinction between the two zones was largely psychological, a matter of human perceptions rather than actual topography. Indeed, one of the most striking features of the political geography of the water world was just how close to shore the outer seas were thought to lie.

Although Map 2 has no scale, it shows where Chinese cartographers and officials believed the outer ocean lay. Places no farther from shore than the Ladrone Islands at the mouth of the Pearl River were placed in the *wai-yang*. For all practical purposes, that is to say, the outer ocean began just beyond where the eye could see. In effect this meant that all outlying areas were virtually unknown.[11] They were also of little concern. For example, although the Chinese made sweeping claims to the Spratly and Paracel islands, they made little attempt to incorporate them into their empire. As late as the nineteenth century cartographers still disagreed about their exact location, and Confucian literati regarded them as little more than "a series of navigational hazards [at] the eastern edge of China's maritime gateway."[12]

Accordingly, the narrow zone of the inner sea marked the farthest seaward extent of active Chinese governance. In choosing not to make coastal control a high priority, Chinese officials forfeited the oppor-

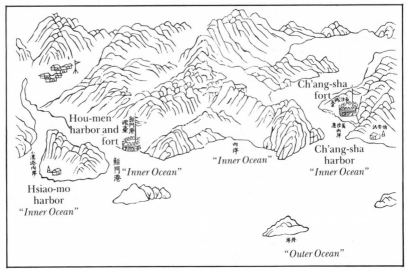

Map 2. The "inner" and "outer" oceans off Kwangtung province's south coast. Note how close to land the Chinese of the day thought the "outer" (largely unknown) ocean lay. Officials tended to perceive the "inner" ocean as the farthest extent of their authority. From *Kuang-tung hai-fang hui-lan*, comp. Lu K'un and Ch'eng Hung-ch'ih, n.d., Vol. 1.

tunity to seize the military initiative in maritime China. As a result, theirs was a weak and passive presence in the heart of the water world.

Petty Piracy in Practice

Much as the Ch'ing desired to keep a tight rein on the coast, they were unable to do so, and it was where the official and real worlds failed to converge—among the inshore islands and along the international border—that piracy most naturally arose. Moreover, the Ch'ing were unequipped to cope with the rise of borderland headquarters like Chiang-p'ing. In swift, short raids Chinese pirates could sail from Vietnam, attack targets in South China, and be back in port before the Chinese water forces could either assemble their boats or instruct the Vietnamese to mobilize from their side.

So successful were Chinese pirates in playing borderland hide-and-seek that by 1790 piracy rather than fishing was the mainstay of Chiang-p'ing's economy. By then the city functioned primarily as a Sino-Vietnamese equivalent of Jean Lafitte's Barataria, its markets brimming with the proceeds of pirate commerce.[13] Pirates found a warm welcome there, for most of Chiang-p'ing's 2,000-odd households were eager to sell them provisions and market their prizes. Once on sale in Chiang-p'ing, pirate booty often found its way into the hands of Chinese merchants who had come there to purchase it. Among the more zealous participants in this exchange were traders from the nearby provinces of Kwangtung and Kwangsi.[14]

Although the center of the Sino-Vietnamese pirate world was firmly established at Chiang-p'ing, the Vietnamese coastal cities of Nghe An, Doan Mien, and Hue, and sometimes even the port of Hanoi, served as pirate centers.[15] These cities were ideal spawning grounds for piracy. Not only did they have well-protected harbors and accommodating inhabitants, but they overflowed with ready recruits. Among these were the Chinese outlaws who streamed steadily "across the border" to seek asylum in Vietnam. Desperate for any means of survival, such men were quick to enlist in pirate gangs. Those fleeing from justice enjoyed a double avenue of escape on the coast, for if they chose to remain in China, they could lose themselves in the floating congestion offshore where, in the words of a contemporary, "there would be a considerable difficulty in apprehending a delinquent if once hidden among the intricacies of the mass of floating huts which cover the water for some acres."[16]

Besides fishermen and criminals, Chiang-p'ing, and to a lesser extent other coastal towns, attracted sizable numbers of urban failures and social misfits, people who, for whatever reasons, had been unable to make ends meet. Once in these centers, they too were often drawn to piracy in order to eat.[17] A typical case was Wu Hsing-hsin, who had run a store at Pai-lung-wei. When his business failed, Wu made his way to Chiang-p'ing and finding himself with no other option, became a pirate.[18]

Although the larger share of pirates mentioned in the sources were fishermen, their gangs were frequently filled out by unsuccessful merchants, porters, and hired laborers, men like Wu Hsing-hsin who failed to establish themselves upon the shore. More than a third of the 93 pirate volunteers of known occupation fell into this category: merchants (9), porters (8), hired laborers (8), peddlers (7), and grasscutters (4). Most of these 36 pirates had worked in Vietnam, and 19 could be specifically linked to Chiang-p'ing (Table A.1, Appendix A).

The occupations of 26 nonfishermen captives-turned-pirates show a similar range. More than half were rice dealers or peddlers of commodities of one sort or another (10), porters (3), or grasscutters (2); one was a shoemaker. Of these 16 people nearly all (14) had had dealings in Vietnam, but what ties they had with Chiang-p'ing, if any, are unknown (Table A.4).

As a gathering point for the flotsam of the earth, the water world

attracted those who could make it nowhere else in society. Their only
recourse was to prey on the establishment in any way they could. In
their adaptive strategies, the line between legal and illegal often
blurred. The gambling parlors, opium dens, and floating bordellos
that dotted the coast were, in part, the products of their endeavors to
survive. For some, piracy was an extension of these endeavors in an
environment where water was ubiquitous, and the knowledge of how
to get around on it universal. In a region virtually outside government
control, piracy was a plausible income-generating option.

Within the water world struggling fisherman, together with down-
and-outers, desperadoes, and malcontents, formed a pool of potential
pirates from which at any moment an actual gang might emerge. And
when that moment came, would-be leaders, relying on networks of
family, friends, and voluntary associations, seldom had trouble recruiting followers for given missions. We may regard the experience
of Ch'en A-ch'ang, a fisherman-pirate in Chiang-p'ing, as typical.[19]

On September 15, 1795, Ch'en A-ch'ang's cousin Ch'en A-yang of
Yang-chiang county, Kwangtung, came to Chiang-p'ing on a visit. No
sooner had he arrived than A-ch'ang told his cousin how, as a member
of Tien-pai Ta's gang, he had attacked junks at sea and received a
share of their booty. He then invited A-yang to become a pirate too.

A-yang agreed and joined his cousin A-ch'ang and the eight other
men that he and leader Tien-pai Ta had assembled on board ship.
The group was still too small, however, so they went into town and
quickly recruited Huang T'ang-yu. Two days later (September 18)
they set sail and in the inner ocean near Ch'in Chou, Kwangtung, attacked T'a Ting-ch'iu's boat. They tried to persuade T'a to join the
gang, but when he refused, he was imprisoned in the hold and forced
to bail water. Later that same day, in the inner ocean off White
Dragon City (Pai-lung-ch'eng) in Ho-p'u county, Kwangtung, the pirates attacked another vessel and took as their captive Hsia T'ien-
jung. He too refused to join the gang and was imprisoned and forced
to boil rice.

On September 20, in the outer ocean of Cow's Head Bay in Ch'in
Chou, the pirates took a junk, and Ch'en A-ch'ang raped its male
owner, Li Sheng-k'o. Later that same day they captured and imprisoned Ch'en Wei-nung, who was forced to boil tea. Two days later, now
in the inner ocean of San-ch'a-k'ou in Ho-p'u county, the pirates attacked still another junk and induced Su Ch'i-hsiao to join them. They
then headed back to Chiang-p'ing where, on October 7 and 8, they
added five more people and two more junks to their original forces.

Recommencing their activities on October 10, they captured a rice boat in the harbor of Hanoi and raped its proprietress. Five days later, in the ocean around Hanoi, they seized a second cargo of rice. On October 19, still in Vietnam, the pirates robbed a vessel laden with pepper and captured Ch'en San-ch'iu who, on refusing to join the gang, was imprisoned. By November 10 the pirates were back in China, where they seized a cargo of pigs and ducks from a boat in the harbor of Hai-t'ou in Sui-ch'i county. Five days later the Ch'en cousins' pirate career came to an abrupt end when, blown by a storm into the harbor at Mu-lan in Wen-ch'ang county, their boat bashed against the rocks and they were arrested.

Like many of the pirates of the South China coast, Ch'en A-ch'ang started out as a fisherman plying the waters of the South China Sea. Unable to make ends meet, he took up piracy in company with Tien-pai Ta, whose gang before long wound up in Chiang-p'ing. There, in search of accomplices, Ch'en turned first to his cousin and, after winning him over, next sought recruits among his friends and acquaintances, and finally to a man enlisted in town. With that accomplished, a gang of ten was ready to set out.

Once a decision was made, pirate gangs could be assembled with uncanny speed. In the case of Ch'en Ya-hui, another fisherman from Sui-ch'i, only one day elapsed between his decision to become a pirate and his first heist the following evening, when his band of 13 attacked a privately hired ferry boat.[20]

While at sea pirates often increased their effective manpower through the labor—either voluntary or forced—of captives. Thus, for example, when Ch'en A-ch'ang's group, on its second day out, seized a vessel whose captain refused to join them, they imprisoned the man, though they might have left him behind. In being forced to boil water and clean the hold, he shared a fate common to scores of other captives who recoiled at the thought of becoming pirates.

Many times, however, captives chose to join their captors, and in doing so provided welcome support. Outstanding captives who found favor with gang leaders might even be catapulted into leadership positions. Such promotions usually grew out of homosexual relations initiated by a gang leader, who would then reward the captive by commissioning him as the boss or skipper (*lao-pan*) of a newly taken craft.[21]

Pirates like Ch'en A-ch'ang tended to carry out short, swift missions. They typically remained at sea only a few days before returning to Chiang-p'ing or their home base to dispose of booty and divide the proceeds. On their first foray, Ch'en and his men appear, after less than a week of operations, to have turned for home on September 22 and to have remained in port at Chiang-p'ing nearly two weeks disposing of their plunder and rounding up additional recruits. Then, on October 8, they set out again for another quick strike and managed to stay intact another month before smashing up against the rocks.

After a successful haul, many gangs dispersed, never to come together again, but some, like Liu Ts'ai-fa's gang, carried out sporadic activities over a period of several months. Liu, who decided to supplement his fishing income with piracy during the fall of 1795, demonstrated the ease with which the two careers could be carried on almost simultaneously.[22] After recruiting a band of 14 and setting out, Liu was immediately thwarted in his first foray by a patrol squadron. Although a number of his colleagues were arrested, Liu himself escaped, and after obtaining another vessel, he resumed his career as a fisherman. But a few months later, on December 9, 1795, he was at it again, suggesting to his fellow fishermen Liu A-t'ing and Ch'en A-ch'i that they try their hand at piracy. Both agreed, and with two other recruits, they headed at once for Feng-yü, where they bore down on a vessel, boarded it, and seized 30 baskets of dried fish. After selling their spoils for 20 silver dollars (*yüan*), the gang members divided the money up and went their separate ways. (On currency and measures, see Appendix E.) Six weeks later, again eager to test his luck, Liu persuaded his two former colleagues to rejoin him. This time they assembled a band of 18 and, on their first day out, they seized two small junks laden with bean bran. These they ransomed for 130 *yüan* of silver, netting them 7.2 *yüan* each. Emboldened by his success, Liu set out on yet another run, whose haul of 40 *yüan* was shared by 10 gang members.

Although Liu managed to stay in the pirate business for a relatively long period of time, the commodities he seized resembled those of other water-world pirates, consisting primarily of everyday items in constant circulation along the coast. The remuneration from such ventures was usually modest. For example, a man who participated in all three of Liu Ts'ai-fa's raids would have taken in only slightly over 15 *yüan* of foreign silver.

After a successful strike, gangs commonly sailed to the outer ocean, where they could sell their prizes through known networks to other "fishermen." It was in this way that the 13-member gang of Ch'en Ya-hui disposed of the spoils from its one-time endeavor, the attack on a privately hired ferry. In addition to currency amounting to 15 *yüan* of foreign silver and 4,500 copper *cash*, the gang took in 25 pieces of clothing and felt, which, with the exception of a woolen robe, were sold at sea for 3,000 copper *cash*.

Once prizes had been taken, gangs faced the task of allocating proceeds among themselves. Describing the practice that prevailed among his 13 men, Ch'en Ya-hui recalled: "We next divided the booty we'd obtained into 15 shares. I came up with the idea that Mo Ya-kuei as the provider of a junk and I as head of the gang should each receive a double share. Everyone else would receive a single share. Each share amounted to 1 silver *yüan* and 500 copper *cash*."[23]

The granting of double shares to gang leaders and those who, like Mo, contributed extra "means of production" (such as boats in the case of pirates) was conventional among both bandits and pirates.[24] Grain and other edible prizes might be retained and divided into commodity shares or sold through the regular channels, or both. In 1801 Huang Wen-sheng's gang sold 35 of its 100 piculs of rice to a fishing junk for 180 *yüan* of silver and divided the rest into shares of three piculs each. Similarly, a gang led by Lin Chang took 150 packages (*pao*) of white sugar, 40 *chin* of fresh fish, and two captives from a merchant junk; this haul, including the captives' ransom, fetched 100 *yüan* of silver. Another gang got 45 *yüan* of silver and 2,300 copper *cash* for its 33 piculs of dried bean curd and 40 piculs of fish.[25]

On the basis of very limited data, it appears that members of small gangs might earn something in the range of 10 to 15 silver *yüan* apiece per venture. In December 1796, for example, 15 pirates each received 13 *yüan* of foreign silver after a three-day foray in the Sino-Vietnamese border region, and in 1797 two other pirates each received ten *yüan* for booty sold in one of the Vietnamese border towns at the end of a similar foray.[26]

In terms of the wage standard of the day, individual shares from these gangs' hauls were approximately equivalent to ten months' salary for a soldier, three and a half months' salary for an agricultural laborer, and one and a quarter months' salary for a skilled worker in Canton.[27] So, although not phenomenal by any means, such returns probably did enable piracy on this scale to pay, particularly since it tended to be a relatively low-overhead, low-risk operation. Because so many pirates were fishermen first, access to a boat, the most expensive tool of a pirate's trade, would have been almost automatic. The simple weapons they wielded—knives, pointed bamboo pikes, and cutting blades—were standard equipment on most craft. Moreover, fishermen-pirates were thoroughly at home on the water, familiar with every trick of wind and tide, every sand bar and hidden rock. For most pirates, then, outfitting an expedition amounted to little more than recruiting accomplices, readying weapons, and procuring provisions.

Once under way, such bands, provided they did not become too greedy or too ambitious, probably ran relatively little risk of apprehension. Their guerrilla-like tactics consisted of striking swift blows and then retreating before stunned victims could recover their senses or offer resistance. By the time constabulary forces reached the water, the pirates had usually vanished without a trace, and the proximity of the international border, as we have seen, considerably reduced their chances of being taken by any government patrols in the area.

Although pirate gangs might come together and disperse several times, each functioned at any given time as a single, independent unit unaffiliated with other gangs or groups. Their targets were almost always single craft moving in shallow seas, though they occasionally attacked a residence on land. Unprepared to engage in a real battle, they could usually be driven off by the appearance of an imperial war junk. Because this was a small-scale phenomenon that posed no threat to maritime commerce as a whole, many of the most successful petty pirates probably eluded the Chinese authorities, and hence the historical record, completely.

The Impetus for the Growth of Petty Piracy

By the late eighteenth century demography was catching up with China. At this stage "social problems were overwhelming the organized capacities of the Ch'ing bureaucracy to deal with them. Central among these was the ratio of resources to population."[28] In the course of the century, and with the extended peace of the Ch'ien-lung reign,* the population of China had doubled from approximately 150 million to 300 million, resulting in a pressure on the land that became noticeable even to contemporaries as the marginal border regions filled up.

Kwangtung was one of the hardest-hit provinces. In terms of total area, Kwangtung was sparsely populated in 1787. But with only 1.67 *mou* (0.25 acre) of cultivable land per person, it was one of the most land-hungry provinces of the empire. Within a quarter century it became overpopulated in absolute terms as well; by 1812 its population had grown 30 percent since 1787, well above the national average of 24 percent.[29] Exacerbating the problem was the absence of any significant economic or political growth. As a result, competition for resources and the means of livelihood intensified.

*In the eighteenth and nineteenth centuries, China was governed by a complex bureaucratic system that culminated in the person of the Emperor, who combines in himself supreme legislative, administrative, and judicial authority. During the years covered by this study, two Emperors were instrumental in determining the course of action taken against the pirates: the Ch'ien-lung Emperor, who ruled from 1736 to 1795, and the Chia-ch'ing Emperor, who ruled from 1796 to 1820. The seat of imperial power was located in the Imperial or Forbidden City of Peking.

Population growth probably accounted for much of the increased commerce and seaborne trade of the second half of the eighteenth century as those denied employment on land turned to the water. It also led to emigration and produced new commercial contacts and opportunities for trade. Despite the Ch'ien-lung court's unsympathetic attitude toward the fate of Chinese who chose to reside abroad, people from Kwangtung and Fukien emigrated throughout the eighteenth century. After 1785, when the British East India Company began recruiting Chinese artisans and peasants for work in Penang, the government could do nothing to stem the exodus.[30]

At the same time local, interregional, and international trade increased steadily. The eighteenth century was a benchmark for the coasting trade, with north–south shipping flourishing along the entire seaboard. Interregional trade with Southeast Asia thrived as well. As early as the 1740's the number of trading junks setting out for Southeast Asia from Kwangtung and Fukien was estimated at no fewer than 110 a year. The value of the commerce was estimated in the millions of taels.[31] Not long after, Kwangtung's trade was given an enormous boost when, in 1756, Canton was made the sole port for international, and especially Western, commerce. The effect was almost immediate, with a discernibly steady increase in the number of foreign trading ships putting in at Whampoa, Canton's harbor, beginning in 1760.[32] The number of European ships alone rose from just under a dozen in 1720 to 60 or 80 per year between 1780 and 1800. The tonnage of the individual ships doubled as well.[33]

As the increasing competition for resources and land forced those at the margins of society to seek their livelihood through whatever means they could, it was only natural that this rich supply of goods afloat tempted the more enterprising to help themselves. Moreover, the laws governing the Sino-Vietnamese trade made their enterprise seem worthwhile.

The legitimate trade between China and Vietnam was a highly regulated activity conducted entirely by Chinese. The flow of goods from China originated primarily in T'ai-p'ing and Chen-an prefectures in Kwangsi and in Shao-chou, Hui-chou, Ch'ao-chou, and Chia-ying prefectures in Kwangtung. Coolies hired to transport goods by land were supposed to reside in Ning-ming, Kwangsi, and could only be employed for specified periods. Merchant junks were supposed to be carefully inspected at their point of embarkation, so their routes, the size of their crews, and the length of their stay could be clearly spelled out.[34]

Once across the border, merchants from the Middle Kingdom conducted business almost exclusively with their compatriots in the Vietnamese market towns. As foreign traders, however, they were at the mercy of Vietnamese officials, who inflicted severe and often arbitrary assessments on them. The Vietnamese commonly taxed large junks more heavily than small ones, regardless of their cargo. Rates charged at the different ports varied as well. For example, junks calling at Saigon paid more tax than those calling at Quang Nam, and those at Quang Nam more than those at Hue. Junks from Ch'ao-chou and Hainan were taxed at a lower rate than those from the rest of Kwangtung.[35]

The tradeable commodities were also limited by restrictions on both sides. The Chinese could legally export only satin thread, certain kinds of cloth, paint pigment, stockings, stationery, tea, white sugar, and medicine. They could legally import only cardamom, *shu-liang* (a kind of plant used to produce brown dye), zinc, and bamboo. All other products were off limits and not to be exchanged without special permission.[36] In addition to the plethora of official restrictions, border trouble during the 1770's led to an embargo on overland commerce, and the chaos of the Tay-son rebellion after 1770 further reduced the opportunities for trade.[37]

These problems were compounded by the fact that the items in greatest demand on both sides—Vietnamese rice and Chinese iron—were officially classified as contraband. The rice surpluses of Vietnam were important to a Cantonese population unable to feed itself, but Vietnamese law forbade the exportation of rice. At the same time the Chinese were banned from exporting the iron so greatly desired across the border that Vietnamese officials often waived their own regulations for Chinese junks that brought it in by reducing or eliminating the customary port duties and allowing them to take back cargoes of rice. For each 100,000 catties of iron entering the country, Vietnamese officials permitted 300,000 catties of rice to leave.[38]

Although each country needed the other's products, open trade in most items was not possible. The result was a well-established smuggling operation, conducted by the Chinese and covertly sanctioned by the Vietnamese. It fed yet another element into the pirate pool at Chiang-p'ing, where smugglers worked hand in glove with fisherman-pirates and shared their underground networks.[39]

By 1790 piracy was on the rise as a survival strategy in the water world. But this was still the petty piracy of individual enterprises undertaken on a short-term basis. Overpopulation and increased maritime trade had changed the frequency of piracy, but not its methods of operation. In fact, piracy at this stage manifested little potential for growth. Leaders, scarcely distinguishable from their followers, lacked the means or the will to consolidate individual bands into a larger organizational framework, and the rank and file demonstrated little interest in perpetuating their enterprises beyond a successful strike or two. In this form piracy represented a type of collective action well suited to an environment where the government was too weak to suppress it, but still strong enough to prevent it from escalating out of control. Lacking the means to transform their operation from within, the pirates' catalyst for expansion would have to come from without.

3

The Effects of the
Vietnamese Rebellion

In the years after 1790 what for centuries had been a petty enterprise
suddenly burgeoned out of control. Since the potential for growth
had long existed in a world little touched by officialdom, why was it
not until then that piracy increased so spectacularly? The answer lies
not in the increasing population pressure and trading opportunities
of the period, though they certainly contributed their share, but in
political changes that significantly altered the balance of power, first
in Vietnam and later in China, and thus allowed maritime troublemakers to move from hit-or-miss, small-time operations to full-blown
professional piracy.

During the late eighteenth century Vietnam was wracked by the so-
called Tay-son Rebellion, which took its name from the native village
of the three rebel leaders, the brothers Nguyen Van Lu, Nguyen Van
Nhac, and Nguyen Van Hue. The Nguyen brothers, merchants engaged in betel commerce with the hill people of Binh Dinh province,
gathered a band of followers, and in 1773 the rebels succeeded in seizing the provincial capital of Qui Nhon (see Map 3).[1]

This coup, capping several decades of upheaval in Vietnam, was
one of the major episodes in eighteenth-century Southeast Asian history. It resulted in a short-lived program of cultural experimentation,
which saw, among other things, classical Chinese replaced as the official language by the indigenous *nom* (a system of characters developed
by the Vietnamese for the written forms of non-Chinese words).[2]
More important, it altered the political order of the water world by
bringing unity to a country that had been divided for nearly two cen-

turies, but at the same time opening the door to foreign interference in its affairs as both Chinese military adventurers and European interlopers tried to restore dethroned monarchs.

Since the sixteenth century Vietnam had been nominally under the rule of the late Le dynasty, but the country had long been effectively governed by two rival families: the Trinh in the north, at Hanoi, and the Nguyen in the south at Hue.* As the Tay-son Rebellion spread outward from Binh Dinh, it centered first on the southern patrimony of the Nguyen. In late 1773 the rebels triumphed in Quang Ngai and Binh Thuan provinces. The Trinh rulers, taking advantage of the confusion, then sent an army against their rivals. In 1775 they evicted the Nguyen from their capital at Hue and forced them to flee to Saigon. But that proved a doubtful haven, for the Tay-son rebels then shifted their sights there in an attempt to dislodge them.

By 1778 the Tay-son had succeeded in forcing the Nguyen heir-apparent, Nguyen Phuc Anh, to seek temporary refuge on an island in the Gulf of Siam. For the next six years the fighting between the Nguyen and Tay-son forces continued in the south, and Saigon changed hands seven times. In the end the Tay-son emerged victorious. After a disastrous defeat at My Tho in early 1785, Nguyen Phuc Anh once more was forced to take refuge in the islands near Bangkok.[3]

With the south temporarily in hand, the Tay-son immediately turned their attention to the north. In 1785 they drove the Trinh from Hue, then moved on to Hanoi, which they entered the next year. At this point the Le Emperor requested aid from China, and in 1788 three Ch'ing armies invaded Vietnam to restore him to his throne.[4] At the same time Nguyen Phuc Anh and his followers began launching a comeback by attacking the Tay-son in the south.

In this critical period Tay-son military power reached its zenith. The rebels met the Chinese challenge by declaring their most able leader, Nguyen Van Hue, the Emperor of Vietnam and totally routing the Ch'ing expedition. The Ch'ien-lung Emperor, recognizing that the Tay-son had become masters of the country, quickly legitimized their rule by officially investing Nguyen Van Hue, the Tay-son Emperor Quang Trung, as the King of Annam (An-nan kuo wang).[5] With this, the first phase of the rebellion came to an end.

---

*The Nguyen at Hue should not be confused with the Nguyen who led the rebellion. The "Nguyen" brothers were actually members of a family surnamed Ho. In the hope of legitimizing their cause, they had adopted the Nguyen surname at the outset of the rebellion.

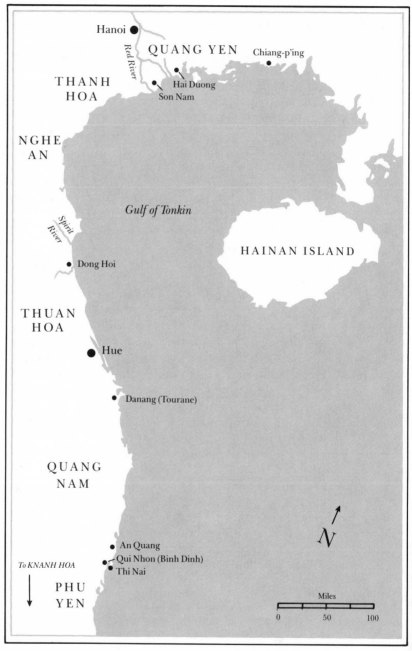

Map 3. Sites of pirate activity in Vietnam under the Tay-son. In many cases, the provincial seat bore the same name as its province.

Chinese Pirates in the Tay-son Forces

People in high places were not the only ones affected by the uprising. It directly influenced the fortunes of the pirates as well. As opportunists, always eager to get ahead by whatever means they could, it did not take them long to realize that the Tay-son's need for resources provided opportunities for their own advancement. The result was a partnership in which significant numbers of Chinese pirates served the Tay-son as privateers.[6]

Two of the Tay-son's earliest allies, Chi T'ing (Tap Dinh) and Li Ts'ai (Ly Tai), Chinese businessmen-turned-pirates, joined forces with the Tay-son in late 1773.[7] After the rebellion erupted, Li Ts'ai recruited a band of Chinese volunteers to the Tay-son cause, a group subsequently known as the Harmonious Army; another group, led by Chi T'ing, constituted the Loyal Army.

During January 1774, in the course of the Tay-son's advance on Binh Dinh, the Chinese troops hid in ambush and killed many of the enemy, enabling the Tay-son to take Quang Ngai. The next year they put to flight the troops of Nguyen Cuu Dat, who was in charge of defending Hue. But a short while later the Loyal Army was routed in its attempt to retake Hue from the Trinh, and the Harmonious Army fled to Binh Dinh. After his Loyal Army's defeat, Chi T'ing made his way to Kwangtung, where he was later caught and executed by the governor-general. Li Ts'ai did not fare much better. In the spring of 1776, now in Hue, he joined a former Tay-son ally, Prince Duong, in staging a coup against the Tay-son and seizing Saigon. A bloody clash between the erstwhile allies resulted in the defeat of the coup and the death of Prince Duong. In revenge for the treachery the Tay-son troops massacred every Chinese they encountered in Saigon. More than 10,000 people were killed and their bodies thrown into the river. The collaboration between Chinese pirates and Vietnamese rebels appeared to be over.

A second, more fruitful period of cooperation was to follow, however. Desperate for manpower, the Tay-son were not daunted in their attempt to secure allies. Outright seizure brought into their service another pirate, Ch'en T'ien-pao, who proved an extraordinarily able leader.[8]

A fisherman by profession, Ch'en usually worked the waters of Lien-chou county, Kwangtung, in the company of his wife and two sons. But when, in October 1780, his boat was blown to Vietnam by a storm, he stayed there, fishing in the area around Hanoi. In 1783 the Tay-son captured the entire family, commissioned Ch'en as a brigade-general (*tong binh; tsung-ping*), and forced him (or so he later claimed) to participate in the campaigns against the Trinh lords. Ch'en was joined in these enterprises by his former helmsman, Liang Kuei-hsing. Both men again fought at the side of the Tay-son in 1785 and took part in the campaign that drove the Trinh from Hue. For his endeavors, Liang Kuei-hsing was given the title Total Virtuous Marquis (Hiep Duc Hau; Ho-te-hou) and presented with a chop bearing the words "allowed to grow the hair" (*hsü-yu t'ou-fa*).

It was the simultaneous invasion of Vietnam by the Chinese from the north and Nguyen Phuc Anh from the south in 1788, however, that precipitated Ch'en Tien-pao's rise to a position of *primus inter pares* among the pirates in the Tay-son's service. Beset on all sides, they turned to Ch'en, made him a marquis, and presented him with a "barbarian permit" (*i-chao*), authorizing him to recruit other pirates. Now bearing the full title "General Pao, Virtuous Marquis" (Tong Binh Pao Duc Hau; Tsung-ping Pao Te-hou), he was entrusted with the command of six armed junks and 200 Vietnamese soldiers.

Ch'en set to work at once and during the next few months recruited all those who would emerge as powerful pirate leaders under the Tay-son. Among them were Liang Wen-keng and Fan Wen-ts'ai. Liang, a fisherman from Hsin-hui, had already joined the pirate gang that captured him in 1786. Ch'en commissioned him as a lieutenant (*thien tong; ch'ien-tsung*). Fan, a fisherman from Lu-shui, Kwangtung, who had also been a pirate since 1786, was made a commander (*chi huy; chih-hui*).

Later in 1788, as the Tay-son's situation became even more critical, they gave Ch'en 16 additional junks and a second document, authorizing him to recruit even more pirates. In response Ch'en enlisted Mo Kuan-fu and Cheng Ch'i in the Tay-son cause. Mo, a native of Sui-ch'i county, came to piracy in 1787, after being captured while cutting wood. The next year found him collaborating with another pirate, Cheng Ch'i. Both were approached by Ch'en, who commissioned them as generals. Thereafter, Ch'en recalled, "They went out to sea and fought several times, and afterward returned to Vietnam and presented me with silk gowns, cotton, and foreign silver."

The pirates' service to the Tay-son did not end with the triumph of 1788–89 that transformed their sponsors from rebels to rulers. For with this event the uprising merely entered its second phase. The new Emperor, beset by difficulties on all fronts, had little time to take his ease or enjoy his power. On the military front he was continuously harassed in both the north and the south by the still-loyal partisans of the former Le Emperor and the Nguyen. On the domestic front his program of cultural experimentation brought little relief to the peasants, whose support of the movement faltered.[9]

The most urgent problems facing the new Emperor, however, were financial ones. The long years of war and military expenditures had drained the treasury. Large stretches of farmland and hundreds of villages had been abandoned as peasants fled the fighting, throwing the entire tax structure into chaos. After the massacre in Saigon, Chinese merchants in the north who had financed the revolution gradually withdrew their contributions. Since most of the Chinese in the south had remained steadfast in their loyalty to the Nguyen, this defection served only to increase the Tay-son's suspicion of all Chinese. Customs revenue became practically nonexistent as chaotic taxation policies in the ports prevented shippers from trading first near Hue and later along the rest of the coast as well.[10]

In 1792, with his situation becoming more critical each day, the Quang Trung Emperor sent his navy on a mission to China. His fleet, consisting of 100 junks, was organized into three divisions, each headed by four brigade-generals he had personally invested. Although the ostensible purpose of the mission was to levy taxes for war, its actual purpose was to recruit privateers from the "scum" of the coast. In June and July the Emperor commissioned 40 Chinese pirate junks to conduct expeditions along the coasts of Kwangtung, Fukien, and Chekiang provinces. Thereafter Chinese pirates participated in every major Tay-son naval encounter.[11]

Between 1792 and 1799 the military action was determined by Nguyen expeditions timed around the monsoons. Each year in June, when the winds were dependable, a Nguyen squadron would leave Saigon and a well-provisioned army would set out by land. Converging at a designated spot, the two forces would engage the Tay-son, occupy territory, garrison the most easily defended points, and then, with the onset of unfavorable winds, return to their base in the south. The Tay-son responded by using the changed winds to launch their own expeditions into Nguyen territory, so that by the mid-1790's a rhythm had been established: the southwest monsoon signaled the advance of the Nguyen and the retreat of the Tay-son; the northeast monsoon saw the advance of the Tay-son and the departure of the Nguyen. The principal theaters of action were in the south, and although the *campagnes de saison* did not follow this pattern year after year, they were the means by which Nguyen Phuc Anh gradually extended his power base to the north.[12]

The first monsoon campaign, in 1792, resulted in the almost total destruction of the Tay-son navy at Thi Nai, the port of Qui Nhon.

There the Emperor's brother, Nguyen Van Nhac, had anchored a fleet of war junks he had just finished building in preparation for an invasion of the south. When the news of their intended mission reached Nguyen Phuc Anh, he sent out an expedition of his own under the command of two Frenchmen. With the wind in its favor, the force quickly reached Thi Nai, found the Tay-son vessels bottled up in the port, and entered the harbor, where the troops promptly disembarked and seized the forts. The Tay-son general and his forces fled, leaving behind their vessels and arms. Among the participants in this battle were the 40 pirate ships recruited by the Quang Trung Emperor. Three of them were captured by the Nguyen, along with 75 other vessels from the new fleet of the Emperor's brother.

For the Tay-son the defeat was devastating: only nine galleys of their new armada remained intact. Further disaster was visited on them soon after, for the Emperor died that November. Quang Trung's ten-year-old son was installed as the Emperor, Quang Toan, but the Tay-son had lost their most able leader. Thereafter, their power increasingly faltered in the south, where they continued to lose popular support.[13]

The pirates, however, persevered in their allegiance to the Tay-son. In 1794 they recruited T'ang Te, of Wu-ch'uan, into their forces. The next year Ch'en T'ien-pao was promoted again, assuming the title Military Governor (*do-doc; tu-tu*).[14] Two years later, in 1797, they were at the side of the Tay-son when Nguyen Phuc Anh mounted a new threat. Phuc Anh, with a fleet of nearly 600 vessels, had embarked on April 25 for an invasion of Qui Nhon. En route, however, he changed his mind and went instead to Tourane (Danang), where he remained for several months. During this period he had numerous encounters with the Tay-son and their pirate allies. In June his forces, under the command of his subordinate, Vu Tieu Sanh, set out from the military post at Dai Chiem and were attacked by a pirate squadron led by Military Governor Nguyen Van Ngu. Vu Tieu Sanh defeated the pirates and captured 30 of their junks. Three of the pirates involved, Ch'en Kuan-hsiang, Cheng Ya-pao, and Tsung Chin, later confessed that they had left Hue in February specifically to fight the Nguyen and did not return until July.[15]

In May Ch'en T'ien-pao, receiving yet another accolade from his sponsors, was presented with a dagger and a seal bearing the inscription "great governor-general who controls each branch of the shan-ts'ao unit" (*t'ung-shan-ts'ao-tao ko-chih ta-tsung-tu*).* He was also

---

*The meaning of the *shan-ts'ao-tao* (or shan-t'sao unit) is unclear, but because the *ts'ao* was a type of cargo carrier, the term probably refers to some kind of fleet.

given the authority to coerce back into action any pirate whose interest in the campaign flagged.[16] This seems to have triggered greater systemization within the Tay-son's pirate ranks, for each pirate boss (*lao ban; lao-pan*) was now made a "General of the Black Junks" (*o tao tong binh; wu-ts'ao tsung-ping*) and placed under Ch'en's authority.[17] (*Wu-ts'ao*, literally "black junk," was a generic term for Vietnamese pirate junks.) According to Ch'en's adopted son, Chang Kuan-hsing, all the pirate groups in Vietnam came under Ch'en's control at this time.[18]

Ch'en T'ien-pao himself led the advance on the coast of Khanh Hoa province in July 1797. The Nguyen countered by spreading their soldiers along the shore, using their junks to surround one of the harbors, and launching an attack from both land and sea during which they killed many of the enemy. In 1798 Chinese pirate junks were again in evidence off the coast of Khanh Hoa. When the commander of the nearby garrison at Dinh Khanh heard of their presence, he set out in pursuit and seized two of their junks.[19]

In 1799 the fighting centered around Qui Nhon, which Chinese pirates once more tried to defend. The first phase of the campaign took place in Hue, where an advance guard of Nguyen infantry, artillery, and elephants, under the command of General Tong Phuc Luong, were met by Fan Wen-ts'ai (who by this time was also a "general"). The battle was fierce, but in the end Fan's forces proved no match for the Nguyen. The successful Tong Phuc Luong then returned to Qui Nhon, where he and Nguyen Phuc Anh forced their way into the port over the opposition of the pirates. These two defeats, combined with the earlier setbacks at Khanh Hoa, considerably weakened the power of the pirates and led to numerous defections.[20]

The worst defeat was yet to come. In July the Nguyen forces, after gaining the approach to the citadel, conquered Qui Nhon, which they renamed Binh Dinh. There they remained until November 1799, when the death of Nguyen Phuc Anh's longtime military adviser, the bishop of Adran, Pigneau de Behaine, forced them to send their main forces back south. A fleet under Brigade-General Vo Tanh was left to defend its port, Thi Nai, from the pirates.[21]

Unresigned to defeat, the Tay-son reopened the struggle for Qui Nhon (Binh Dinh) early the next year by dispatching a huge fleet to Thi Nai. There is little information concerning its origin, but most of the vessels seem to have come from the pirates, for the Liang-kuang Governor-general reported that more than 100 pirate junks from Kwangtung were then in Vietnam.[22] To meet this challenge, Nguyen Phuc Anh assembled a force of some 1,200 vessels and 80,000 men. With four European ships, 40 large war junks, and over 300 galleys, it was the most formidable navy ever seen in the region.[23] The Tay-son laid siege to Qui Nhon for nearly a year. Although they never managed to retake the city itself, they succeeded in capturing the nearby town of Phu Yen and, as a result, were able to establish 48 fortified posts and recruit men from the area. Their control of Phu Yen was only brief, however. Thanks to treason on the part of a former Tay-son official, the town was soon lost again to the Nguyen.

As a part of this Tay-son thrust, 12 Chinese pirate junks were sent south to invade Yen Cuong Uc (Cloud and Water Bay; also known as Van Phong or Hon Khoi), but their mission was aborted when Nguyen troops prevented them from landing. In July the pirates seized a number of merchant vessels and salt junks, including a boat carrying Nguyen ammunition and supplies. When news of these incidents reached Nguyen Phuc Anh, he immediately ordered Nguyen Van Truong and his fleet of 50 vessels to set out in pursuit. A few months later 11 pirate junks, blown to sea by a storm, were destroyed by gunboats.[24]

Chinese Attempts at Suppression

Participation in the *campagnes de saison* was only one of the pirates' services to the Tay-son. Of equal importance were their raids into China to procure revenue in the form of booty. These had been crucial to the Tay-son from the very start of the rebellion. It was for this reason that the Quang Trung Emperor provided pirate leaders with junks and weapons, authorized them to confer military ranks and titles in their enlistment campaigns, and legitimized their operations with a series of passes, permits, and seals. After conducting activities in the Middle Kingdom, the pirates returned to Vietnam and surrendered their prizes to the Emperor. In return they received a safe harbor and a percentage of the profits.

Two descriptions of this system have been preserved in the Chinese sources. The first is an eyewitness account of two former pirates, Ch'en Kang and Ts'ai Shih-chüeh, who surrendered to the Chinese government and joined the army. According to them, when Nguyen Van Hue, the future Quang Trung Emperor, was plotting against the Le, the agents he relied on most were the pirate leaders Mo Kuan-fu and Cheng Ch'i. He gave them titles, vessels, and weapons, and addressed them as *ts'ao-chang* (junk captains). Each year they and other pirate leaders called together their gangs in the third or fourth lunar month and went east to plunder in China until the ninth or tenth month, when they returned to Vietnam. To the petty pirates of Kwangtung, Fukien, Chekiang, and Kiangsu, Nguyen Van Hue was the "Big Boss of Yüeh-nan" (Yüeh-nan ta-lao-pan), who sold their booty and gave them between 20 and 40 percent of the profits. The big pirate gangs also benefited from the Emperor's rule, because he not only allowed them to anchor in the border area to gather recruits and steal food, but also let them use Vietnam as a "nest" to which they could retreat. These pirates accepted the Emperor as their master because under his authority they were able to reap great profits from the sea.[25]

The second account was written by Wei Yüan, a noted Chinese historian and geographer of the mid-nineteenth century. According to him, after Nguyen Van Hue usurped the throne, both his soldiers and his funds were soon exhausted. He therefore recruited the "scum of the coast" and gave them vessels and official rank. To help pay the recruits' wages, he ordered them to rob merchant junks in China. The pirates usually arrived in Kwangtung during the summer and returned to Vietnam during the fall, but their exact comings and goings were not fixed. They caused great harm in Kwangtung and from there penetrated deeply into Fukien and Chekiang provinces, where they collaborated with the local bandits (*t'u-tao*).[26]

As the pirates' military performance in Vietnam faltered, their success in raiding China grew. Strike after strike brought forth rich cargoes of badly needed commodities. They were able to get away with such conduct largely because the height of their Vietnamese sponsorship came at a time when the Ch'ing government's ability to deal with them was at a low. Just as the changing balance of power resulting from the Tay-son Rebellion caused piracy to escalate on the Vietnamese side of the border, so a succession of domestic upheavals in China allowed it to flourish there as well.

The first of these upheavals occurred in early 1795, when Miao tribes living in the mountainous border regions of Kweichow, Hupeh, and Szechwan provinces rebelled. They seized several small towns, drove out the local officials, and murdered a number of Chinese. Fu-k'ang-an, the governor-general of Yunnan and Kweichow, was sent to quell the disturbance, and the ensuing campaign lasted several years.[27]

With even more serious consequences, a dissident group called the White Lotus Society (Pai-lien-chiao) rose up in late 1795, and within a few months had set off a rebellion that spread from Hupeh to Honan and Szechwan. This rebellion lasted more than nine years and before it ended, encompassed parts of Shensi province, as well as Honan and Szechwan.[28] Farther to the south an uprising of the Triad Society in Po-lo county, Kwangtung, kept provincial authorities occupied for several months in 1802.[29]

What looks like indifference to the similarly disruptive activities on the south coast is not difficult to explain. In fact the Manchus, especially in light of their experiences in attempting to pacify non-Han regions in the seventeenth century, regarded the coastal region as an area where disturbances might erupt at any time. But they were even more sensitive to land-based uprisings that might threaten the capital. Predictably, then, the Ch'ing court responded with far more concern to the possible spread of dissident movements like the White Lotus Society than to the pirates in Kwangtung, who seemed far removed from the lifelines of Peking.

The following exchange between Liang-kuang Governor-general Chi-ch'ing and the Chia-ch'ing Emperor illustrates Peking's priorities.[30] In 1800 Chi-ch'ing, charged with the responsibility of combating pirates in Kwangtung, wrote the Emperor seeking permission to use 216,000 taels from uncommitted salt revenues to build 80 war junks and pointed out that the authorities in Kwangtung could then muster only 80 vessels for the defense of the province. The Emperor's response to a project of such dimensions was a resounding "No." Because Kwangtung already possessed what seemed to him a large number of vessels, he allowed Chi-ch'ing to use no more than 86,000 taels to construct 28 additional craft. Worse still, from Chi-ch'ing's point of view, the Emperor reminded him of the heavy cost of suppressing insurrection in Szechwan, Hupeh, and Shensi provinces and ordered him to hand over the rest of Kwangtung's surplus revenues, hence the bulk of its potential pirate-suppression fund, for use in the southwest.[31] Thus, as new sectarian, minority, and secret-society movements emerged to challenge the political order in the Chinese heartland, pirates along the coast were able to exploit the political vacuum to their own advantage.

The government's dilatory response was fed by another consideration as well: the delicate nature of Sino-Vietnamese relations. Although it was clear to the Chinese that the source of the pirate problem lay in Vietnam, they were extremely reluctant to solicit Tay-son cooperation against them. Indeed, sensitivity to the international situation and fear of the Vietnamese had circumscribed their actions since the defeat of their expedition to save the Le Emperor in 1789. This situation was, in part, a result of the special relationship between the two countries; except for certain periods, Vietnam had been a tributary vassal of China since the tenth century.

To be sure, by the time of the Tay-son Rebellion, China's relationships with its vassal states had become largely ritualistic, a matter of the tributaries honoring China by sending missions, requesting the investiture of their Kings, and adopting the Chinese calendar.[32] Nevertheless, this made the situation with the Tay-son particularly delicate, for the pirates—China's enemies—not only were being protected by the vassal kingdom of Vietnam, but were also officially serving in its navy.

Under the circumstances, Ch'ing officials were reluctant to request Vietnamese assistance in handling the pirates and even considered communicating with the Tay-son a last resort.[33] But their reluctance seems to have been owing at least as much to a fear of provoking a conflict or perhaps even a war with the Tay-son. Memories of 1789 were still vivid, and they now had reason to be wary of Vietnamese irredentism, for there is evidence to suggest that Quang Trung wished to reconstitute the ancient kingdom of Bach Viet or "Hundred Yüeh," which before 221 B.C. had encompassed the Red River to Chekiang province, and was in the process of constructing a fleet for this purpose at the time of his death.

But by 1796 Chinese officials could no longer shut their eyes to piracy. In Vietnam a lull in the fighting allowed the Tay-son to deploy their "navy" across the border; or, in the words of one participant, "The black junks [*wu-ts'ao*] were sent out to rob."[34] The increasing evidence of seals and certificates on captured pirates documenting Tay-son sponsorship finally goaded the Chinese into action.[35] The arrest of Lo A-i, a Chinese from Fukien who was dressed like a Vietnamese (barbarian) and who had in his possession three such seals, provided the immediate catalyst.[36] The evidence for Vietnamese inducements to Chinese pirates was irrefutable. Deciding that it was time to take a stand, the Chinese Emperor ordered the Grand Council to draft an edict pointing out that pirates were ravaging Kwangtung, Fukien, and Chekiang provinces as a result of the Vietnamese government's unwillingness to restrain them. The Emperor announced that henceforth any Vietnamese pirate arrested in China would be immediately executed and instructed the council to seek Vietnamese assistance in destroying the pirates' places of assembly.[37]

The Tay-son obliged by launching an attack on the pirates and, during the course of several encounters, captured 63 of them. At the same time they commissioned a naval officer to destroy their lair at Chiang-p'ing. After burning more than 100 residences, he left behind a mop-up contingent of four junks and 200 soldiers. As a consequence, by the time a Chinese tour of inspection reached the border on April 10, 1797, to meet with a Tay-son representative, he could inform its members that the Vietnamese Emperor, influenced by the moral power of China, had already ordered his subordinates to attack the pirates. Satisfied, the Chinese inspectors held a feast for the Tay-son and rewarded them with 1,000 strings of *cash*, 30,000 catties of rice, and an assortment of silks, writing tablets, cattle, pigs, and sheep. The 63 pirate-captives, along with their junks, weapons, and banners were handed over to the Chinese. By June the team was back in Canton, captives in tow. There they were interrogated by the governor-general, who had been instructed to forward all important leaders to Peking. As it turned out, however, the pirates were all small-timers from Fukien, who were dealt with on the spot.[38]

This endeavor can be regarded as little more than a token display of Vietnamese cooperation. The formal and ceremonial relationship between the two countries in no way inhibited the Tay-son from simultaneously pursuing other policies (such as sponsoring Chinese pirates) in their own interest, even at the risk of antagonizing China.[39] In any event the effects of the Tay-son raid at Chiang-p'ing were short-lived. Within a matter of weeks the pirates had moved into new quarters and resumed their operations. If anything, piracy flourished even more than before. The most powerful leaders, Ch'en T'ien-pao, Cheng Ch'i, and Mo Kuan-fu were left untouched, their gangs intact.

Scarcely two months after the raid Chinese officials reported that the Tay-son were once again employing pirates to fight on their behalf. The first to do so was the Liang-kuang Governor-general, who sent a memorial to the throne on July 1, 1797, complaining that despite the campaign, the most formidable pirates remained in Vietnam, gathering in Chiang-p'ing and allying themselves with coastal inhabitants.[40] Further confirmation of the mission's failure came a few weeks later, when the provincial commander-in-chief, Sun Ch'üan-mou, was dispatched with a squadron of gunboats to cruise near Chiang-p'ing. Reporting from the border, Sun affirmed that the pirates had not really scattered, and that their most powerful leaders were still at large.[41]

At this point the Emperor decided on a new course of action. Overriding his officials' preference for "sea defense" (*hai-fang*), he called instead for "sea war" (*hai-chan*) and launched a vigorous extermination campaign from the Chinese side of the border.[42] This policy, predicated on the assumption that repeated examples of Ch'ing severity would ultimately dissuade pirates from entering the country, called for vigorous borderland offensives and head-on confrontations at sea. Chinese military officials were prohibited from pursuing the pirates into Vietnam but were admonished to destroy them as soon as they sailed into Chinese waters. Once apprehended in China, pirates were to be dealt with swiftly. Those from Vietnam were to be imprisoned

and executed, not repatriated, and Chinese who had disguised themselves as Vietnamese were to be treated as rebels and sentenced to
death by slicing (an excruciating punishment reserved for traitors and
other serious offenders). Native Chinese who had received investiture
from the Vietnamese were also to be considered rebels and put to
death by slicing.[43]

According to the Emperor, pirate cases were too serious for the
punishment to be delayed by lengthy legal proceedings or by sending
each offender to Peking. On arrest, pirates were to be interrogated,
tried, and summarily executed before they had a chance to escape or
cause trouble of any kind. It became the standard procedure that
after investigating a case and interrogating the offenders, the gover-
nors-general and other concerned provincial officials would report
their findings to the Emperor and simultaneously invoke the power of
royal authority (*wang-ming*) that allowed them to carry out executions
without awaiting instructions from either the Court of Revision or the
Son of Heaven. But important ringleaders, as always, were sent on at
once to Peking.[44]

To execute the new sea-war policy, squadrons of gunboats led by
such experienced combatants as Brigade-general (*tsung-ping*) Huang
Piao and Lin Kuo-liang, Colonel (*fu-chiang*) Ch'ien Meng-hu, and
First Captains (*tu-szu*) Wei Ta-pin, Ho Ying, and Hsü T'ing-kuei were
repeatedly sent out on attack missions. But in the end they accomplished little, for piracy continued unchecked in both China and Vietnam. The pirates' strength and bravado had much to do with this lack
of success. Despairing officials increasingly complained that soldiers,
afraid of the pirates, refrained from arresting them. If, during a patrol or inspection, one or two gunboats suddenly encountered several
pirate junks sailing together, the soldiers would simply fire their cannon as a way of warning the pirates to make their escape.[45]

By 1799 the pirates had so successfully withstood all attempts to destroy them that provincial officials called for the replacement of extermination (*chiao-fu*) with a policy of pardon and pacification (*chao-an*,
chao-fu), historically used by the Chinese in suppressing rebellions.[46]
Pacification and pardon centered on weakening a dissident movement
by creating divisions within its ranks, pitting troublemaker against
troublemaker instead of troublemaker against soldier, and isolating
leaders from their followers. A favored method was to allow the followers, but not the leaders of a movement, to surrender to the authorities without penalty. On occasion, however, followers were required
to demonstrate their "sincerity" by presenting government officials
with the heads of their former leaders.[47]

The use of "pacification" with regard to the pirates had first been suggested by Governor-general Ch'ang-lin. On assuming office in 1794, he had proposed amnesty for pirate-captives who contrived to escape and turn themselves in. He further suggested giving rewards of silver taels to those who were able to capture other pirates or could point out their gathering places. Objections to the proposal were immediately raised by Grand Secretary A-kuei, who contended that, far from curbing piracy, this program would encourage it by allowing officials to become lax and thus leading to new disturbances. Condemned as a "worthless" policy, pacification was not tried at that time.[48] However, by 1799, in the face of decreasing military effectiveness, Ch'ing officials had little choice but to turn to this ancient expedient and to proclaim a general amnesty for those who would willingly "return to allegiance."

As it worked out in practice, each pirate who turned himself in was examined to determine the sincerity of his intentions. If his case was convincing, he was then given the option of joining the army, being returned to his village in the custody of a relative, or being settled farther inland. He was also awarded ten taels of silver to give him a fresh start in life.

As an inducement to turn informer, pirate leaders who agreed to enter the army were often commissioned sergeants (*e-wai wai-wei*), ensigns (*wai-wei ch'ien-tsung*), or sublieutenants (*pa-tsung*), and given the appropriate buttons of rank. Ordinary "reformed" pirates were often enrolled in the army and sent to battalions far from the coast, where it was hoped that under strict discipline they would not again cause trouble. To demonstrate their sincerity, those who intended to surrender were encouraged to capture or kill members of their former gangs; on presenting dismembered ears or heads at the time of surrender, they were rewarded with money or rank. Former pirates were warned that they could not again expect such leniency from the state, and that on the slightest future provocation they would be severely punished. In accord with the new policy, native Vietnamese were now to be repatriated at once.[49]

But Ch'ing expectations were shattered again, for pirates were increasingly able to manipulate the new policy to their own advantage. In the end the procedure became little more than a racket through which the more enterprising of them enriched themselves at the expense of the state. One of the favorite methods of exploiting the process was to surrender more than once to government officials.[50] Before long, even pirate leaders themselves were capitalizing on pacification as an opportunity to procure official rank, and by 1800 so many pirates were surrendering that it was becoming difficult to settle them in widely scattered places.[51] Although more than 1,700 pirates turned themselves in, the policy seems to have had little effect in reducing their total numbers, because on July 16, 1800, a disappointed Emperor grudgingly admitted that piracy in Kwangtung was still increasing.[52]

Ultimately, it was not policies in China but the military situation in Vietnam that substantially altered the pirates' circumstances. Their fate was inextricably tied to that of the Tay-son, and by 1800 the tide of battle was slowly turning against pirate and patron alike. For the first time Nguyen Phuc Anh, instead of returning to the south, remained at Qui Nhon, then under siege. After nearly a year with no decisive results, he chose to shift his attack to Hue. First, however, he had to destroy the Tay-son navy at Thi Nai. The result was a very costly battle on February 21, 1801. According to a French participant, J. B. Chaigneau, "the campaign was the bloodiest that the Cochin Chinese had ever known."[53] The Tay-son took heavy casualties, losing some 50,000 men, most of their fleet, and 6,000 cannon, and the pirates were devastated when three of their most formidable leaders— Mo Kuan-fu, Fan Wen-ts'ai, and Liang Wen-keng—were captured.[54]

With the emasculation of the Tay-son navy and the reduction of its pirate supporters, Nguyen Phuc Anh was able to unleash a northern advance that eventually gave him control of most of the country. On June 5, 1801, his junks left Qui Nhon, and ten days later he took Hue. The young Tay-son Emperor Quang Toan fled to Hanoi, leaving behind the seals and brevets of his Chinese investiture. Hard on his heels in flight were the pirates who had been seeking shelter in the coves along the coast. A few weeks later, in early July, 50 junks suddenly appeared in Kwangtung, where Ch'ing officials surmised that the defeat, in leaving the pirates without a safe harbor, had caused them to sneak back into China.[55]

In Hanoi the Tay-son Emperor began making plans to assemble another fleet and retake Hue. By this time, however, the Chinese pirates' enthusiasm for fighting in a losing cause had waned. Cheng Ch'i showed little interest in returning to Vietnam, but persuaded to do so by Ch'en T'ien-pao, he arrived in Hanoi early in 1802. Somewhat reluctantly, he presented his fleet of 200 junks to the Tay-son and received the rank of "Master of the Horses" (Dai Ty Ma; Ta-szu-ma).[56] In the meantime, the man who had secured his services, Ch'en T'ien-pao, had opted out of the fighting by surrendering, along with his family and 30 followers, to the Chinese authorities in late November 1801.[57]

Soon after Cheng Chi's arrival, the Tay-son Emperor launched his campaign. Dividing his army into two wings, he dispatched one to Tran Ninh and the other to Dau Mau and then sent his navy to the mouth of the Spirit (Gianh) River. More than 100 pirates were deployed at Nhat Le, a port near Dong Hoi. The Nguyen took command at Dong Hoi and engaged the pirates in battle on February 3, 1802. A sudden northeast wind enabled the Nguyen to capture more than 20 enemy vessels, and once more the campaign ended in disaster for the pirates, who fled to Tien Coc in Quang Binh province, only to be attacked again.

By this time the Tay-son were nearly finished. Their final battle occurred at Hanoi in 1802, and once again Chinese pirates were at their side. For this encounter approximately 40 of Cheng Ch'i's junks were recruited to guard the port, but this measure was of no avail. The denouement was swift and sudden: the Nguyen forces attacked Hanoi on July 13; the Nguyen navy reached Son Nam on July 16; and a victorious Nguyen Phuc Anh entered Hanoi on July 20.[58] His vanquished foe, the Emperor Quang Toan, was captured, imprisoned, and paraded through the city in a cage. With this action, the rebellion that had gripped Vietnam for 30 years came to an end.

When victory had appeared imminent, the triumphant Nguyen Phuc Anh dispatched his first tribute mission to China. His "tribute" included the three pirate leaders Mo Kuan-fu, Liang Wen-keng, and Fan Wen-ts'ai (captured the year before), who were sent to serve as living proof that a new era had dawned and that the presence of Chinese pirates would no longer be tolerated in Vietnam.[59] Now, as the Gia-long Emperor, one of his first acts was to attack the pirate strongholds in An Quang province. Six weeks later his officials dealt the pirates yet another stunning blow by capturing and beheading their most formidable leader, Cheng Ch'i, and destroying the base at Chiang-p'ing. The result was an immediate exodus of survivors across the border into China and a temporary lull as the pirates regrouped.*

The Development
of Piracy Under Tay-son Sponsorship

Despite the ultimate failure of the rebellion and the pirates' endeavors on its behalf, Tay-son sponsorship was a great boon to piracy. Viet-

---

*Although the defeat of the Tay-son put an end to the major pirate activity in Vietnam, it by no means curbed it completely, for each year between 1803 and 1808 Chinese pirates either continued to prey on ships along the coast of Vietnam or joined remnants of the former Le and Tay-son ruling houses in instigating domestic uprisings.

namese ships, with masts more than 80 feet tall and sides protected by layers of ox-hides and nets, were larger and sturdier than any pirates could obtain on their own. With cannon weighing up to 4,000 catties, they were also much better armed. But perhaps most important of all was the asylum they obtained from the Tay-son. Safe headquarters and protected bases of operation allowed piracy to flourish in both Vietnam and China.

No longer forced to expend so much energy on survival, the pirates could now turn some of their attention to organization, for once some of them received official sanction to recruit gangs and plunder at will, it was not long before their gangs expanded and new leaders emerged. For the most part these were ambitious and ruthless men whose services were deliberately cultivated by Tay-son officials. Unsurprisingly, many of them, like their predecessors at Chiang-p'ing, formed their groups on the basis of kinship and family ties. For example, Cheng Ch'i, as the most prominent offspring of a family that had engaged in piracy for more than a century, had a number of kinsmen who, though not pirates themselves, stood ready to help him. Among the most interesting was his nephew Chang Lien-k'o, who posed as a fish seller while spying out potential victims.[60]

But pirate gangs eventually grew so big that even the largest families could not staff them entirely. At that point patron-client relations became the means by which nonrelated newcomers were incorporated into the group.

Ties of native place frequently served as the foundation on which close patron-client relationships were built. One pirate who used this strategy to his advantage was the "Pirate King," Mo Kuan-fu, of Sui-ch'i, Kwangtung. When, in 1794, Mo and three friends from Sui-ch'i decided to become pirates, they set off at once to round up accomplices from their home town.[61] Mo managed to recruit seven acquaintances and his companions rounded up eight. Two days later the gang of 19 set out.

A more personalized form of patron-client relationship was established through fictive kinship. It was not uncommon for pirate leaders to adopt young gang members as sons. Such was the case with Chang Kuan-hsing, who joined Ch'en T'ien-pao's gang in 1789. As time went on, Ch'en grew fond of Chang and adopted him.[62] On other occasions pirates tried to reinforce professional ties with familial ones by presenting their subordinates with wives. In 1789 Li Ya-hsing joined the gang of Mo Kuan-fu, who subsequently put him in command of a stolen junk and gave him as a bride the captive Miss Kuo. Similarly, in 1795 Cheng Ch'i captured Ho Sung, a lad of 19, whom he first adopted and then appointed as his adjutant (*hsien-feng*). Later, when he was in need of Ho's help in Fukien, Cheng Ch'i entrusted him with 7,000 taels of silver to garner support there and presented him with a female captive to wed.[63]

Patron-client alliances between people of unequal status and resources remained operative only so long as the two parties had something to offer one another and only so long as the patron or leader could satisfy his clients' demand for remuneration. In the pirates' case direct personal contact between leaders and followers was of crucial importance in maintaining these relationships.[64]

When the demand for recruits outstripped the number that could be procured as volunteers, pirate leaders often rounded out their gangs with captives. Many of these were either induced or forced to join the pirate "family" by means of sexual assaults. We have already seen this in the case of the pirate Ch'en A-ch'ang who, on capturing Li Sheng-k'o, forced him to engage in sodomy. Another pirate leader, Ch'en A-hsia, sexually assaulted the fisherman I A-yu; and still another, Ya-tsung, brought three male captives into piracy by this means.[65] Pirate leaders also made catamites of handsome boys, like the youthful captive Su Ya-pao, who caught the eye of Ch'en Ya-t'ien.[66]

It is difficult to say to what degree pirate leaders forced homosexuality on others as a means of initiating them into a gang, and to what degree it was freely engaged in by the two participants. One must bear in mind that the information on this practice comes from the testimony of men on trial for piracy, and that under Ch'ing law the punishment for homosexuality was 100 blows of the bamboo (but in fact only 40 blows) plus three years of penal servitude (*t'u*), whereas the punishment for piracy was beheading. During a trial a man would obviously have improved his chances by contending that he had been forcibly raped and detained against his will instead of confessing that he had become a pirate voluntarily. In any event homosexuality seems to have been a frequent practice in pirate gangs. Twenty-two memorials submitted from Kwangtung between 1796 and 1800 cite 50 instances of such conduct.[67]

Pirate leaders also used gifts of money and weapons to induce recruits to join them. One observer reported that pirates gave the young men along the coast "silver to support their homes" (*an-chia-yin*) and in this way lured them to the sea. In 1797 Boss Mai Ying-pu paid Liu Ya-chiu four *yüan* of foreign silver to join him, and Li Ya-ch'i paid Fu Pang-ching three *yüan*. Mo Kuan-fu tried unsuccessfully to recruit his younger brother with the promise of 100 *yüan* of foreign silver.[68] It was through such gifts that followers of Lin Shuang-wen, whose rebellion on Taiwan was suppressed in the spring of 1788, were incorporated into the pirate organizations after they fled to Vietnam.[69] The association with the Tay-son gave pirate leaders other means of incorporating outsiders into their organizations. The ability to confer status through the granting of titles that were recognized by the government was an important recruiting tool, and one that greatly aided the progress of piracy throughout the water world. The practice began in a small way, with Ch'en T'ien-pao.

As *primus inter pares* among the pirate leaders, he was empowered to recruit other leaders, and in the manner already described, induced Liang Wen-keng, Fan Wen-ts'ai, Mo Kuan-fu, and Cheng Ch'i to join the Tay-son. By the 1790's would-be pirate leaders were approaching Ch'en on their own, seeking his authorization to form gangs. Aspiring pirate leaders used such authorization to gain legitimacy for themselves and recognition for their organizations. To cite one case, in March 1796, four men who were working as hired laborers at Chiang-p'ing approached Ch'en, who gave them a "barbarian permit" (*i-chao*) that enabled them to become leaders, build junks, and recruit accomplices. The following month they set out with 109 men and eight junks.[70] Similarly, when Feng Ya-szu, a native of Wu-ch'uan county, Kwangtung, who fished at Chiang-p'ing, wanted to become a pirate, he went to Ch'en T'ien-pao and was given two documents that allowed him to join the leader Fan Kuang-shan.[71]

Just as the Tay-son later expanded this practice and more and more often bestowed titles, ranks, and "operating licenses" on their most trusted collaborators, so pirate leaders began to follow their lead by presenting their subordinates with documents of accreditation. Lucky recipients gained increased prestige for themselves and official sanction for the organizations they were forming. For example, Mo Kuan-fu, after successfully attacking the Fukienese pirate Huang Sheng-chang and killing 600 of his men, was invested by the Tay-son with the title "King of the Eastern Seas" (Dong Hoi Vuong; Tung-hai-wang).[72] This apparently carried with it the authority to confer titles on subordinates, because when Chang Ya-liu and ten of his friends were captured by Mo and agreed to join forces with him, Mo first commissioned Chang as a "head man," or captain (*t'ou-mu*), and later as a "boss" (*lao-pan*).[73]

Consequently, one result of Tay-son sponsorship was a pirate gang of substantially greater complexity. Whereas earlier gangs had been mobilized for the purposes of temporary predation on a "one leader, one gang" basis, the most able pirate heads (*tao-shou* or *ta-tao-shou*) now began to secure control over lesser chiefs (or captains, *t'ou-mu*)

CHENG CH'I

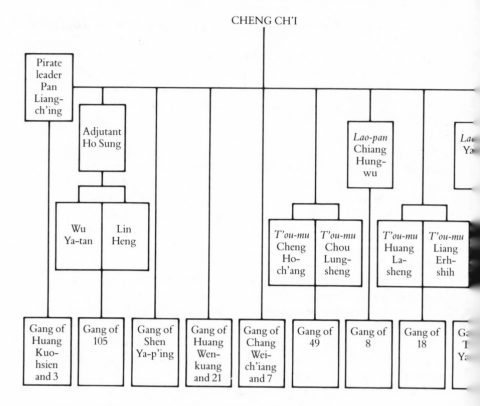

Fig. 1. The structure of Cheng Ch'i's pirate association, ca. 1800

and bosses (or boat owners, *lao-pan*), who then recruited bands of their own.

Among the most successful of these new organization builders was the pirate leader Cheng Ch'i. As early as 1795 he and his associates Huang Ta-hsing and Ch'en Ch'ang-fa had formed a gang that operated out of Chiang-p'ing and was active in both Vietnam and Kwangtung.[74] From there he reached out in several directions, until at his peak he had at least nine different groups under his command. His colleague Mo Kuan-fu was equally successful, building a force of 17 junks and 1,000 men by 1796.

Still, Cheng Chi's organization, diagrammed in Figure 1, was composed of discrete units, each of them linked directly to him through bonds of personal loyalty. Such units in turn tended to be vertically organized, with authority flowing from the top down and loyalty from the bottom up. Horizontal bonds linking groups for cooperative ventures were tenuous and poorly developed. Each group interacted with its leader on a one-to-one basis, and there was little attempt to join what were still essentially independent gangs into more sophisticated, laterally cohesive units. At this stage pirate gangs, however large, still bore a close resemblance to the small gangs from which they derived.

Holding these associations together required knowledgeable, charismatic leaders capable of retaining followers. Because the ties binding leader and follower were based on direct personal alliances, and group cohesiveness emanated from the top, a major preoccupation of every leader was securing loyalty through the creation of personal relationships, or what the Chinese called *kuan-hsi.*

Under Tay-son sponsorship, moreover, these leaders were able to make contact with one another and became accustomed to cooperating in joint ventures. In September 1801, for example, the enterprising Cheng Ch'i and Mo Kuan-fu joined forces to launch a surprise attack on a fort in Wu-ch'uan county, which almost resulted in its capitulation. The sublieutenant (*pa-tsung*) in charge of its defense carried cannon down to the beach, constructed a fortification, and made a stand against the pirates. Although his soldiers wanted to run, they withstood the most critical advance of the pirates, who finally withdrew. Angry but undaunted, the pirates then disguised themselves as villagers and crept up on the fort from behind. In the ensuing battle, they killed the sublieutenant and desecrated his corpse.[75]

Two days later Cheng Ch'i joined forces with three other leaders, Wu-shih Erh, Cheng I, and Mo Kuan-fu, to seize an entire fleet of 18 salt junks from the Shui-tung Harbor in Tien-pai district, Kwangtung. Similarly, in December 1801 a force of 30 junks under the command of Cheng Ch'i and other pirate leaders blocked the port of Shan-mei in Hai-feng county. After overcoming the resistance of the salt commissioner's hired braves,* they too seized 18 salt junks, along with the five fishing vessels accompanying them.[76]

Tay-son sponsorship dramatically upgraded the combat skills of pirates who participated in battle. There they gained valuable experience in confronting an enemy head-on, developed a degree of discipline, and learned how to wield weapons and make stands at sea.[77] No longer were they smash-and-grab outlaws. Tay-son sponsorship created pirates with plans, pirates who had learned to join forces and to

---

*Braves (*hsiang-yung*) were small, ad hoc companies of mercenaries mustered to meet local emergencies. They were usually hired by district magistrates, though in imes of great duress they might also be hired by local gentry. The employment of such units was most often resorted to only when regular forces proved unable to handle a given situation or crisis.

sail each spring from Kwangtung and return each autumn to Vietnam. Further, now working on a more or less fixed scheduled, they
were able to cooperate with bandits on the shore as well. As the Ch'ing
official Wei Yüan later complained, "When we fight the pirates, then
the local bandits recklessly rob; and when we fight the local bandits,
the pirates assist them."[78]

Perhaps the biggest boon of all was that, in creating privateers, the
Tay-son legitimized piracy and thus radically transformed the standing of its underworld practitioners, elevating them from "scum of the
sea" to "sailors in a King's navy." Suddenly the most flagrant depredations, because they were conducted on behalf of the Vietnamese Emperor, became the legitimate undertakings of a sovereign state. As a
result piracy now attracted others from the water world, people who
saw it as a way of advancing themselves not only economically, but also
in status, power, and prestige. For most of those who became pirates,
entry into the upper reaches of society was beyond the realm of possibility; they could expect to live out their lives as social "nobodies," vulnerable to the demands and exploitation of superiors. But within pirate brotherhoods this underclass had a chance at social mobility.
Through their own efforts and military prowess, they could become
"somebodies." They could receive rank, honor, and recognition, and
attain the prestige denied them onshore.[79]

For this reason the conferring of titles was an integral part of the
Tay-son's appeal to pirate recruits. From the Tay-son point of view it
was appealing as an inexpensive way to reward performance. It may
also have served as a way to designate which pirates could operate
where, as suggested by the inscription on the seal Lo Ya-san received,
which read "Control and Defend Cassia Bark Mountain" (Quan Thu
Que Bi Son; Kuan-shou kuei-p'i shan).[80] Recall also that Ch'en T'ien-
pao's title specified that he was the military governor of the Shan-
ts'ao unit.

Tay-son titles seem to have been of two types—those conferring
status and those conferring military rank—and many pirates ended
up holding one of each. Ch'en T'ien-pao was both a military governor
and a marquis, and Mo Kuan-fu both a general and the "King of the
Eastern Seas."

The most frequently granted status-conferring titles were King and
marquis, often with a further gloss. Thus T'an A-chao was the "King
Who Pacifies the Waves" (Binh Ba Vuong; P'ing-po wang), and Liang
Kuei-hsing the "Marquis of Total Virtue."[81] The top military titles were
military governor and master of the horses. Besides brigade-general
(*tong binh; tsung-ping*), other titles of command were generalissimo

(*dai nguyen soai; ta yüan-shuai*), deputy generalissimo (*phuc dai nguyen soai; Fu ta-yüan-shuai*), and deputy leader. Wu-shih Erh was the "Deputy Leader Who Pacifies the Sea" (*Ninh hoi phuc tuong quan; Ning-hai fu-chiang-chün*), and Cheng Liu-t'ang held the title "Military Minister."[82] Liang Wen-keng and Fan Wen-ts'ai joined the Tay-son as lieutenant (*thien tong; ch'ien-tsung*) and commander (*chi huy; chih-hui*), respectively. Individual gangs were led by "heads," "bosses," or "skippers" (*lao-pan*), and there were times when the Tay-son seemed interested in militarizing this rank as well. Recall their attempt to transform pirate *lao-pan* into "black junk generals" (*o tao tong binh; wu-ts'ao tsung-ping*).

Less easy to document is the extent to which pirates were ideologically committed to the Tay-son cause. As the marauders of Chiang-p'ing became the mariners of Tonkin, it is possible that some of them saw the Tay-son goal of conquering South China and reestablishing the former Bach Viet domain as in their own best interest. As we have seen, the first Tay-son Emperor, Quang Trung, seems to have been set on restoring this ancient kingdom and had reportedly begun building "great war junks to transport Vietnamese war elephants to Canton, as the first step toward the necessary reconquest of Kwang-tung and Kwangsi."[83] He is also said to have aided the rebel Triad Society (T'ien-ti hui) in Kwangsi province with this goal in mind.[84] The Emperor died before his elephants could reach Canton, and the reincorporation of South China was in any case no more than a pipedream. But assuming that the plan reached pirate ears at all, it might have provided a rallying cause.

In the absence of diaries or other accounts written by the pirates themselves, it is almost impossible to ascertain their motivation for any undertaking. Yet it does appear that the Tay-son affiliation had the effect of broadening the scope of piracy from a temporary survival strategy to a kind of mobility strategy for the more ambitious of those who were shut out from prestigious careers onshore. For most, the motivation no doubt remained economic as always, but some, particularly those who later became leaders, must also have been attracted by the opportunities for status, and a few may even have been inspired by the chance to fight for an ennobling cause.

In providing an experience on which they could draw to found larger and more complex associations, the Tay-son enabled fishermen-pirates to take a crucial step in their transformation. Although the days of the independent petty pirate were by no means over, by the mid-1790's part-time operators were increasingly being overshadowed by professionals for whom piracy was a full-time career.

Without the uprising in Vietnam, petty pirates would probably have remained little more than "struggling banditti" in the offshore islands. Even Ch'ing officials came to recognize that it was Tay-son sponsorship, more than anything else, that allowed piracy to develop to the scale it reached during the late eighteenth and early nineteenth centuries.[85]

The result was a system of piracy so well established in the water world that not even the defeat of the Tay-son could eliminate it. The pirates were simply too organized to melt inconspicuously back into the society from which they had come. Thus, the defeat of the Tay-son, like their rise, stands as a critical turning point in the evolution of Chinese piracy. For, deprived of asylum in Vietnam, the pirates' only recourse was to return to their homes. Once back across the border in China, their survival as enemies of the state in an increasingly hostile environment would depend almost entirely on their ability to develop new forms of leadership and organization. But in 1802, with the loss of their primary headquarters and three of their most important leaders, their prospects appeared none too good.

4

The Professionalization
of Piracy

In returning to China, pirates who had been more or less allied
under the Tay-son suddenly found themselves engaged in a life-and-
death competition for resources. Within an atmosphere of strife and
disaffection, remnant bands turned on one another and killed each
other in bloody battles that sapped their energies and drained their
resolve. Meanwhile, the national dimension of their endeavor broke
down, as pirates from Kwangtung and Fukien went their separate
ways. Even within Kwangtung, where 12 contenders for leadership
battled among themselves, the likelihood of coordinated action seemed
remote.

In 1805, however, an organizational breakthrough ended the free-
for-all, as leaders from Kwangtung came to see that their best strategy
for survival lay in collaboration instead of confrontation. In July five
of the challengers withdrew from the competition, and the other
seven formed a confederation by signing an agreement (*li-ho-yüeh*) in
which each sacrificed some of his autonomy for the greater good. The
seven signatories were Cheng Wen-hsien, Mai Yu-chin, Wu Chih-
ch'ing, Li Hsiang-ch'ing, Cheng Liu-t'ang, Kuo Hsüeh-hsien, and
Liang Pao. In putting their chop to this document, they perhaps little
realized that they would become the predominant power holders
along the South China coast for the remainder of the decade. Their
contract read as follows:

The seven persons entering into the agreement—Cheng Wen-hsien, Mai Yu-
chin, Wu Chih-ch'ing, Li Hsiang-ch'ing, Cheng Liu-t'ang, Kuo Hsüeh-hsien,
and Liang Pao—have discussed it among themselves and have agreed openly
and publicly to record its provisions [so that there will be no grounds for mis-

understanding]. We know that if orders are not severe, then they are not sufficient to make the masses obey, and that if evil practices are not abolished, then
commercial intercourse cannot take place. We who have agreed to join forces
have now made a list [of regulations] that will set an example to be followed.
Only if each regulation is strictly written down, clearly laid out, and impar-
tially enforced can people be induced to obey.

The physical characteristics of each branch are not uniform; the abilities of
its men are not the same. If not forcefully controlled, people will neglect the
laws. [These physical differences no longer matter now because] we have discussed and set down strict laws, each of which must be obeyed for our own
good. Since we are of one will, it matters not whether our strength is great or
small, we must not cling to internal petty grievances. If there are those who,
from positions of strength, exhibit no compassion for those less able to defend themselves and who would willingly withhold provision from them, their
cases will be investigated and handled by the entire group. But these are
matters that cannot just be discussed. Thus we have drawn up seven documents that must be distributed to the flagship of each branch.

The regulations are as follows:

1. We have agreed that our seagoing vessels, both large and small, will be
arranged in seven branches: T'ien, Ti, Hsüan, Huang, Yü, Chou, and Hung.
Each will be registered according to the regulations. Each fast boat [*k'uai-
ch'uan*] must have its name and registration number inscribed on the side of
the bow and must fly the branch's banner on its foremast. [If there is a junk]
whose bow bears no registration number and whose foremast has a banner of
the wrong color, then the junk and its weapons will be immediately confiscated and distributed in accord with our rules.

2. Each branch has its own banner [and registration number]. If there are
those who fake another branch's flag or color, as soon as the act is discovered,
the junk and its weapons will become the property of the whole group; those
who have not wholeheartedly carried out the law must await punishment
from the whole group.

3. If a fast boat disobeys the regulations and hinders a junk with [one of
our permits] to the point of damaging it, selling its cargo, or robbing it of its
money and clothes, the value of the booty must be estimated and [the injured
party] indemnified. The offending junk's weapons and anchors will be confiscated. In accord with our regulations and the circumstances of the case, we
will decide the punishment. If the booty is of such value that the offender
cannot pay the indemnity himself, then the amount will be deducted from the
branch's future shares.

4. In an attack, a cargo ship will become the property of the junk that
strikes it first. If there are others who seize it from the original captors by
force, they must estimate the value of the booty and indemnify the original
captor with a sum greater than the original value. If there are those who do
not obey, then the entire group will turn against them and attack.

5. No matter which branch's fast boat pulls out [i.e. stops] a junk with a
pass, those who witness the action . . . and come forward to apprehend the

wrongdoer will be rewarded with 100 silver dollars. If, in the process, any of our brothers is wounded, the whole group must be responsible for his medical care. Moreover, the group will measure the merits of his action and decide on a fitting reward. Those who are sitting at the side and see such an event, but do not come forward and take action, will be punished as co-conspirators.

6. If there are [fast boats] that sail without permission to the various oceans and harbors to rob, they, along with all the small boats accompanying them, irrespective of any documents or money in their possession, will be subject to seizure. As soon as a branch's patrol boats capture them, they will be burned, their weapons confiscated, and their bosses [*lao-pan*] executed.

7. If there are merchants on either land or sea who have connections with our enemies and who not only make no effort to cover this fact and hide, but are bold enough to come back and forth to do business, we must restrain our anger and overlook their actions even though we may not be pleased. We cannot use our power as a pretext to seize or persecute them on the grounds that they are townsmen of our enemies. Once these kinds of violations are discovered, they will be handled as crimes of false implication.

8. If [two] flagships meet at sea with something to discuss, they should hoist a flag on their foremast, and the big bosses (*ta-lao-pan*) should come to confer. If a branch leader has an order to transmit to his own fast boats, he should hoist a flag on the third mast, whereupon all junks must assemble and listen to the order. Those who do not assemble will be held in contempt.

Chu-kung has ordered that a copy [of this document] be sent to each flagship so that it can be respectfully obeyed.

Heavenly Circle [T'ien-yün] *Reign, I-ch'ou year, sixth month* [July 1805].
Drawn up by Secretary Wu Shang-te.[1]

The provisions of the agreement, as we see, fall into three broad categories: those regularizing internal procedures, those prescribing members' conduct at sea, and those outlining procedures for business transactions with outsiders. To bring order to the confederation, each vessel was to be registered with one fleet and clearly identified. Because the stability of the confederation would be threatened by individual junks switching affiliation or by fleet leaders encouraging them to do so, anyone caught tampering with the identification process was subject to punishment. Provisions prohibiting pirates from fighting one another for prizes already taken or from undertaking unauthorized activities on their own sought to prevent internal conflict. Because the leaders envisaged that much of their income would come from the sale of protection to other members of water-world society, their ability to extract protection fees depended on all members honoring one another's contracts of sale. Harsh punishment was therefore prescribed for those who even passively allowed breaches to occur. Implicit in the document is the pirates' view of their confederation as an ongoing organization with a future as well as a present;

witness their provision for deferred payments by confederation members who lacked the cash for indemnities or other internal obligations. In reserving for the confederation as a whole the right to distribute confiscated property and punish offenders, the founders created an organization that functioned as a final unit of accounting and an ultimate "court" of arbitration. Although tightly regulated in theory, the confederation proved to be flexible and loosely structured enough to accommodate fluctuations in size and number. Moreover, it made sense organizationally because it represented no radical departure from the existing situation by simply consolidating the seven fleets that were already in place.

The Structure of Command and the Commanders

Shortly after the confederation was founded, Cheng Liu-t'ang surrendered to the state, so in the end it had only six branches. These branches, comprising between 70 and 300 vessels each, were commonly referred to as the Red, Black, White, Green, Blue, and Yellow Flag fleets. The Chinese terms for these units varied, but they were most often called either "great fleets" or "fleets" (*ta-pang* or *pang*).[2] The six fleet leaders retained considerably autonomy. At least five of them (and possibly all six) had fought in Vietnam and been commissioned by the Tay-son. Their followers either referred to them as "branch bosses" (*ta-lao-pan*) or called them by the titles they had received in Vietnam; Westerners usually referred to them as "admirals" or "chiefs of the flag"; and Ch'ing officials used several terms: "great pirate heads" (*ta-tao-shou*), "great heads of the fleet" (*ta-pang-tao-shou*), and "chief pirate heads" (*tsung-tao-shou*).[3]

An entire fleet sailed together for large undertakings, but most activities were carried out by smaller units known as squadrons (*ku* or *ta-ku*). These units were formed out of the independent gangs (*huo*) that had once flourished at Chiang-p'ing and had later constituted the basis for the fleets of the Tay-son. As intermediary units between the fleet command and the individual junks, the squadrons were the major building blocks of the confederation. Consequently, the squadron commander played a crucial role in the chain of command: he appointed all the officers on the junks in his squadron, relayed to them his fleet leader's orders, and was accountable for their conduct. Squadron commanders were referred to by Westerners as "inferior chiefs," by pirates as "great heads" (*ta-t'ou-mu*), and by government officials as "robber heads" (*tao-shou* or *tsei-shou*).[4] The size of the fleets fluctuated constantly over the life of the confederation, so it is impossible to give meaningful figures for the number of squadrons either in the confederation as a whole or in a given fleet. The squadrons themselves comprised from 10 to 40 vessels, but 40 was rare. One of the largest had 36 junks, crewed by 1,422 men and 34 women.[5]

The structure of command at the most basic level varied. Most junks were under a *lao-pan*, who acted as a skipper or boss. Since *lao-pan* had long functioned as commanders of the petty pirate gangs at Chiang-p'ing, it is not surprising that they continued to play an important role in the confederation. *Lao-pan* were often responsible for several ships. They were also assigned to newly captured craft and when their crews were willing to turn to piracy, the *lao-pan* frequently supplied them with weapons and rice.[6]

Each vessel also had a headman (*t'ou-mu* or *t'ou-jen*), who shared responsibility for its management with the *lao-pan*. The men Western captives described as "captains," whose authority was respected by the whole crew, were probably *t'ou-mu*. The *t'ou-mu* was readily distinguishable from the rank and file by his better dress and fare, and it was he who took active command of the ship during combat. If he fell in battle, he was usually replaced by one of the gunners, a man who, like him, was a pirate of deep loyalty and long service to the confederation.[7] Although there was usually only one *t'ou-mu* on a ship, there were occasionally two, three, or even four. These might have special names and assignments, such as *tsung-t'ou-mu* (chief headman), *hsien-feng t'ou-mu* (vanguard headman), and *fu-t'ou-mu* (deputy headman).[8]

The pirate *t'ou-mu*'s status was quite different from that of the *t'ou-mu* on merchant junks, who were merely petty officers in charge of the anchor and sails.[9] On pirate junks, these tasks fell to other people, and the *t'ou-mu* clearly ranked above them. Those appointed as *t'ou-mu* were men who had caught their superior's eye and were deemed capable of handling responsibility. On one occasion the pirate leader Cheng Ch'i asked the two sailors Huang Ya-sheng and Liang Erh-shih to join his gang. When they agreed, he commissioned them as *t'ou-mu* and gave them a crew of 18 and a junk of their own. Similarly, when Lo Yung-hu joined T'ang Jen-szu, he was made a *t'ou-mu* and put in charge of a fast boat. On still another occasion the pirate leader Ya Wu commissioned his two captives, Li Wen-pa and Ch'en Jih-shih, to act as *t'ou-mu* on a newly acquired craft.[10] The *t'ou-mu*, in his capacity as "captain," possessed certain powers of appointment and frequently assigned tasks and rank to other crewmen. As *t'ou-mu*, Li Wen-pa and Ch'en Jih-shih commissioned one member of their crew as the helmsman and three as sailors and handed out specific tasks to all the others on board.[11]

The importance of the *t'ou-mu* as authority figures within the pirate hierarchy is evident from the fact that Ch'ing officials, in their reports to the throne, usually based their accounts upon the confessions of those regarded as principal offenders, and in almost every instance these turned out to be *t'ou-mu*. Their testimony and relevant biographical information were sent to the Emperor, whereas most pirates were given only passing mention.

Next in importance to the *t'ou-mu* were the helmsmen (*to-kung*), who were charged with the general management of the sails as well as steering. There were usually at least two helmsmen on a vessel, and they were experienced hands whose orders were attentively executed by others. Helmsmen were sometimes selected from among the pirates themselves, but were more often hired from the outside as specialists. This practice was so widespread that in late 1804 the Liang-kuang Governor-general complained that all the good helmsmen were leaving the navy because the pirates were luring them away with higher wages.[12]

Under the helmsmen were three or four men called *huo-chang*, who were charged with the deck duties. Each vessel also had from two to four people who manned the cannon, threw the anchors, and burned incense. Pursers, designated by the pirates as "accountants" (*chang-mu*), "fellows of the brush and ink" (*t'ung pi-mo*), or "keepers of the treasury" (*sui-k'u*), kept track of protection contracts and booty. Any remaining crew members were charged with hauling up the sails and sculling.[13]

For an illustration of a typical command structure, we can take the case of the pirate P'eng A-chü. When P'eng established himself as the head (*t'ou-jen*) of a junk, he appointed T'ang Shih-jui, Ch'en A-wei, Lin A-chih, Shen A-szu, and Chu A-erh as his *huo-chang*, placed Ch'en A-erh in charge of the cannon, Ch'en I-ching and Ts'eng Chih-kuang in charge of the foremast, Lin Mou-kuang and Feng Pang-chieh in charge of the anchor, and Lin Mou-kuang and Hsieh Ku-shun in charge of the accounts. The 16 remaining crew members hauled up the sails and manned the oars. The boss (*lao-pan*) Mai Ying-pu organized his junk in a similar manner. Ti Tsai, Liu A-chiu, and Ti Ch'ing served as *t'ou mu*; Wu Ch'eng-ch'üan and Huang Piao manned the anchor; Chung T'ien-chien, Wu Ya-san, and Lin Shan-k'uei oversaw the cannon; Su Shih-mou and Chang Yüan kept the accounts; and Chung Hsiu, Wang Chin-hsin, Ho Lao-chien, and Lin Han-chang managed the sails and burned incense. The remainder of the crew assisted with the sails and anchors.[14]

The ability of the pirates to survive and regroup after their flight from Vietnam is a tribute to their extraordinary leadership. Without leaders capable of seeing beyond the immediate chaos to the possibility of building on the Tay-son experience, the confederation would never have come into being. Adding to the pirates' good fortune was the fact that the confederation's principal founder, Cheng Wen-hsien, better known as Cheng I, was a pirate of both pedigree and prowess.

Few, if any, pirates of whatever place and time have brought more tradition to their trade than Cheng I, whose pirate ancestors dated from the seventeenth century (see Fig. 2). The first member of the family to take up the practice was Cheng Chien, the son of an obscure farmer from Fukien. In 1641 Cheng Chien moved the family from Wu-p'ing to Hai-ch'eng (Fukien), and allied himself with the famous pirate patriot Cheng Ch'eng-kung (Koxinga). After the Manchus overthrew the Ming dynasty, Cheng Chien became an active participant in the Ming Loyalist Movement and appears to have served as an officer in Koxinga's army.* He did not accompany Koxinga in his invasion of Taiwan in 1661, however. Because of a delay in marshaling his troops, he was forced to flee instead to Ta-p'eng (Mirs Bay), Kwangtung, where he settled down as a fisherman and woodcutter. To supplement his income, Cheng began demanding fees of passage from the merchant junks entering the bay.[15]

After Cheng's death in 1671 some of his descendants moved to Hsin-an, where they joined a pirate gang. They defeated the troops of the Chieh-shih Brigade in 1678 and in ensuing years preyed on the coastal trade. By the end of the Yung-cheng period (1723–35), two of Cheng Chien's great-grandsons, Cheng Lien-fu and Cheng Lien-ch'ang, had become the pirate leaders of Hsin-an county. Cheng Lien-ch'ang (1712–75) positioned his stronghold on Devil's Peak in the narrows of Li-yü-men at the eastern end of Hong Kong, where he could keep a lookout on all ships entering the harbor. When, in 1753, he built a Sea Goddess temple, it was no accident that he put it at the most strategic point on the shore, for its real purpose was to serve as the administrative headquarters of his pirate activities.[16]

Meanwhile, his elder brother, Cheng Lien-fu (1706–61), established his base atop Big Chicken Mountain (Ta-chi-shan) on Lantao (Ta-yü-shan), an island 15 miles west of Hong Kong. In siring his seventh son, Cheng Lien-fu assured the family's predominance among the pirates of the late eighteenth century, for this son, Cheng Yao-huang, better

*The Ming Loyalist Movement was the term used to describe the activities of the large number of Chinese who remained in opposition to the Manchu government to the end of the seventeenth century. Throughout China their movements rose and fell in rapid succession.

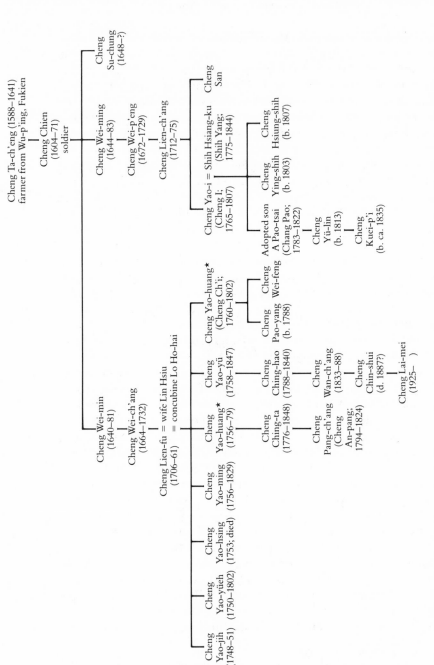

Fig. 2. The Cheng family genealogy. The Chinese characters for the two asterisked names are identical. Cheng I (Cheng Yao-i) was also known as Cheng Wen-hsien. Source: Hsiao Wan-om, "Research in the History of the Pirates on the China

known by his nickname, Cheng Ch'i (Cheng Seven), was none other than the Tay-son-sponsored pirate leader of Chapter Three. At some point Cheng Ch'i moved from Kwangtung to Hanoi, because he was there at the outbreak of the Tay-son Rebellion. By 1786 he was already well launched on his career as a pirate, and in 1788 he joined the Tay-son. For the next 13 years he looked after his own interests as well as those of his sponsors, working to increase his power even as he waged war for the Tay-son.

After his defeat at Qui Nhon in early 1801, Cheng Ch'i fled back to China and took up residence in Kwangtung.[17] There he remained, raiding forts and seizing salt junks until January of the following year, when, at the summons of the Tay-son court, he sailed once more to Vietnam. With a 200-junk armada, he made an all-out attempt to recover Hue. After that mission failed, the Tay-son retained about 40 of his junks for their last-ditch defense of Hanoi. On their defeat, Cheng Ch'i fled to the border, where he was killed during the Gia-long Emperor's attack on Chiang-p'ing. In the ensuing brief interregnum, leadership changed hands several times, until Cheng Chi's cousin Cheng I finally emerged as the man in charge.[18]

Cheng I, the eldest of temple-builder Cheng Lien-ch'ang's seven sons, was five years younger than Cheng Ch'i. Like him, he fought for the Tay-son and returned to China in 1801. His early days back on his native soil are lost to history; we know only that he settled briefly in Tung-hai (a village on the island at the southern end of Kuang-chou Bay) and married the prostitute (*yüeh-chi*) Shih Yang (also known as Shih Hsiang-ku).[19]

Cheng I served as the principal leader of the Kwangtung pirates for five years, nurturing them through the critical period following the Tay-son defeat and ultimately bringing about their unification. His foremost collaborator in this achievement was another Vietnam veteran, Mai Yu-chin, the leader of the Blue Flag Fleet. Mai was more commonly referred to by his nickname Wu-shih Erh, after his place of residence in Wu-shih (Black Stone) village, Hai-k'ang county. Wu became a pirate after having been captured, and early in his career made his living by extorting blackmail in the ports of Kwangtung. After joining the Tay-son, he was first given the title "Vice Admiral Who Pacifies the Seas" (Ning-hai fu-chiang chün) and later made "Great Admiral Who Pacifies the Sea" (Ch'ing-hai ta-chiang-chün).

After the Tay-son defeat at Hue in June 1801, Wu accompanied the Quang Toan Emperor in his flight to Hanoi, where he soon struck up an alliance with Cheng Ch'i to attack the salt fleets at Tien-pai. On Cheng Ch'i's death, Wu-shih Erh continued his association with the family by cooperating with Cheng I and joining him in raids. He rose to become a figure second in importance only to Cheng I and ultimately became the master of the entire Lei-chou Peninsula. At that point he also possessed a fleet of junks that operated in eastern Kwangtung, near the Fukien border. No estimate of his total force has survived, but as early as 1805 he was reportedly in command of 160 junks, equally divided between points east and west.[20]

Fleet leader Wu-shih Erh relied heavily on the assistance of his elder brother, Mai Yu-kuei, also known as Wu-shih Ta (Wu-shih Eldest), and their younger cousin (*t'ang-ti*) Mai Yu-chi, also known as Wu-shih San (Wu-shih Third). One of Wu's principal *t'ou-mu* was Chou T'ien of Jao-p'ing county, whom he captured and recruited in 1807; Wu immediately promoted Chou and entrusted him with 18 junks. Others in his service were Yang P'ien-k'e and Ch'en Ya-kuang, both of Sui-ch'i county; Lung Yüan-teng of Hai-k'ang county; and Cheng Yao-chang (origin unknown), who managed a squadron for him in eastern Kwangtung.[21]

An organization as large as Wu's required record keeping. For this purpose he employed a number of accountants, including Yang Wei-meng and Sung Kuo-hsing, who kept track of the silver, rice, and gunpowder allocated to his subordinates, and P'eng Ch'ao-hsiang, who kept track of his salt junks.[22] Huang Ho, a degree-holder of Hai-k'ang, joined Wu after having been dismissed from office and thereafter served the fleet as counselor, strategist, and spy. Huang also managed Wu's blackmail lists and wrote placards to frighten the country folk into submitting to the pirates' demands. With the aid of these assistants, Wu managed to take in several thousand taels a year. Thanks to a reputation for dealing fairly with villagers and for paying high prices for their goods, he was never wanting for supplies.[23]

Like Wu-shih Erh, the leaders of both the Yellow and the White Flag Fleet had made the acquaintance of Cheng I in Vietnam and had served under Tay-son leadership. Wu Chih-ch'ing, the leader of the Yellow Fleet and a native of Tung-hai village, Kwangtung, was also known as Tung-hai Pa (rendered in the Chinese sources variously as Tung-hai Eight, Tung-hai Uncle, and Tung-hai Scourge). His principal deputy was Li Tsung-ch'ao. The leader of the White Flag Fleet, Liang Pao, had been a Tay-son "general" and was consequently referred to as Tsung-ping Pao. On board his flagship Liang Pao was joined by his father and by his adopted son, Liang Ya-k'ang. His deputies included his captive and willing convert Wen A-ku and his *t'ou-mu* Yeh Ya-wu. Because his own fleet was very small, Liang often sailed with Cheng I.[24]

The leader of the Green Flag Fleet, Li Shang-ch'ing (Li Hsiang-ch'ing), was also an acquaintance of Cheng I's, but whether or not he fought for the Tay-son is unrecorded. Li, who was also known as Chin Ku-yang and sometimes, more colorfully, as Hsia Mo-yang (Son of a Frog), often sailed with Wu-shih Erh.[25]

Kuo Hsüeh-hsien, leader of the Black Flag Fleet, was Kuo P'o-tai to his peers. The son of a Tanka family from P'an-yü, Kuo had been abducted by Cheng I at age 14 and forced to become a pirate. As a favorite of Cheng I's, he rose through the pirate ranks until he commanded his own fleet. He then joined Cheng I in serving the Tay-son and reached a high enough position to be allowed to dispense cannon to his subordinates. At its peak his Black Fleet had more than 100 vessels and 10,000 men. Kuo's major subordinates were Feng Yung-fa, Chang Jih-kao, Kuo Chiu-shan, Wang Ya-san, and Ya-kan. His wife, Cheng Wang-jen, may even have been a relative of Cheng I's. Unlike most of his peers, Kuo P'o-tai was literate, and the hold of his flagship was said to have been filled with books that he read during moments of leisure.[26]

The leader who helped form the confederation, only to drop out, had also become a pirate after having been captured. Cheng Liu-t'ang, also known as Liu T'ang-pai, was a fisherman from Chiang-men, Kwangtung, who had been captured by Cheng I in 1794 and placed in charge of eight junks. For the next ten years he carried out missions at sea, but by 1805 the 50-year-old Cheng had had enough of life at sea. An injury that obliterated half of his face prompted him to "return to allegiance" shortly after he signed the contract establishing the confederation. His 388 followers joined him in his surrender.[27]

As the confederation's principal founder, Cheng I commanded the largest and most powerful unit, the Red Flag Fleet. Cheng's original fleet consisted of 200 junks (with between 20,000 and 40,000 men), but by 1807 he had more than 600 junks operating in the Li-yü-men region of Hong Kong alone. Cheng I's major commanders were Liang P'o-pao, Hsiao Chi-lan (also known as Hsiang-shan Erh), Hsiao Pu-ao, Cheng Kuo-hua, Ch'en Wu, Ya Hsüan Sao, Ch'en Ya-nan, and Ta P'ao-fu.[28]

Cheng I tried to strengthen his position within the confederation by placing his relatives as squadron leaders in the fleets of his colleagues. His younger brother, Cheng San, for example, sailed with Wu-shih Erh. When the supply of male relatives ran short, Cheng I relied on the females to extend the family network. His favorite strategy was to give them to other pirates as wives. In this way his younger sister became the bride of the pirate Chou Ho-sheng.[29] Other fleet and squadron leaders also relied on family members to strengthen their positions.

In the absence of real family ties, Cheng I and his colleagues, like the leaders who preceded them, established fictive kinship relations by adopting younger pirates or by presenting female captives to them as brides. Ties of place also bound their fleets together. Leaders frequently operated in close proximity to their homes and tended to draw a majority of their recruits from these areas.[30]

Through the confederation, the pirates were able to overcome their personal rivalries and cooperate on a scale that had previously been impossible. At the same time, the small petty pirate gangs that had once stood at the forefront of pirate organization were now increasingly being superseded. Most newcomers, instead of forming gangs of their own, affiliated with confederation units. Many were in fact actively recruited by confederation members.

Expansion and Consolidation

Cheng I not only unified the pirates; he also gave them new permanent headquarters in China. As their first base of operation he chose the Lei-chou Peninsula, an ideal location because of the long narrow channels of Kuang-chou Bay and the peninsula's relative isolation from strong administrative centers. The pirates rounded out this stronghold by taking possession of Nao-chou and Wei-chou, two little-frequented islands that flanked the peninsula and gave them easy access to both the salt fleets of Tien-pai and the vessels passing through the narrow strait of Hainan.[31]

It is a mark of the pirates' willingness to join forces, divide territory, and allocate resources that they were soon able to establish a second headquarters in the east, on Lantao Island. Lantao, which stretched from Victoria Harbor to the mouth of the Pearl River, provided access to the major seaways of the region. To the east was Capsingmen, the narrow strait at the western entrance of Victoria Harbor. On the northwest was the Pearl River estuary, with the island of Lintin, which had been an important center for the opium trade since 1800. Midway along the northern shore of Lantao, at the village of Tung-yung, the coastline dipped to form a well-protected bay bounded on the north by the tiny island of Ch'ih-li-chiao (Chek Lap Kok). Today a well-preserved fort used as a school stands in the foothills behind the village. But in the early nineteenth century Tung-yung was an undefended site that provided the pirates with an excellent anchorage and rendezvous point.[32]

Lantao also appealed to the pirates as a source of potential recruits. In 1800 most of its settlers were fishermen and boatmen whose ancestors had intermittently engaged in piracy since the tenth century.[33] In time Lantao became the pirates' main headquarters. On November 19, 1805, the Russian ambassador to China, Captain Adam von Krusenstern, reported seeing approximately 300 vessels lying at anchor south of Lantao. Supposing them to be fishing boats, he sailed quietly by, only to learn afterward in Macao that what he had seen were pirate ships.[34]

From Lantao the pirates soon extended their operations to the small unfortified islands along the coast, where some conveniently situated harbors (identified by contemporary Westerners as Sattye, Loompako, or Lunpachou, and Wanchunchow, or Wong Chun-chou) fell under their control. At these bases the largest vessels refitted while the others conducted missions in the adjacent countryside.

By 1804 Cheng I had even established anchorages within the two major passages of the Pearl River. The first, known as the Outer Passage, ran east of Macao, through the Bogue, past the first and second bars, and on to Whampoa. It was the principal route to Canton. To cover it, Cheng I established anchorages at San-men, located just south of Lantao Island and at Lung-hsüeh (Lung Keio) and San-chiao (Samcock), located in the middle of the river northwest of Lintin. The Bogue, or Bocca Tigris (Tiger's Mouth; Hu-men), was the main entrance to the Pearl River. It was a small strait formed by four tiny islands on which four famous forts were built. Once past the Bogue and its forts, a vessel was considered to have entered China's inner waters (*nei-ho*).[35]

The second route, known as the Inner Passage, was more frequently used by small craft and was guarded by Cheng I from Chu-chou, P'ing-shan, and Mo-tao.[36] It followed the channel of the Pearl River that ran west of Macao through the "broadway and flats" to Hsiang-shan, where it was fed by a host of tributaries that led to Canton (Map 4).

A major consideration in determining who operated where seems to have been the fleet leader's native place. Wu-shih Erh, Tung-hai Pa, and Li Shang-ch'ing, for whom the Lei-chou region was home territory, remained there for the most part and drew the majority of their recruits from such western cities as Sui-ch'i, Yang-chiang, Wu-ch'uan, Hai-k'ang, Ho-p'u, Ch'in Chou, and Shih-ch'eng.[37] Cheng I's roots were planted more firmly in the east. His uncle Cheng Lien-fu had had his base on Lantao Island, and his father Lien-ch'ang had controlled the strategic pass at Li-yü-men just east of Hong Kong. In addition, both his wife and his most powerful colleague came from

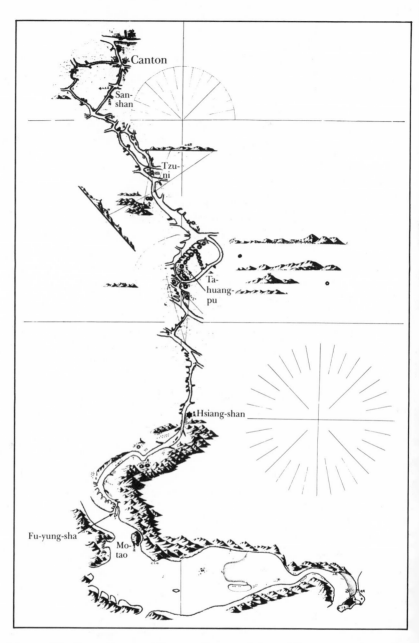

Map 4. The Inner Passage, Macao to Canton. Adapted from a map drawn by Messrs. Reeves in the 19th century (British Museum Add. Misc. 31,348C), based on a Spanish chart. The original map identifies some 60 cities and towns by Chinese characters in the margin; these have been deleted and romanizations provided only for places mentioned in the text.

the center of the Pearl River Delta—his wife, from Hsin-hui, and his colleague, Kuo P'o-tai, from P'an-yü. Consequently, in pioneering the territorial expansion from western to eastern Kwangtung, Cheng I took advantage of hometown connections whenever he could.

Cheng I, however, was not destined to sail much longer. He died suddenly in Vietnam on November 16, 1807, at the age of 42. According to one account he was blown overboard and drowned in a gale; according to another, he was struck by a cannonball while fighting in an attempt to recapture Vietnam on behalf of his former Tay-son allies.[38]

Though some of Cheng's co-founders must have had ambitions to command the confederation's largest fleet, power passed virtually uncontested into the hands of his widow. A former prostitute and mother of two of Cheng I's sons, the woman known to her associates as simply Cheng I Sao (Wife of Cheng I) could truly be called the real "Dragon Lady" of the South China Sea.[39]

On Cheng I's death, Cheng I Sao, who had participated fully in her husband's piracy, moved at once to create personal relationships that would legitimize her status and allow her to exercise authority. Aware of the need to quell opposition before it erupted, she first obtained the support of her husband's most powerful kinsmen: Cheng Pao-yang, his nephew, and Cheng An-pang, the son of his cousin Cheng Ch'i. Then she set about balancing the factions around her, building on the loyalties owed to her husband and making herself indispensable to all the other fleet leaders in order to override any centrifugal tendencies.

What ultimately secured her position, though, was her decision to find someone to assist her in the management of the Red Flag Fleet. With a force of more than 300 junks and 20,000 to 40,000 men to command, she needed someone who could handle its daily operation and who would win the acceptance of the rank and file while at the same time remaining absolute in his loyalty to her.

From her perspective there was but one suitable person—her young favorite, Chang Pao, a fisherman's son, who had joined the pirates at age 15 after having been captured by her husband. As Cheng I's protégé, initiated by him into piracy by means of a homosexual liaison, Chang Pao rose rapidly through the pirate ranks and eventually became Cheng I's adopted son. At some point he was invested by the Vietnamese as a "Great Generalissimo" (Ta yüan-shuai).[40] Once Cheng I Sao had made her decision, she acted quickly to seal the alliance through a sexual relationship of her own. She and Chang Pao became lovers within weeks and, later, they became husband and wife.

With her position secured, Cheng I Sao next turned to the task of consolidating her fleet. To this end she issued a code of laws that regularized the operation of its squadrons and transformed personal relationships into more formal power relations.[41] The code was severe. Anyone caught giving commands on his own or disobeying those of a superior was to be immediately decapitated. Pilfering from the common treasury or public fund (*kung-hsiang*) and stealing from villagers who supplied the pirates were also capital offenses. No pirate could retain any goods taken as booty without first producing them for group inspection. Such goods were to be registered by the pirates' purser and distributed by the fleet leader. Customarily, 20 percent of the booty was returned to the original captor, and the remainder, referred to as the "public fund," was placed in a joint treasury, or storehouse (*k'u*).[42] Currency was to be handed over to the squadron leader, who would turn over a certain portion to the fleet leader and return a slight amount to the captor. The rest was to be reserved for purchasing supplies and provisioning vessels that were unsuccessful in their own pursuits.[43]

In theory, then, failure to cooperate in the surrender of booty might bring the death penalty. In practice, however, the punishment was sometimes softened. Philip Maughan, first lieutenant of the HC *Bombay Marine*, reported that first-time offenders who withheld only a small portion of their booty were whipped severely on the back and then released. He hastened to add, however, that repeating the offense or concealing a large amount of goods would bring certain death.[44] Other offenders paid dearly, too. For deserting or being absent without leave, a man's ears were cut off, and he was then paraded through his squadron. If a pirate raped a female captive, he was put to death. If the two fornicated by mutual consent, the man was beheaded and the woman cast overboard with a weight attached to her legs.[45]

In principle women captives were to be released, but J. L. Turner, a British captive of the Red Fleet in 1807, indicated that the pirates customarily took their most beautiful captives as concubines or wives, returned the ugliest to shore, and ransomed all the rest. According to him, once a pirate had chosen a wife from among the captives, he was obliged to be loyal to her; no promiscuous sexual activities were supposed to occur.[46]

On more than one occasion Westerners saw pirates who had violated the code flogged, put in irons, or quartered. According to Richard Glasspoole, the pirates' code was strictly enforced and transgressions punished with an efficiency that seemed "almost incredible." Such severity, he concluded, gave rise to a force that was intrepid in attack, desperate in defense, and unyielding even when outnumbered.[47]

Chang Pao

As commander-in-chief, Cheng I Sao conducted her transactions with businesslike perspicacity. Only after receiving her permission could an operation be carried out. When she spoke, the pirates obeyed. But she also recognized that the fleet needed to be given ideological inspiration as an antidote to too much "legalism." For this, she once again turned to her more colorful subordinate, Chang Pao. Among the pirate leaders, no one was more charismatic than the stout commander of the Red Flag Fleet. A flamboyant man, whose habitual dress was a purple silk robe and a black turban, Chang nevertheless appealed to those around him as a man of dignified manner, sound discretion, and temperate habits.[48] He was a flexible leader not given to the wanton killing of captives, a practice that earned him the loyalty of his subordinates.

Like the other boat dwellers of the South China Sea, the pirates never set sail without praying to their gods. Before each foray the gods were faithfully consulted, and if the omens were bad, the pirates would not go forth. To facilitate these practices, Chang Pao ordered the construction of a temple aboard his largest ship, and there the fleet's most important leaders would assemble before each major undertaking to burn incense and inquire about their chances for success. Miraculously enough, whenever Chang Pao conferred with his priests beforehand, as he often did, the oracles always seconded his desires.[49] Chang Pao also set himself up as a protector of religion. In the company of his men, he frequently visited the temples on shore and made donations to the priests. Seldom if ever did he destroy a temple or harm a priest.[50]

In time a kind of supernatural prowess became associated with his name. The story is told about a temple in Hui-chou whose deity was so famous for its miracles that the pirates routinely stopped to visit the temple and pay their respects whenever they passed by. One day several of the leaders decided to carry the deity's image away so that they could always have it aboard ship with them. But despite the most strenuous efforts, no one could budge it from its pedestal—no one, that is, except Chang Pao. As soon as he touched it, the image rose easily from its stand and accompanied the pirates to their junks as though "blown by a wind."[51]

Unfavorable reports from the gods sometimes constrained even

Chang Pao. On one occasion, after anchoring alongside four mud guardhouses defending a town, he waited quietly for two days. On the third day, when the forts opened fire, he failed to return a shot and withdrew down the river during the night. The Joss (gods), he said, had not promised success.[52] Similarly, in 1809, after an attack in which 300 of his men had been killed, Chang Pao inquired of the Joss what course to follow. The omens were inauspicious for victory in battle but favorable for retreating and breaking the attackers' blockade. So Chang called off the counterattack, and the following noon a strong southerly wind arose, allowing his men to break the blockade and sail away just as the Joss had predicted.[53]

Bold in all endeavors, Chang Pao still treated his own men with justice and impartiality, as the following anecdote attests. When the father of a man named Liu died shortly after having been captured by pirates, Liu blamed Chang Pao. Bent on revenge, Liu purchased a long-bladed knife and steeped it in poison day and night. When at last he thought it was ready, Liu concealed the knife on his body and begged permission to join Chang Pao's fleet. One day Chang Pao noticed a strange expression on Liu's face and ordered him tied up. When the concealed knife was brought to light, Chang, with no trace of anger, elicited the reason for its existence. After explaining to Liu that he had had nothing to do with his father's abduction, Chang commended the man for his bravery and rewarded him with four silver dollars.[54]

On other occasions Chang Pao prevailed in settling disputes. Two pirates planning to run away were overheard, flogged, and put in irons by their captain, who then presented them to Chang, asking that they be put to death. When Chang refused, the angry captain and some of his crew seized their weapons and insisted that their demand be carried out. But Chang Pao held firm, and drove the captain and his men out of the fleet.[55]

Always mindful of the requirements of his profession, Chang Pao was deeply interested in the Europeans with whom he came into contact. He eyed their cannon and ships with curiosity and made the most of every opportunity to profit from their naval expertise.[56] One incident that typifies his resolve to learn from the foreigners occurred during an attack on the British brig *Baracoutta*, lying at anchor for repairs at Lintin Island. As the pirates bore down, the ship fired a broadside of 24-pound shot that so alarmed them they retreated in fear. On closer examination, Chang Pao expressed astonishment at the size of the ball and bragged that it would not be long before he, too, possessed such shot. His assertion proved no idle boast, for within a few months his flagship sported a 24-pounder of its own.[57]

A final quality that Chang possessed was vision. It was said that as his success grew, so did his ambition—to the point where, in the words of Glasspoole, he openly spoke of "his intention of displacing the . . . Tartar family from the throne of China."[58] Other Westerners heard the same story: "He proclaimed to all his partisans how by consenting to the barbarian dynasty on the throne the empire suffered tyrannical oppression. He pointed out to them how easy it would be to depose [the Ch'ing], reestablish China, and make each one of them rulers of the empire. Such was his skill in both piracy and persuasion that his followers were undivided in their desire to restore the dignity of the country."[59]

Although Chang Pao may not have been alone among the leaders in invoking the rhetoric of rebellion from time to time, there is no way of knowing whether the rank and file subscribed to such ideas. Nowhere in the pirates' confessions or other pirate records is there any suggestion, let alone mention, that they were at all interested in either rebellion or overthrowing the dynasty. Moreover, government officials did not see them as rebels either. Throughout the period, they appear as sea bandits (*hai-fei* or *yang-fei*) in official sources, not rebels (*ni-fei*). It is true that in 1808, after some pirates killed a provincial commander-in-chief, a few officials began referring to them as rebels, but others did not pick up the usage, and the *hai-fei* label was still very much in vogue throughout most of 1808 and 1809.

Even more difficult to determine is the precise relationship between pirates and secret societies. Some modern scholars have suggested that the pirates may have been inspired by the Ming Loyalist activities of Kwangtung's secret societies, and that by invoking the "overthrow the Ch'ing, restore the Ming" ideas often associated with such groups, they were able to transform operations for profit into noble-sounding political adventures.[60] Archival data, however, do not support this hypothesis. In the first place, it is not clear to what extent pirates even belonged to secret societies. They were almost never called *hui-fei*, the term most often used for Triad or secret society members in official sources, and one finds few examples of men known to have been active in both secret society and pirate circles. The most that can be said, then, is that pirates worked with and were influenced by secret societies. In any case, even if we had conclusive proof that pirates were members of secret societies, this would still not necessarily indicate that they were involved in subversive activities. None of the archival documents contain any references to "overthrowing the Ch'ing" or "restoring the Ming" as a goal of the secret societies of Kwangtung during the late eighteeenth and nearly nineteenth centuries. The secret societies there functioned primarily as fronts for robbery and extortion. Sworn brothers sought economic gain from these associations, not restorationist inspiration.[61]

In sum, it was the charisma of pirate leaders more than the rhetoric of secret societies that inspired men to fight and share their prizes. To breathe life into the confederation and motivate the rank and file to give it their loyalty required energy and skilled leadership. Moreover, that leadership had to be earned and continually demonstrated. It is a tribute to the quality of the pirate leaders that the confederation doubled in size in four short years. Beginning with perhaps 800 junks in 1805, it expanded to at least 1,800 junks (and 70,000 men) by 1809, and at its height comprised a force twice as large as the combined forces in 1588, when the English fleet met the Spanish Armada.[62]

Everyday Life at Sea

Like their counterparts at Chiang-p'ing, most of the rank and file of the pirate confederation were impoverished fishermen at the bottom of society. In dress they were hardly distinguishable from other lower-class members of the water world, except that in place of hats they wore dark-colored cotton turbans.[63] Their motivations for taking up piracy were mixed. Some were clearly eager to secure rank and status within the hierarchy, and others must have sought the adventure denied by their drab lives onshore. Many, it seems, were driven by the wish to escape the tyranny and exactions of Ch'ing officials,[64] for in a declaration posted throughout Canton and Macao, we find some of the pirates claiming that they had taken up this life because the "mandarins, being persons of tyrannical hearts, sought for nought but money." In this document (reproduced in Appendix B) some of the pirates expressed their anger at the forced labor and taxes exacted from them, while others were more disturbed by the incompetence of those in charge of defending them from the predations of criminals and bandits.

The confederation also included a few men of "decent appearance" who had joined it with money in hand. One even spoke a little English and claimed to have visited England.[65] These were the exceptions, however, for the majority who came to piracy were in search of profits. By 1806 recruits were flocking to the confederation in numbers "hardly to be credited," in groups of five, ten, or even 30 at a time. Fishermen joined by the hundreds.[66] At first volunteers appear to have been at liberty to come and go as they pleased, and some remained with the pirates only a month or two. But by 1807 the pirate leaders refused to admit anyone who did not agree to stay at least eight or nine months.[67]

Captives continued to be a significant source of manpower under the confederation. People were captured almost daily, and the pressure brought to bear on them could be excruciating. Even the usually forebearing Chang Pao would resort to force when he was balked. On one occasion, after seizing nine rice boats, he informed the men on board that he would allow them to become pirates by taking an oath before the Joss. When three or four refused, he tied their hands behind their backs, ran a rope from the masthead through their arms, and hoisted them three feet from the deck. His assistants then flogged the captives into unconsciousness and raised them to the masthead, where they were left hanging for almost an hour. The entire process was repeated until the unfortunate victims either died or submitted.[68]

The crews of captured fishing junks were obliged to serve the pirates without the slightest prospect of release. Young boys were highly esteemed as prizes; they were usually brought up by the pirates as servants or adopted as sons.[69] Kidnapped victims, unable to ransom themselves, were imprisoned and obliged to assist in manning the vessels or handling the booty. They were never allowed to go ashore unless accompanied by an armed guard. If caught trying to escape, they were tortured or killed. Sometimes, after four or five years of captivity, they were given the choice of liberty, but by then most of them were too afraid of being recognized as pirates to leave.[70] So numerous were captives among those arrested for piracy that in 1805 the Liang-kuang Governor-general estimated they constituted more than half of the entire pirate force.[71]

In the hope of being trained in the use of Western guns, the pirates frequently spared the lives of European and American prisoners. The crews of a Portuguese brig and an American schooner managed to preserve their lives this way. And so did Turner and Glasspoole. Both lived to tell their tales only by teaching their captors how to prepare cartridges and use muskets. One Armenian captive served as the pirates' physician for over a year in exchange for his life. The purser of the junk on which Turner was kept was a captive who, having failed to procure the money for his ransom, was able to save his life by keeping records for his captors.[72]

Women participated fully in the life of the confederation, though in theory, at least, they were not allowed aboard ship unless they were married to one of the men. Many had no permanent residence onshore and lived with their children in horribly cramped conditions afloat. It was not uncommon for pirate leaders to share their quarters with as many as five or six wives, but the crews tended to be made up of unmarried men. Despite the strictures against promiscuity, Turner noted that each vessel usually carried eight or ten women who were "intended to please all the society indiscriminately and to do the work of their sex."[73] Yet it seemed to him that "the greater part of the crew [were] satisfied without [them]," probably because the pirates "committed almost publicly crimes against nature."[74]

Aboard ship the women worked as hard as the men. As was traditional throughout South China, the handling of sampans fell to them. These pirate women, however feminine and flirtatious they might have seemed at first glance, were tough and aggressive. With unbound feet they were active and mobile, able to hold rank and command entire junks themselves.[75] In the heat of battle, they sometimes even fought side by side with their husbands. During an engagement in 1809, one pirate wife managed to wound several assailants while holding fast to the helm and defending herself with a cutlass.[76]

Living conditions on board ship were always crowded. While the captain and his wives occupied the relatively spacious quarters of the poop, the rest of the crew crammed into the cargo holds under the main deck. In theory each pirate and his wife occupied a small cabin of their own. But space was at such a premium that a man and his family might sometimes share only a small berth, about four feet square. Captives and recruits usually bedded down on the deck, unsheltered from wind or rain.[77] Turner had to make do with a sleeping space that was at most four feet long and one-and-a-half feet wide. If he happened to extend beyond his limits, he was quickly reminded of his error with a swift blow or a kick. Glasspoole was obliged to weather even the heaviest rain on deck with no covering but an old mat, which was frequently taken from him during the night by the pirates on watch.[78]

The ship's galley consisted of a small wooden shed on the afterdeck, where the wooden casks for storing fresh water were also kept. The pirates' diet, except when they seized cargoes of pork or poultry, usually consisted of coarse red rice and fish, but in times of scarcity they sometimes lived for weeks on caterpillars boiled in rice or on the rats encouraged to breed in the dirty, vermin-infested conditions of the hold.[79]

Life afloat, however, was not all work and hardship. Above all else, the pirates were fond of gambling, and many spent most of their leisure at cards. Indeed, at least one group continued playing even during battle. When one of the players was struck and killed, the others, undisturbed, merely pulled his mangled body aside and resumed their play.[80] The pirates also whiled away their leisure hours smoking opium and fitted out their ships with all the necessary paraphernalia.[81] Such moments of leisure must have become increasingly rare, however, as the confederation became more ambitious in its endeavors.

5

The Confederation
in Action

With the signing of the agreement and the establishment of the confederation, piracy in the water world became a big business. More
than anything else, the confederation allowed pirates to conduct their
activities on a scale that made their enterprise pay.

The Pirates' Tactics

Unlike the uncoordinated assaults of the petty pirates at Chiang-
p'ing, attacks were now planned in advance and systematically executed. The first rule was never to attack unless victory was virtually
assured. The pirates' favorite tactic was to take their enemy by surprise. Rather than confront a target caught in a calm head on, for example, they generally closed in silently, caught their victims unaware,
and overpowered them in hand to hand combat.[1]

To approach their enemies unseen, the pirates had to sail inconspicuously amid the vessels of the water world. In 1800 China had no national flag that could be raised by a private boat. The use of the imperial banner, a yellow triangle with a green dragon, was reserved for
the Emperor and institutions such as the army and navy that received
their authority from him. The flags over private shipping were as varied as individual taste and fashion decreed. As a result, the pirates'
kaleidoscope of flying ensigns not only allowed them to identify one
another, but also helped them to blend into the surrounding traffic.[2]

Unlike pirate ships, government vessels always had identifying
characters on their sails. Also, imperial fleets were almost entirely
composed of large junks, whereas pirate fleets always included large

numbers of small rowboats, which were propelled by a combination of sail and human muscle power. But at a distance it was difficult to distinguish between the two fleets in full assembly because of the similar shape and appearance of their large junks' sails. Ships that made the mistake of taking a pirate squadron for a naval squadron usually paid the price. Just as often, pirate ships were mistaken for fishing vessels until they were right on top of their unsuspecting prey. It was because Richard Glasspoole and his seven companions mistook a large fleet of anchored vessels for fishing craft that they were captured from the cutter of the HCS *Marquis of Ely* on September 21, 1908.[3]

Once their victims had been singled out, the pirates came into battle with cutlasses slung over their shoulders and knives sheathed under their arms. When they could not board an enemy ship directly from their own junks, they took to the water. In one instance 200 or 300 exasperated pirates, blocked from entering a harbor by impediments sunk at its entrance, ran along the shore until they came abreast of their quarry. Then, with swords lashed under their arms, they plunged into the water to attack the junk from the sea.[4]

On some occasions the pirates fought with cannon, but they seldom fired until they were close to their prey. In launching assaults through shallow harbors or streams, the largest vessels stood by to give covering fire for the smaller sampans that actually led the charge. At such times the pirates erected large flags on the decks of the sampans and armed themselves with halberds, tridents, hooks, and sabers.[5]

When moving in on an intended victim, the pirates usually concealed most of their ships behind a point or promontory and sent out two or three as decoys. Then, after contact with a likely target had been made, the remaining pirates would suddenly emerge and surround the boat. The pirates habitually hired the people on fishing junks or other small vessels to scout out victims. Fish selling provided a pretext for pulling up alongside an intended victim and assessing its strength; news of its condition was then quickly forwarded to the pirate employers.[6]

The pirates also capitalized on the psychological effects of terror by deliberately cultivating a reputation for fierceness that would make local groups more amenable to their demands. To this end they subjected the crews of private junks who resisted them to the harshest treatment. The most common torture was to strip resisters of all but their trousers, tie their hands behind their backs, hoist them from the deck, and beat them with rods of twisted rattan; in some cases the victim was then left dangling by his hands for almost an hour. But the greatest cruelty was reserved for the crews of naval vessels, who were routinely put to death even if they had surrendered without a fight. In most instances they were either cut to pieces and cast overboard or disemboweled. The more unfortunate ones had their feet nailed to the deck with large spikes, were beaten until they vomited blood, and left in that state for some time until the pirates decided to end their misery by cutting them to pieces.[7]

To coordinate their movements in battle, the pirates established a few basic signals, such as recall and chase, but their small rowboats could deliver messages so expeditiously that a more elaborate system was unnecessary. In combat the leader's junk set an example for the rest. The hoisting of his mainsail was a signal for the fleet to get under way. Whenever the flagship attacked or retreated, the rest of the fleet followed suit.[8]

To fortify themselves for combat, the pirates sometimes drank a mixture of wine and gunpowder that sent them into battle with faces aflame and eyes aglow. On other occasions they bolstered their courage by eating the hearts of vanquished foes. Once engaged, they sprinkled themselves repeatedly with garlic water as a charm against shot.[9]

The vessels most vulnerable to pirate attack were the passenger boats, cargo transports, and fishing craft of the Nan-hai. From them the pirates obtained mostly everyday commodities: betel nut, sugar, fish, vegetables, oil, rice, firewood, rushes, brass utensils, cotton quilts, cloth, porcelain, iron nails, tea leaves, liquor, and occasionally even fresh water. From time to time these ships also yielded modest amounts of specie. Occasionally the pirates even struck it rich, as on the day when Cheng Ya-lu seized more than 8,000 taels of silver from a cargo carrier at Ch'eng-hai.[10]

The pirates' tactics succeeded marvelously against the coasting vessels of the Nan-hai, but their most desired prey were the large ocean-going junks of the Nan-yang. Although the pirates were equipped to carry out operations in the deeps, like most other Chinese mariners, they preferred to confine their activities to less-treacherous coastal waters, and thus waited to tackle such craft until they neared the shore. But even then success was by no means guaranteed. These large junks were heavily armed, and their high sides made boarding problematical. Their hulls, protected by meshes of fishnet and hides, repelled shot, enabling their crews to fend off adversaries who outnumbered them. For all this, any of these vessels that anchored short of the entrance to the Pearl River was almost certain to find itself the target of a pirate attack.[11] Indeed, so desirable were these ships that once the pirates had them in their sights they would go to any lengths to take them. On one occasion, after failing to capture two large ocean junks from Ch'üan-chou, Fukien, they converted their smallest vessel into a fire ship, then placed it windward alongside the enemy junks, lit the train, and allowed the flames to do the rest.[12]

When unable to overcome large ocean junks by force, the pirates often resorted to subterfuge, as in their seizure of the *P'eng-fa*, a heavily laden junk that was returning from Vietnam to China in September 1808. Knowing that they could not attack it directly, the pirates seized two ferry boats, concealed some of their men on board, and ordered them to pretend that they were being attacked. The spurious passengers-in-distress then hailed the junk and asked for assistance. When the crew of the *P'eng-fa* allowed them to approach, the "passengers" lumbered up the sides and revealed their true intentions. By that time several of the pirate vessels had closed in, and the *P'eng-fa* was taken.[13]

The capture of an ocean junk was usually worth the effort. Those returning from Batavia and Malaysia carried valuable cargoes of birds' nests, specie, bêche-de-mer, and rice. One successful venture near Macao in October 1805 yielded the pirates 30,000 piculs of rice and a cargo valued at more than 20,000 taels of silver.[14] In tackling such craft, the advantages of scale paid off, for these junks had been well beyond the reach of the petty pirates.

Confederation not only made such ventures possible, but allowed the pirates to operate freely in the inner waters of the coastal strip. It was only a matter of time before they began coming ashore more and more frequently to plunder villages, markets, and rice fields. A favorite onshore enterprise was raiding government forts for weapons. On March 16, 1805, some 300 pirates attacked the fort at Ch'ih-ao (in Hui-lai county). Although the soldiers defending the fort opened fire, they were soon overwhelmed by pirates pressing in from two directions. Before long the pirates set fire to the barracks and seized the main gate, at which point the commanding sergeant fled from his post in terror, his troops hard on his heels. With this, the attackers transferred a sizable cache of cannon and gunpowder to their junks.[15]

Two months later the pirates took another fort, at Ch'ao-chou in eastern Kwangtung. In this case 20 junks took advantage of the early morning fog to reach an anchorage close to the Ta-chi-mu-ao fort. From there they sailed to shore in sampans, seized the hill overlooking the fort, and from its heights discharged a barrage of rocks that wounded five soldiers. Despite a stout defense by the fort's 80-man force, the pirates held their own until braves (*hsiang-yung*) from the nearby guardhouses arrived.[16]

By coordinating their assaults with local bandits (*t'u-fei*), the pirates came in time to operate with almost as much facility on land as they did at sea. Besides guiding the pirates to prime targets, bandits often enlisted recruits to bolster their combined forces once an attack had begun. By late 1805 pirate-bandit raids took place regularly, and the supercargoes of the British East India Company reported seeing the results in the many charred villages along the river between Canton and Macao.[17]

The points of contact between the two groups were the gambling dens along the coast. Although proscribed by law, the dens flourished and even proliferated because their owners paid yamen attendants generously to turn a blind eye to them. Nan-hai county alone had 70 or 80, and nearby Fo-shan more than 40.[18] Some were even operated by the pirates themselves, and all provided space where pirates and bandits could plot strategy and split proceeds.

Pirates and Profits

With confederation, the ransoming of captives and vessels became a thoroughly profitable business. Vessels of no use to the pirates were ransomed at standard rates: 50 *yüan* of silver for fishing junks, 130 *yüan* for cargo carriers.[19] On one occasion, however, the pirates got a fat fee of 3,000 Spanish dollars from the customs office in Canton for the release of a chop boat that they had already plundered of birds' nests, bêche-de-mer, and specie.*

Ransoming human captives was less straightforward because it required extended negotiations with the victim's family. The pirates set the ransom by what they thought the families could pay and typically demanded two or three times as much as bandits. They seldom released anyone for less than 90 taels, compared with the 25 or 30 taels the bandits frequently accepted.[20]

Greed sometimes led to outlandish demands, as in the case of 250 women who were captured on October 1, 1809. On this occasion Richard Glasspoole looked on as the women's village, located on the Pearl River, was attacked. With their bound feet, few could walk unassisted or put up any kind of resistance, and at least 20 who struggled were "hauled on board by the hair and treated in a most savage manner." Customarily, when women were captured, the commander of

*CanCon, Nov. 26, 1804; Secret Consultations, Nov. 24, 1804; Dalrymple, *Memoir*, p. 32. Chopboats were small Chinese government vessels used to convey the personnel of the East India Company back and forth between Macao and Canton and to transship merchandise between the European vessels at Whampoa and the warehouses of Canton. Because of their shape they were called water melons (*hsi-kua*) by the Chinese. Hunter, '*Fan Kwai*', pp. 33–34.

the vessel interrogated them to determine their circumstances, recorded their answers in a register, and assigned them to separate quarters in the hold, where they remained until their ransom was forthcoming. In this instance the pirate leader decided the women were worth between 600 and 6,000 Spanish dollars each, rates that Glasspoole thought "exorbitant." After relaying these demands to the villagers, the leader ordered the women to berth on deck at the rear of the vessel where there was no shelter, and proceeded upriver. Ten days later he returned to the village, anchored for five or six days, and in the end ransomed only 100 of the women. The other 150 he sold to his men for 40 dollars each.[21]

In negotiating for the ransom of villagers, the pirates did not hesitate to use terror. They often severed the fingers or ears of promising captives and delivered them to relatives who hesitated to meet their price. But on receipt of the payments, the pirates faithfully released their prisoners; there are no reports of cases in which ransomed victims were not freed. Ransom funds were turned over to the fleet or squadron leaders for allocation.[22]

The confederation also made it possible for the pirates to extract payments from foreigners and thereby challenge Westerners, something their predecessors had never been in a position to do. Most vulnerable were Portuguese sailors on the brigs from India and the Philippines. Americans, too, fell prey to the pirates; eight were seized from the small schooner *Pilgrim* in 1808.[23] Englishmen, Dutchmen, and Armenians were also taken from time to time. We have already met J. L. Turner, chief mate of the country ship *Tay*, who was captured along with his crew of six Lascars on December 7, 1806. A whole series of negotiations followed, which before their end involved the captain of the ship, the ship's agents, the supercargoes of the British East India Company, the Chinese Hong merchants, the head of the customs office at Canton, and the Liang-kuang Governor-general. After five months of discussions in which the pirates skillfully played off one side against the other, they were rewarded for their efforts with a settlement valued at 7,150 Spanish dollars. Approximately half was contributed by the provincial authorities in Kwangtung (3,500) and half (3,650) by the private subscription of Europeans in Asia. The payment was made in kind and cash. Of this amount, the pirates actually received 6,160 dollars' worth of specie and goods: 2,800 dollars in cash, three chests of opium valued at 2,760 dollars, and mats for sails valued at 600 dollars. (The remainder of the money was used to compensate the Chinese who had arranged the ransom, to hire a boat for the transfer of the prisoner, and to remit back pay to Turner.)[24]

It was two years later that the pirates captured Richard Glasspoole. Again the pirates bargained persistently and exacted handsome payments from both the Chinese and foreigners. Glasspoole's total ransom was 7,654 Spanish dollars; the British paid 5,200 and the Hong merchants the rest. Of this amount, 212 dollars was used to compensate the fishermen and officials who had assisted in the negotiations, and 44 dollars for chops and duties, but the pirates walked away with a haul worth 7,398 dollars: 4,320 dollars in cash, along with two chests of opium and two bales of broadcloth valued at 3,078 dollars.[25]

The pirates of Kwangtung differed most strikingly from those at Chiang-p'ing in the breadth of their financial undertakings. With small, ad hoc groups, the petty pirates were always dependent on the chance seizure of vessels at sea. But in an organization of thousands, survival required more than chance encounters, so the pirates were forced by sheer necessity to look for a source of dependable income. They found it close at hand in the provincial salt trade.

In the early nineteenth century Kwangtung had 22 salterns, the majority of them located in the southernmost prefectures—Kao-chou, Lei-chou, Ch'iung-chou, and Lien-chou. The richest of these, including the important T'ien-mou field, were concentrated in the northeast corner of the peninsula near Tien-pai. Since most of the fields were located near the sea (many were in fact surrounded on three sides by water), the bulk of the salt was transported by junk. Four times each year large fleets gathered at Tien-pai to begin the 400-mile voyage to Canton.[26]

Pirates had begun interfering with the salt trade as early as 1796, when small gangs periodically seized a junk or two.[27] Later, as their groups became more organized and skilled under the Tay-son, they were able to amass 70 or 100 junks for raids against entire salt fleets. By 1801, with an armada of 300 junks, they were bold enough to attack the vessels before they even left Tien-pai.[28]

With their new headquarters in Kwangtung, the pirates were in an even better position to prey on the salt trade because their base on Nao-chou Island afforded easy access to Tien-pai. As more and more salt junks fell into their hands, the pirates forced the crews to continue hauling salt on their behalf. By 1805 they had increased their hold over the traffic to the point of domination. Throughout Kwangtung the price of salt skyrocketed, and though the Emperor ordered militia placed aboard all salt junks, the measure was of little avail. Salt merchants soon found it more expedient to negotiate directly with the pirates and to hand over large sums for the safe passage of their junks.[29]

With the help of local secret societies, the pirates succeeded in regularizing the practice to such a degree that every vessel setting out for Canton found it necessary to purchase protection. The standard rate was 50 *yüan* of silver for each 100 *pao* or package of salt. Sometimes the pirates even undertook to provide an escort. In 1805 a fleet of salt junks paid 200 Spanish dollars apiece for a pirate convoy to Canton.[30] Through the collection of set fees, the pirates established a system that yielded predictable profits from season to season.

What made the system work was the pirates' demonstrated willingness to destroy junks that would not submit. When countered, they reacted ruthlessly. Resistance resulted in the burning of 70 government junks at Ta-chou field on June 28, 1805, and 110 others a few days later.[31] On September 13, 120 pirate junks attacked and burned 90 vessels in the harbor of Tien-pai. By the end of the year only four of the government's junks remained independent of pirate control.[32] As the payment of fees continued, the pirates' ties to the salt merchants strengthened. Eventually the merchants even began conveying provisions and ammunition to them.[33]

The pirates may have exercised a similar hold over the opium trade. Although the trade had not yet taken on the dimensions it would later acquire, by 1800 the Chinese were importing about 4,500 chests of opium annually. The first evidence of pirate interference dates from 1793, with the report that the British opium vessels in Lark's Bay "frequently suffered at the hands of the pirates."[34] By 1795 pirates had brought the trade in eastern Kwangtung to a halt, and in 1803 the supercargoes of the East India Company complained that they were interfering with the opium sales west of Canton.[35] Between 1803 and 1815, however, there are no references at all to pirate interference, despite the fact that many pirates, including their most powerful leaders, were opium smokers. In this period, then, the pirates may have installed another system of protection in which opium traders paid dearly for the privilege of carrying out their commerce unmolested.

The pirates reached the pinnacle of their power when they were able to extract protection payments from every type of vessel afloat. Merchants, boat owners, pilots, and fishermen alike were forced to buy protection before setting out on any voyage. In return for specified sums (variously referred to as *hao-shui, kang-kuei, yang-shui,* and *le-shui*), purchasers received documents (or passports, as Westerners called them) signed by the pirate leaders.[36]

In general these protection fees were collected annually, although special temporary certificates could be purchased for specified periods. Protection was expensive. In some areas merchant junks (*shang-ch'uan*) were assessed by the value of their cargoes at rates ranging from 50 to 500 *yüan* of foreign silver per trip. In other areas the price for an oceangoing merchant junk was 400 Spanish dollars on leaving the port and 800 on return, and it was not unheard of for wealthy shipowners to pay several thousand taels for a single voyage.[37]

The protection system took root in western Kwangtung with such success that by late 1803 the trade west of Canton "was annihilated except with passes from [the pirates]."[38] A year later they had extended their reach to the Pearl River Delta, with 70 large vessels on station near Macao that were sent out each day to seize unprotected junks in the islands to the east. By 1806 all craft were at risk, and few dared venture forth without a pass.[39]

The pirate leaders were scrupulous in abiding by the terms of these documents, which were supposed to be universally respected throughout the confederation. On being intercepted, vessels had merely to produce their documents as proof of payment and were then to be allowed to proceed on their way. Discipline was such that when breaches occurred, the leaders successfully compelled subordinates to make restitution. On one occasion, when a division leader mistakenly seized a protected fishing vessel, he was not only forced to restore the vessel to its owner, but ordered to pay him an additional 500 Spanish dollars for his trouble.[40]

At their peak the pirates were able to sell protection on land as well as sea. Along the coast, all settlements except those in the vicinity of large forts or on high hills were considered fair game, and recalcitrant villages were often destroyed. At San-shan pirates retaliated against those who refused their levy by killing some 2,000 residents and capturing large numbers of women and children. In most cases, the villagers, well aware of the pirates' ways, quickly met their demands.[41]

During September 1809 Richard Glasspoole accompanied the pirates on one of their fee-collecting cruises. The fleet, composed of 500 junks of different sizes, set out at daylight, and entered the Pearl River west of the Bogue the next day at noon. Three or four miles upriver, as they passed a large town under their protection, the inhabitants saluted them with shots. At this point the force separated. Around midnight some of the boats, including Glasspoole's, anchored close to a village and prepared for an attack. The crews burned the customs house and assembled their rowboats, but held off from further action while their messenger went into the village to demand a payment of 10,000 dollars per year. When this demand was refused, the pirate threatened to murder all the inhabitants. After hard bargaining, the two sides finally agreed on a "fee" of 6,000 dollars, to be paid upon the pirates' return downriver. On October 5 the Glasspoole fleet proceeded up another branch of the river, stopping at several small vil lages to receive payments in specie, sugar, and rice. They were also given a few large roasted pigs as presents for their Joss. Meanwhile, the other half of the fleet, anchored in the middle of the river, extracted 10,000 pieces of money (probably taels) from the inhabitants of Tzu-ni and 2,000 more from a nearby hamlet.[42]

The pirates' protection documents were widely available from their leaders aboard ship and from their agents onshore. As their activities expanded, the confederation established financial offices along the entire coast and even set up a tax office (*shui-chü*) in Canton as a collection for their fees. The headquarters of their financial operation appears to have been at Macao, where assistants sold protection and supplied pirates with weapons and ammunition. Thanks to their success in this enterprise, the confederation had no want of money, for its flagships often carried sums of 50,000 to 100,000 dollars in hard cash.[43] More than anything else, it was the pirates' ability to regularize their finances that effected their final transformation into true professionals.

Allies and Armaments

Like other maritime residents, the pirates were ultimately dependent on well-established links to coastal inhabitants. Necessities such as rice, gunpowder, tung oil, and water could only come from the shore, and certain prizes could only be disposed of there. Without allies willing to participate in this exchange, the pirates would have starved.

By 1805 the pirates had such allies throughout the province. From suppliers in Fang-ch'eng, Tien-pai, Tung-hai, Nao-chou, Lei-chou, Sui-ch'i, Wu-ch'uan, Hsin-an, Hai-k'ang, Jao-p'ing, and Hsin-ning they got rice, wine, tung oil, and wood; from others, in Hsiang-shan, P'an-yü, Lien-chou, Hai-k'ang, Hai-yang, Hainan, Kao-chou, and Wu-ch'uan, they got iron, cannon, and ammunition.[44] The arrest of 500 of their suppliers in 1805 scarcely affected their operations at all.[45] As the governor-general exclaimed in distress, "On land the 'traitors' [*chien-fei*] exchange news with the pirates and arresting [them] has no effect."[46] Since pirate leaders often assured their sources of supply by paying above-market prices and forbidding their subordinates from plundering their provisioners' shops, they seldom lacked for necessities.[47]

Besides enlisting private individuals to fence goods and furnish supplies, the pirates collaborated with secret societies for business purposes. Before the nineteenth century Triad societies had been known only in Chekiang, Fukien, and Taiwan. Around the turn of the century, however, they began to spread rapidly in Kwangtung, so rapidly, in fact, that 1802 saw a Triad-led insurrection in the province.[48] Individual lodges were theoretically affiliated with the parent Hung League (Hung-men) through such agencies as the Three Dots Society (San-tien hui), the Three Harmonies Society (San-ho hui), and the Heaven and Earth Society (T'ien-ti hui), but the movement was far from monolithic. Rather, it was made up of regionally divided, decentralized chapters united by a common ritual and a vague sense of brotherhood. In an organization so amorphously structured, underworld entrepreneurs found the means for the running of gambling dens, prostitution rings, and other illicit operations, and at the same time profited local officials, who were routinely bribed with "rebates."[49] Secret societies were prevalent throughout Kwangtung by 1804, at which time the pirates must have had well-established links with them, for within only a few weeks of the Tay-son defeat in Vietnam, the Liang-kuang Governor-general reported, "We have secretly investigated the T'ien-ti hui and indeed there are instances of conspiracies with the pirates."[50]

Secret-society members served the pirates in all kinds of ways: keeping them abreast of what was taking place in Macao and Canton, procuring goods for them, and helping them dispose of their booty. Such were their links that the pirates were moved to incorporate some of the societies' titles of rank into their own organization.[51] Many secret-society members took an even more active role in the pirates' doings by joining forces with them in onshore raids. This seems to have been a frequent occurrence, judging by the complaint of an imperial censor in 1802. He reported that although the pirates might bring only 100 or 200 men to an attack, they would be joined by so many allies that by the time they reached their destination the force was several times its original size.[52] Finally, and probably most important to the pirates' cause, was the assistance the secret societies gave them in setting up the protection rackets that supported the confederation.[53]

The pirates were occasionally joined by the very authorities whose job it was to arrest them. Local officials and yamen personnel sometimes assisted them as secretaries and accountants, and many clerks, runners, and soldiers willingly provided information for a healthy fee.[54] Alexander Dalrymple, a hydrographer for the British East India Company, reported in 1803 that for years the pirates had shared their profits with government officials. By 1809 even the Emperor was complaining that yamen in Chekiang, Fukien, and Kwangtung were full of officials who openly received payments from the pirates.[55]

One local official who collaborated with the pirates was Lin Pan, also known as Lin Ch'eng-jui. After purchasing the rank of a first-class department magistrate, Lin prospered by opening a shop and building a fleet of merchant junks that traded to Siam and Vietnam. In 1803, on learning that a pirate vessel laden with plunder was at hand, he jumped at the opportunity to buy 100 *pao* of black pepper from its captain for 520 *yüan*. A year later, when the pirate leader Cheng Lao-tung came to Chang-lin, in Ch'eng-hai county, Lin Pan searched him out, hoping to curry his favor and further secure the safety of his fleet. Lin presented the pirate with two *piculs* of gunpowder and a number of hogs and sheep, and Cheng reciprocated by sending 12 elephant tusks to his new "friend," who then purchased 100 more himself. A few weeks later Lin again sought to befriend Cheng. Learning that the pirates were in need of cannon, he presented Cheng with two of his own.[56]

The pirates were also assisted by Lin Wu, a wealthy official in Chang-lin. Lin Wu was a clansman of Lin Pan's who had purchased his post and amassed enough money to build a fleet of ships. In 1804 the pirates captured one of his junks. Deciding that his only recourse was to submit to their demands, he arranged to ransom the junk for 100 *pao* of rice. The following month Cheng Lao-tung intercepted another of Lin's junks. This time he had to pay 7,500 *yüan* of silver in ransom. Lin decided at this point to go into business with the pirate and later worked for him onshore by selling passports to other merchants.[57] Eventually, even the magistrate of Ch'eng-hai county took to collaborating with the pirates.[58]

The Confederation's Ships and Weapons

Most of the pirates' ships were acquired through capture; only in rare instances was a ship made to order. As a result, they differed little in either construction or appearance from the other vessels of the water world. To tackle the craft of the Nan-yang, the pirates needed a fleet of large, oceangoing junks (*yang-ch'uan*). Among their favorites were those built at Ch'üan-chou, Fukien—strong, sturdy vessels that mounted 30 cannon or more. The previously mentioned cargo carrier *P'eng-fa*, captured en route from Vietnam to China, was such a vessel. That prize, with more than 40 cannon, became Chang Pao's flagship.[59] The pirates also liked the "redheaded" (*hung-t'ou*) cargo carriers of Kwangtung and seized them whenever possible. Built to withstand the stormiest seas, these vessels were constructed of ironwood and often ran more than 150 feet in length. The name redheaded derived from the fact that all junks from Kwangtung were required to have red bands on their hulls.[60]

In 1809, at the peak of the confederation's strength, 200 of its 2,000

(a)

Fig. 3. Pirate junks. (a) A type of seagoing trawler or fishing junk resembling
the boats of the fishermen-pirates. (b) A trading junk from Hainan. (c) South
China cargo carrier. Since pirates generally sailed captured prizes, the cargo
carrier and the trading junks are probably typical examples of early-19th-
century pirate vessels. Source: Maze Collection of Chinese Junk Models, Science Museum, Kensington, England.

(b)

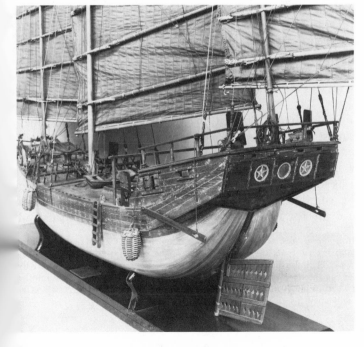

(c)

junks fell in the oceangoing category. Capable of carrying 300 to 400 men and mounting 20 to 30 cannon, these vessels were comparable in size to the British country ships that sailed between India and China.* But though by pirate standards, the crews of those ships were small, seldom exceeding 150 men, the pirates rarely attacked them. Because they rode high in the water, they were hard to board from the sea, and their sturdy construction rendered them resilient to shot.[61]

Since most of the pirates' activities were carried out in the coastal waters of the Nan-hai, the bulk of their ships were smaller, seagoing craft (*hai-ch'uan*). Most were captured merchant junks approximately 40 feet long and 14 feet wide.[62] The type most commonly used in Kwangtung was the black-and-white-hulled junk called the *ts'ao-ch'uan* or *ts'ao-pai ch'uan*, which was used to transport passengers and goods. Its name reflected its shape, something like that of a horse trough (*ts'ao*). (For technical information on this and other pirate craft, see Appendix C.)

There were between 600 and 800 junks of this class in the confederation's armada. At most they carried 200 men. Their 12 to 25 cannon fired mostly 8- to 16-pound shot. Above water they appeared to a seaman's eye as "rudely constructed," but their bottoms, well cleaned and oiled for speed in chase, were admirably suited to the coastal waters. For protection, the pirates often placed fishing nets and ox hides along the sides to prevent boarding and repel spears.[63]

In terms of the Western vessels then on the scene, the pirates' seagoing junks were most comparable to the American schooners or the Portuguese brigs and snows—all of which were two-masted ships of less than 200 tons. These were a favorite target, relatively easily taken because the pirates could outman their crews if it came to hand-to-hand combat.[64]

The pirates also had a fleet of river junks that plied the inner waters. Foremost among them were the swarms of small rowboats that accompanied the fleets and squadrons. These junks generally had one or two sails, 14 to 20 oars, and crews of 18 to 30 men. They were armed with six to ten wall-pieces and were well stocked with boarding pikes and swords. The pirates used them mainly for communication between ships and for going ashore at night to destroy the farms and

*Country ships (*kang-chiao*) were the English trading ships that sailed between India and China under license from the East India Company, as opposed to the ancestor-house ships (*tsu-chia*) that sailed from English ports. "Country traders" were strictly controlled: they operated only between Canton and India, and were allowed to import opium and raw cotton into China and tea and silk into India. Lo-shu Fu, *Documentary Chronicle of Sino-Western Relations*, pp. 598–99.

villages that did not pay them protection fees, but their crews were not above kidnapping people who crossed their path. Rowboats were most often found clustered at the mouths of rivers. Although they sometimes left a fleet for two or three days, they usually departed about an hour before sunset and returned the following noon.[65]

Among the specific types of rowboats employed by the pirates were the "long dragons" (*ch'ang-lung*)—"serpent boats" or "snake boats" in the European lexicon—which were used for navigating and fighting in the rivers.[66] Sampans, or "three-board boats," were also widely used, being especially well suited for fighting in shallow water or mounting an onshore attack. They were unmasted sculls with raised sterns that formed a platform on which the pilot and helmsman rode, and with a mat roof in the middle of the deck for shelter. Crew members and women usually alternated sculling with keeping watch.[67]

Over the years the pirates accumulated an impressive store of arms. In 1806 the flagship of the Red Flag Fleet mounted ten cannon: two long 18-pounders and eight small 6-pounders.[68] By 1809, however, with the capture of the *P'eng-fa*, Chang Pao's flagship mounted 38 cannon on one deck alone; moreover, two of them fired 24-pound shot, and at least eight fired 18-pound shot.[69]

The country ships mentioned above had only ten to 15 cannon, and the largest fired only 12-pound shot. But those ships had much the advantage over the pirates, whose cannon, like those of the Chinese war junks, were simply mounted by "a rope rove thro' a hole in the gunnel and made fast to the muzzle of the gun."[70] Although some could be directed fore and aft with handspikes, the majority could not be positioned at all. Thus, in battle, the pirates were obliged to maneuver their ships to fix their prey in their sights. Before engaging the enemy, they would elevate or lower their guns, according to the distance between them. The gunners then stood with their matches ready and fired as soon as the aim was right.[71] Having discharged their broadsides, the junks then had to haul off to reload and reposition their guns. When fighting at close quarters, the pirates often fired nails or fragments of iron pots, and sometimes even used copper *cash* for grapeshot and canister.[72]

Pirate cannon generally weighed between 60 and 3,000 catties, although a piece of 6,000 catties was not uncommon. Some were wooden, with an iron bore, but the majority were smelted from varying grades of raw and scrap iron. Many of these were of the type called the turtle-dove (*pai-tzu* or *pan-chiu*), which were roughly cast, poorly constructed, and woefully inaccurate. Their structural deficiencies were compounded by the pirates' inability to fire them effectively.[73]

Armaments came to the pirates from a variety of sources. Some of the largest were acquisitions from the Tay-son that were taken in charge by Wu-shih Erh and Cheng I and distributed among the fleets. A few were salvaged from sunken or disabled vessels. Many were confiscated from captured prizes or seized during raids on coastal forts and guardhouses. But some were simply purchased from the Portuguese in Macao or from illegal smelters in Kwangtung.[74]

The pirates' stocks of small arms usually included the crudely built wall-pieces commonly known as the gingall, or Chinese blunderbuss, a Manchu invention used in the conquest of China. With a barrel seven feet long and a weight of 12 pounds, the gingall resembled the European wall-piece of the early eighteenth century or the elephant gun of the nineteenth. On land it was either steadied on a man's shoulder or mounted on a tripod and fired by two or three men; afloat it was fitted into a rowlock and mounted on the bulwarks. It fired iron scraps or ball of less than a pound. (Interestingly enough, this weapon, which was less likely to burst than other small arms of the period, was still used in China as late as 1945.)[75]

Besides gingalls, the pirates possessed a miscellany of old matchlocks and fowling pieces (*niao-chiang*), many of them of doubtful value, since their owners knew little or nothing about their care and operation. Chinese muskets were "wretched things," crudely made and of small calibers, with touchholes large enough to admit a tenpenny nail. If the charge did not blow out the back, it often escaped forward, because the ball went in without wad or ramming. The pirates' fowling pieces, 60-caliber flintlocks modeled after the Portuguese or European bird guns of the sixteenth century, were not much better. But worst of all were the matchlocks, which were fired by holding a slow-burning cord over the hole. Given such a mélange of weapons, it is little wonder that the pirates frequently forced European captives to assist them with their guns.[76]

This also explains why, in the end, the pirates relied most heavily on their skill in hand-to-hand combat. Their most deadly weapon was a long bamboo pike with a sharp, saberlike blade. The majority were around 14 to 18 feet long, but some ranged to lengths of more than 30 feet. Since they were hurled like javelins, they were always stored on the sampans in large numbers.[77] The pirates also had shorter pikes with shafts of solid wood and slightly curved blades that were sometimes sharpened on both edges. These were used for fighting at close quarters. For fighting their way aboard craft, though, the pirates generally preferred to use a short, heavy sword (*yao-tao*) barely 18 inches long, which resembled a woodcutter's billhook.[78]

The pirates also wielded knives of all sorts. Favorites were the long-handled *ch'ang-ping tao* and the *t'iao-tao* (literally, "knives carried on the shoulder"), which were described as long knives with iron-tipped blades of a "miscellaneous kind." To round out their arsenals, the pirates kept an assortment of bows and arrows, which were deployed on both land and sea. Their only protection against blades of all sorts were tightly woven rattan shields.[79]

Fire was another of the pirates' principal weapons. They often filled large boats with combustible straw and sent them ablaze into the fleets of their adversaries. Smaller firebrands, hurled out of long hollow bamboos, were aimed at enemy sails.[80] Also hurled at enemy vessels were "stinkpots," earthenware containers about the size of 32-pound shot half filled with a combination of gunpowder and Chinese gin (*sam-shew*). Pieces of ignited charcoal were placed in their concave lids, and the pots were then suspended from the masthead in bags. When flung onto enemy decks, the pots shattered and the powder ignited.[81]

The pirates were well supplied with gunpowder and shot. Ammunition was usually obtained from captured ships or stolen from government forts and smuggled to them by agents in Canton or Macao. Sometimes it was even purchased outright at plants that were supposedly manufacturing it for the army. On one occasion Glasspoole actually saw oversupplied pirates refuse 18-pound shot that had been brought to them from Whampoa.[82] On board ship, muskets were stored in the poop near the captain's quarters, and all ammunition supposedly in the hold. In practice, however, the pirates carelessly placed their gunpowder on deck in huge chests on which they sat to relax and smoke. During combat powder lay everywhere, and it was only by constantly wetting down the decks that the pirates kept themselves from being blown up.[83]

With no want of weapons, well-armed fleets took on the appearance of floating fortresses. In 1805, for example, an 11-junk, 301-man squadron had the following items in its arsenal:[84]

6 iron cannon	36 *t'iao-tao* knives (5 with
55 turtle-dove cannon	iron tips)
1 wooden cannon (iron core)	180 long-handled knives
40 lead shells	180 bamboo spears
2 fowling pieces	134 short knives
27 catties of iron bullets	23 rattan shields
55 catties of old lead and	10 iron chains
iron	Assorted sickles
36 catties of gunpowder	

Another squadron, of 5 boats and 489 people, had 100 cannon, 500 catties of gunpowder, and 883 miscellaneous hand weapons and guns. A third, with 10 boats and 669 people, had 127 cannon, 500 catties of gunpowder, and 789 miscellaneous weapons.

One of Chang Pao's largest squadrons, under the command of Huang Cheng-sung, had 36 junks with 1,422 men and 34 women and children. In addition to 1,270 fowling pieces, hooks, sickles, knives, and rattan shields, Huang had 206 cannon. Fully 50 of these were large, heavy cannon: 20 weighed between 600 and 3,000 catties, and 30 between 60 and 500 catties.[85]

Clearly, the pirates did not want for the tools of their trade, and the overall success of the confederation is nowhere better demonstrated than in its ability to not only feed but also royally equip several thousand members throughout most of its life.

Deprived of the benign environment they had enjoyed in Vietnam and no longer able to melt back into the milieu from which they had come, the Kwangtung pirates were forced to rely on their own resources. That they survived at all, let alone flourished, is testimony to their rare perception that their future lay in collective action. Whether or not these sea bandits can be labeled a "protest" group, as their counterparts on land often are, they clearly met the three conditions that theorists have argued are needed to counteract the centrifugal forces inherent in all such collective action groups: (1) the existence of a subculture; (2) the emergence of charismatic leaders; and (3) the creation of an overarching organizational framework.[86]

Yet even as they achieved greater and greater cohesion, the centrifugal forces that could pull them apart were building, namely, the forces of a state that could no longer close its eyes to their activities. Thus, the success or failure of the pirates would ultimately hinge on their military prowess. When pitted in action against enemies from without, how would the confederation fare?

6

The Ch'ing Response

The state did not sit idly by as the pirates grew bolder and bolder: 1805 saw a sharp change in direction toward a tough, new sea-war policy. The stage for this new beginning had been set on December 24, 1804, when the Chia-ch'ing Emperor resolved an extended debate on the merits of the old policy of sea defense by appointing his crack rebel-suppressor to exterminate the pirates in Kwangtung.

There was no one at hand more suited for the job than the man the Emperor chose, 40-year-old Na-yen-ch'eng.[1] Na was a Manchu of the Janggiya clan and a member of one of the Manchus' traditional military units, the Plain White Banner, who had advanced rapidly through the Ch'ing hierarchy. After serving on both the Grand Secretariat and the Grand Council and as president of the Board of Works, Na had begun his career as a rebel-suppressor in 1799, when he was sent to fight the White Lotus rebels in Shensi. His experience in countering dissidence broadened in 1802, when he was sent as an imperial commissioner to investigate a secret-society uprising in eastern Kwangtung. He settled the affair in record time and distinguished himself by a tough stance against the rebel leaders. Two years later his appointment as the governor-general of Shensi and Kansu put him back in the midst of the White Lotus rebels, who occupied his attention until the Emperor again sent him to Kwangtung.[2]

The Forces at Na's Disposal

On arriving in Kwangtung in the spring of 1805, Liang-kuang Governor-general Na found that he had been called on to perform a formidable task with a dearth of resources and an antiquated structure of military command that was a bureaucratic nightmare. For military purposes, Kwangtung had been divided into three districts (*lu*) since 1565. The eastern district ran west from the border of Kwangtung and Fukien provinces to encompass the prefectures of Hui-chou and Ch'ao-chou; the middle district encompassed Kuang-chou prefecture and guarded the heartland of the province; and the western district encompassed the "lower four" prefectures (Kao-chou, Lei-chou, Lien-chou, and Ch'iung-chou or Hainan Island). In principle the officials of these units were responsible for planning the province's maritime defense.[3] But a complex division of military authority made a coordinated effort all but impossible.

At the top of the military hierarchy were the Manchu Banner forces, with a naval contingent of 470 men divided into the Right Flank and the Left Flank. Their commander, a Tartar general, was the highest-ranking military official in the province.[4] Below the Manchu Banners stood the troops of the Green Standard Army. As an indigenous Chinese force, the Green Standard had been relegated to the role of a provincial constabulary by the conquering Manchus and fell under the shared command of civil and military officials.

Besides its military districts, the coastal strip of Kwangtung was divided into a pyramid of administrative units—circuits (*tao*), prefectures (*fu*), independent departments (*t'ing*), independent subprefectures (*chou*), and counties (*hsien*). Green Standard troops were deployed at each of these levels and were divided into various commands. The governor-general, the provincial commander-in-chief, and the governor headed forces of their own, known as the *tu-piao*, *t'i-piao*, and *fu-piao*, respectively. Below them came the Green Standard brigade-generals, whose water forces were allocated into brigades (*chen-piao*), regiments (*hsieh-piao*), battalions (*ying*), patrols or squadrons of the left and right (*shao*), and posts (*hsün*).[5]

During the late eighteenth and early nineteenth centuries, the governor-general's maritime forces were stationed in Chao-ch'ing, whose prefectural seat was Kao-yao, and the provincial commander-in-chief's in Hui-chou. The three "naval" brigade-generals of the Green Standard Army made their headquarters at Kao-chou, Nan-ao, and Ch'iung-chou (Hainan), respectively. It was their troops who manned the forts and guardhouses scattered along the coast. The overlap in the command system was deliberately fostered by the Manchu rulers, who were afraid of concentrating too much military power in the hands of a few Chinese.

Even so, it was theoretically possible for the Green Standard Army to be coordinated for a major undertaking. In practice, however, such coordination seldom took place. A governor-general could exercise

little authority over provincial officials such as the lieutenant governor, finance commissioner, and salt controller, who had troops of
their own. There were other breaks in the chain of command as well.
Below the highest provincial officials were other officials, such as circuit intendants (*tao-t'ai*), who also had their own troops. In some cases
brigade-generals had more strength than their superiors; in some districts civil officials with concurrent military power acted independently; and in some instances local officers had to answer to three or
four superiors. In extreme emergencies Emperors would often ap-
point special imperial commissioners, whose presence did little more
than add to the confusion. Coordinating movement across administrative jurisdictions, let alone across provinces, was almost impossible.[6]

The deployment of troops in small, disparate units along the coast
ensured that little could be accomplished by local units either. Because the Manchus feared the amalgamation of the Green Standard
Army as a threat to their own military superiority, in assigning it to
maintain coastal defense, they took care to keep its units small. The
hundreds of guardhouses (*hsün*) that dotted the coast, at intervals of
three to six miles, looked imposing enough with their watchtowers
and flags, but the small contingents of five, ten, or at most 20 men who
manned them could do little to stave off trouble and were easily overpowered when it arose.[7]

To further exacerbate the situation, fleets and armaments were also
spread thin. Although Kwangtung had 187 shallow-draft sampans
and rowboats to defend its rivers, these were divided among 35 marine battalions, which in turn further divided their five or six boats
among their own units.[8]

So, in contrast to the pirates, who never lacked for men or vessels,
the provincial navy was plagued by shortages of both. On investigation, Na found that at best he had a force of only 19,000 men and
83 rice carriers (*mi-t'ing*) with which to combat a pirate confederation at least three times that size.[9] Theoretically, Kwangtung's naval defense was predicated on having 135 rice carriers in operation at all
times. But the number usually fell far short of that. Vessels destroyed
by weather or attack were seldom replaced, and the rest were often in
such bad repair that they could not be used. Na's further inquiry revealed that only 57 of the province's 83 rice carriers were actually seaworthy; the other 26, sorely in need of repair, had been out of commission for a long time.

Rice carriers, originally designed for transporting tribute rice to the
Emperor, had formed the bastion of Kwangtung's anti-pirate defense
force since 1793. In the early nineteenth century these small vessels

(a)

(b)

(c)

Fig. 4. Rice carriers (*mi-t'ing*). Carriers (a) and (b), originally designed to transport tribute rice to the Emperor, were used as war junks in the attempt to suppress the pirates. Carrier (c), one of several types used locally in Kwangtung province for the transport of rice, is typical of the *mi-t'ing* of Hsiangshan county. Sources: model from the Maze Collection of Chinese Junk Models, Science Museum, Kensington, England; drawings from the India Office Library, London, Add. Or. 1976, 1994 (copied from the library's originals by Thomas A. Murray).

were also used to transport general cargo from Kwangtung to the northern ports. Like most other Chinese craft, they were built with solid transversal bulkheads that divided the hull into separate watertight compartments. They had fenestrated keels, high sterns, and three masts with flat, battened sails, and were capable of close sailing into the wind. Their decks were broad enough to permit the use of large cannon and to accommodate 40 to 80 men. Rice carriers were of three sizes—large, medium, and small. The largest weighed 2,500 *piculs*, the smallest 1,500 (see Fig. 4).[10] Rice carriers compared favorably in size to the majority of pirate junks, but in terms of armament and manpower, they were no match for pirate craft, which typically carried up to 200 men and mounted between 12 and 25 cannon. Moreover, they were often poorly made because dockyard personnel used only a small part of their shipbuilding allocations for construction and pocketed the rest.[11]

One traveler, commenting on the precarious state of maritime defense, remarked in 1805 that the Chinese had no navy to speak of, only a dozen junks that cruised about in the Bocca Tigris under the command of a low-ranking official.[12] Presumably this had reference to the fact that the rice carriers were not equipped to venture forth into deep waters, so that Chinese administrators were unable to extend their suzerainty more than a few thousand meters offshore. For this reason, as we have seen, they repeatedly wrote off incidents in the outer seas (*wai-hai* or *wai-yang*) as beyond the government's jurisdiction and grudgingly allowed large oceangoing junks to carry a limited number of arms for their own defense. This prerogative was seldom, if ever, accorded to the seagoing junks of the Nan-hai.[13]

Na found the state of naval arms fully as bad as the state of the fleet—indeed worse, for the Chinese had no cannon specifically designed for use at sea. Their war junks were haphazardly armed with Dutch and Portuguese fieldpieces of every age, length, shape, and caliber. The native cannon they carried were also fieldpieces and were cast of iron, but their bores were not drilled smooth. War junks seldom carried more than 14 guns and most fired shot of less than 10 pounds. Mounted and lashed with ropes of rattan onto solid blocks of wood, they could fire only point-blank shots.

Chinese gunpowder, of coarse grain and uneven quality, was as deficient as the guns that fired it. The gunpowder abounded in sulphur and decomposed rapidly. With the least exposure to air it caked together in unusable masses. To make matters worse, more than half of the shells did not fit the guns for which they were designed. The navy's knives, swords, and spears were dull and rusty, and its bows and arrows existed only on paper.[14]

The coast and rivers were supposed to be patrolled at all times on a rotation system, in which each of the three military districts sent out its fleet for six months of upper-river cruises and six months of lower-river cruises. Some of these cruising patrols were to be under the command of ranking officers, brigade-generals and colonels, and others were to have been led by captains or at least lieutenants. On designated dates and at designated sites, various units were to rendezvous and submit reports to their superiors.[15] But despite the meticulousness with which all this was set out on paper, the patrol cruises seldom took place, and on the rare occasions when they did, the rules were flagrantly violated, with sublieutenants, sergeants, and sometimes even common soldiers put in charge.[16] In 1800 these abuses elicited an imperial edict ordering all naval officers to go to sea in person, but it appears to have had little effect, for four years later the Emperor renewed his complaint.[17]

On top of everything else, lethargic local military commanders took few measures to protect the rivers or to maintain their fleets.[18] According to Na, throughout the province junks fresh from the shipbuilders were left to become waterlogged as they lay at anchor, and the older ones were allowed to split and rot. Even clear instructions from above were often ignored. When orders came to recaulk, many officials replied that the expense was not worth it; when orders came to go to sea, they complained that they lacked for vessels. If finally goaded into action, they performed their duties as perfunctorily as possible and filled in their fleets by hiring small, useless junks from coastal inhabitants.[19] Worse still, when the pirates attacked, these soldiers sometimes abandoned their stations and fled.[20]

By 1804 the situation had so deteriorated that military personnel, afraid to go to sea at all, resorted to putting their own ships out of commission. Those who could not avoid sea duty sailed with caution, and seldom appeared at any location where the pirates were thought to be until they had already left it. As a result there were few engagements, and almost none that ended in the government's favor.[21]

In October 1803 a leadership crisis occurred when the pirates defeated Brigade-general Huang Piao and Provincial Commander-in-chief Sun Ch'üan-mou in narrow Kuang-chou Bay. With a pirate fleet cornered inside the bay, Huang suggested that the pirates be starved out by blockade. Sun was unwilling, arguing that this would expose the ships to the capriciousness of monsoon storms. When at last Huang prevailed, the jealous Sun gave him only a handful of vessels and ordered him to defend the mouth of the bay alone. No sooner had the blockade been imposed than the pirates, on learning that only a few junks restrained them, charged forth and escaped. For the two men, defeated more by personal animosity than military ineptitude, the result was a personal tragedy: death from grief for Huang Piao, an imperial reprimand for Sun Ch'üan-mou.[22]

The reprimand brought no improvement. On July 30, 1804, the Emperor again criticized Sun Ch'üan-mou for his laxity in stopping the pirates, and the next day he was dismissed from office.[23] His replacement, Brigade-general Wei Ta-pin, proved even less successful, for on January 16, 1805, he lost an entire fleet of 40 gunboats when a navigational error took them into the heart of a storm.[24] On June 9, 1805, he, too, was dismissed from office and demoted to the rank of lieutenant. The next appointment, Hsü Wen-mo, lasted only two months, and finally, on August 2, Ch'ien Meng-hu became Kwangtung's third provincial commander-in-chief within a year.[25]

While incompetence plagued Na-yen-ch'eng's navy at the top, venality undermined it from below. Just as the pirates were often abetted by lower-level Chinese officials, so they were able to find men in the military ranks willing to help them for a price. In 1804 such collusion resulted in the failure of a Sino-Portuguese mission against the pirates, and on March 12, 1805, a warning shot fired by soldiers ruined Governor Sun Yü-t'ing's plan to arrest a pirate leader during a raid of his onshore residence in Lu-feng county.[26]

Na's Program for Local Defense

Na's immediate response to the problems confronting him was to seek the Emperor's permission to repair the 26 disabled rice carriers and construct 33 new ones to give him a provincial fleet of about 120 vessels.[27] But Na could not afford to sit back and wait for the Emperor's reply. Circumstances compelled him to act. So he set out to bolster his navy by other means: the hiring of fishing junks.

In a province-wide proclamation, Na appealed to all fishermen to cooperate in the effort to curb piracy with the promise of rations and silver to those who came forward. Shortly thereafter he extended his appeal to salt transporters (*yen-ch'uan*). The sailors and helmsmen on these vessels were to be issued certificates that authorized them to arrest pirates and rewarded with catties of salt. Anyone who captured a leader or some other important pirate was to receive official rank. Thanks to these efforts, Na was able to recruit a fleet of 120 private junks.[28]

During times of crisis, when regular military forces failed to perform, Chinese administrators encouraged the creation of extralegal, subbureaucratic mutual defense groups among the local populace, organized under the *pao-chia* system. The inspiration for the formation of these groups among the coastal population had come during the Ming dynasty from the official Huo T'ao, who noticed how easily coastal inhabitants in Tung-kuan, Hsiang-shan, and Shun-te counties (Kwangtung) slipped into piracy, and how little the authorities could do to stop them.[29] Huo outlined a program in which military personnel would help county magistrates and prefects establish mutual defense organizations in their jurisdictions. Under this system, 10 households constituted one *chia*, and 100 *chia* one *hsiang* (a subcounty unit or township). Members of a *chia* were to keep one another informed of their comings and goings. On the discovery of a suspicious person or pirate, the entire group was to join forces in arresting him so that the trouble would not spread.[30] Regulations for *pao-chia* as a preventive defense measure remained on the books until the end of the Ch'ing dynasty.

In 1707 inshore fishermen and fishing families who lived permanently on the water were ordered to establish similar units, in this case known as *ao-chia*. Ten junks would form a *chia* and elect a leader called the *chia-chang*. Thirty junks made up a *pao*, headed by a *pao-chang*. Each vessel was required to affiliate with a *chia* (or a smaller unit if there were fewer than ten boats in their locale). When there was an alarm, members were expected to go to the aid of one another. Each such incident was to be recorded, and at the beginning of each month officials were to inspect all records to make sure that everything was in order.[31]

In 1756 the system was elaborated to bring merchant and fishing junks under control. Ten junks constituted a *chia*, and every ten *chia* (or 100 vessels) formed a unit led by an *ao-chang* (fishing unit headman). Districts that lacked the stipulated 100 vessels still had an *ao-chang* placed at their head, and those with as many as 150 vessels had two *ao-chang*. One-masted merchant junks were organized separately from two-masted ones; Tanka and fishermen had separate units with their own *ao-chang*. A year later control of fishing junks was tightened. They were now instructed to return to their home ports at least once a month. Ten-boat units became a *p'ai*, headed by *p'ai-t'ou*; ten *pai* formed a *chia*, headed by a *chia-chang*.[32]

One of the problems inherent in the *pao-chia* system was that it specifically excluded the gentry from leadership positions, and therefore the organizations never got off the ground in many places. Whatever hopes Na may have entertained about *pao-chia* sharing the burden of anti-pirate defense were soon dashed. Despite the best efforts of his predecessor, Governor-general Chi-ch'ing, to activate the *pao-chia* in 1799 as a means of preventing collaboration between shore dwellers and pirates, when Na arrived five years later little progress had been made: mutual surveillance units had not been systematically formed; administration was lax and recordkeeping sloppy.[33]

In times of crisis county magistrates and other civilian officials customarily hired braves (*hsiang-yung*) to fill in for regular army troops. By 1796 such militarization was occurring in Kwangtung, but not on a scale commensurate with the problems. Thus, by 1800 members of the local gentry, usually barred from involvement in local defense, were being empowered to hire braves and mobilize villagers for the protection of their homes.[34]

In cases of extreme emergency the final self-defense units to appear in the Chinese countryside were gentry-led local militia (*t'uan-lien*). The goal of these organizations was to sever the links between dissidents and law-abiding inhabitants by resorting to a strategy known as "strengthening the walls and clearing the fields" (*chien-pi ch'ing-yeh*). Stout walls were erected around selected villages, and grain from the surrounding countryside was brought in and stored there, so that when the area was besieged, people living outside the walls could seek shelter in well-provisioned sanctuaries. Around these fortifications, residents were organized into local defense groups (*t'uan*), each bearing the name of the village to which it was attached.[35]

T'uan-lien were an integral element of Na-yen-ch'eng's defense strategy. As governor-general of Shensi and Kansu, he had used them repeatedly and successfuly in his suppression of the White Lotus rebels. But there were few *t'uan-lien* in Kwangtung when he arrived, and so, once again, Na had to take matters into his own hands. In another province-wide proclamation he called for his own version of "strengthening the walls and clearing the fields."[36] Declaring that "soldiers protecting people" was not so good as "people protecting themselves," and conceding that in any case total defense was impossible under the present system of forts and guardhouses, he exhorted village gentry and elders (*shen-ch'ih*) to form *t'uan-lien* for protection against the pirates.[37] His hope was that, at the beat of a gong, hoe-carrying farmers would be transformed into sword-wielding soldiers.

Under Na's plan, the name of every able-bodied male in each household was to be entered in a register. Households with three or more men were to volunteer one of them for militia training; those with fewer were to cooperate in providing a recruit. For the organization of these militia units, Na turned to the traditional *pao-chia* system. *Pao-chia* officials, such as the *chia-chang* (heads of 100-house units), were to serve simultaneously as training heads (*lien-t'ou*) in the militia. One or two large villages (or three or four smaller ones) were to pool their resources and form a single organization under the leadership of a principal militia captain (*cheng-t'uan-tsung*) or deputy militia captain (*fu-t'uan-tsung*), and as an indication of the seriousness of the problem an exception was made to allow these positions to be filled by the gentry.

The militias were to concentrate on drilling and discipline. During the day they were to send out spies in search of information; at night they were to patrol all strategic locations. They were also encouraged to build stone watchtowers (*tiao-lou*) and prepare signals so that alarms could be quickly transmitted from village to village. According to Na's system, the firing of two cannon would signal the approach of pirates and summon the militia captains to begin preparations. Three shots would signal the pirates' arrival and summon the men to their stations. To ensure the smooth running of the *t'uan-lien* and as a guard against corruption, prefectural and district officials were to go to each village in person, investigate its procedures, and reward outstanding leaders with silver taels or official rank. Cannon could be borrowed from nearby battalions or made locally at the villagers' expense, but were to be surrendered to the county magistrate as soon as the pirates were suppressed.[38]

Since "strengthening the walls and clearing the fields" was effective only for the hinterland, Na developed an alternative for the coast. Settlements near the sea were to be protected by moats surrounded by earthen embankments. The moats were to be 12 feet deep and 20 feet wide, and the surrounding embankments 30 feet tall, too high for any pirate to climb. Wherever possible, the embankments were to be planted with bamboo and surrounded by tile walls 12 feet high and 12 inches thick. (These measurements are all in Chinese feet or inches.) Removable bridges were to span the moat.[39]

In response to Na's proclamation, two gentry, Cheng Min-ta and Liu Yüan-lung, established *t'uan-lien* in Hsiang-shan county. By levying a tax of 0.008 of an ounce of silver per *mou* of land on all county landowners, they accumulated 10,000 taels, and with this they built weirs, bought cannon, constructed guardhouses, hired boats from the people, and recruited a force of several hundred stalwarts (*chuang-yung*).* Funds were also collected in Shun-te county, at a rate of 80 *wen* of silver per *mou* of land; landlords and tenants were to split the cost.[40]

If Na's goal of a province-wide system of local militias was to be realized, however, Kwangtung's spontaneous, ad hoc, and widely diverging local defenses would have to be thoroughly systematized and coordinated. Even under ideal circumstances, this would take time, and in 1805 circumstances in Kwangtung were far from ideal. Not only were the pirates growing bolder, but China had become embroiled in controversies with both Portugal and Britain, and so Na could not expect any aid from either quarter.

The troubles with Portugal began in late March 1804, when pirates occupied the Taypa (Taipa) anchorage of Macao. By April 3 they had reduced the city to a two-day supply of rice, and Macao, defended by fewer than 120 soldiers, was in a state of alarm. To make matters worse, the city had only one small vessel, and it was sorely in need of repair.[41] Portuguese officials quickly purchased the grab ship *Nancy*, then under English colors at Whampoa. During the next several days, as the Portuguese readied their two vessels, the pirates continued to hold their own in the harbor.[42] Finally, on April 11, one of the Por-

---

Chuang-yung were civilian militiamen who were mobilized for local defense by county magistrates or gentry to handle local military emergencies.

tuguese vessels made its appearance and put the pirates to flight. Two weeks later the first of a short-lived series of Sino-foreign expeditions set out to give chase as the Portuguese ships joined 20 Chinese war junks from Hsiang-shan. The mission was a complete failure. Owing to a combination of strong winds and the Chinese navy's practice of "keeping aloof," the pirates escaped into the shallows, and the armada was forced to return to port.[43]

A second attempt at collaboration took place six months later in the autumn of 1804, but this effort also failed. After petitioning the Hoppo at Canton to be allowed to join in the effort to stamp out the pirates, the Portuguese were given permission to prepare four ships at their own expense.* These vessels then joined 100 Chinese junks, which arrived in Macao on September 3. The expedition set out on October 10 and remained at sea until early November.[44] What actually happened is difficult to ascertain, but according to the Portuguese commander, the fault lay with the Chinese, who instead of attacking the pirates, supplied them with provisions from the shore. After several useless protests, the Portuguese returned to port.[45]

The Chinese told a different story. According to their commander, Wei Ta-pin, the mission failed not because of Chinese collusion with the pirates, but because the deep draft of the Portuguese vessels prevented them from pursuing the pirates into the shallows. At all odds, on learning of the joint collaboration, the Emperor was outraged. He dismissed both the governor-general and the Hoppo, and decreed that the Portuguese should never again be allowed to conduct missions with the Chinese. Thereafter, Portuguese ships were to be confined to the waters around Macao.[46]

In 1805 China's relations with the British were hardly better. The British had always proceeded against the pirates with caution. Called on to assess the situation, the select committee of supercargoes concluded that the pirates offered little challenge to His Majesty's ships or Indiamen, but did threaten the lightly armed country ships.† Yet the British hesitated to jump headlong into any endeavor of their own for fear that a setback would result in a national humiliation and loss of face.

---

*Hoppo was the foreigners' term for the superintendent of customs of Kwangtung province, a usage that grew out of their having mistaken this official, who was a member of the Emperor's private "inner bureaucracy," with the head of the Hu-pu, or Board of Revenue of the "outer" (or regular civil service) bureaucracy. In fact the two positions, superintendent of customs and head of the Hu-pu, were totally unrelated.

†The East India Company's select committee of supercargoes consisted of the three senior supercargoes, along with the president, or "taipan." One of its primary tasks was discharging necessary diplomatic duties, since there was no official diplomatic exchange between Britain and China in this period.

Still, they seemed willing to take the risk, for on October 8, 1804, Captain B. W. Page, head of His Majesty's warships, who had been sent to convoy the Indiamen to England, informed the supercargoes that he and Admiral Peter Rainier stood ready to defend Macao and protect local trade.[47] On October 25 the supercargoes relayed this offer to the Hoppo and requested permission for Page's fleet to anchor in the Bocca Tigris. Chinese law prohibited foreign warships from entering the Bocca Tigris, and the British generally acquiesced by anchoring at Macao or Lintin. But by this time the pirates' activities in the Pearl River were making it difficult for the British to supply their ships from Macao, and they wanted a safer anchorage in China's internal waters.[48] The Hoppo, reluctant to alter the traditional arrangement, objected to the move, but he did promise to forward the British offer of assistance to the governor-general. Two days later the Hong merchants (Puan Khequa and Mowqua) informed the supercargoes that the governor-general, ridiculing the idea that the pirates were too formidable for his own defenses, had rejected the British proposal.[49]

In the meantime, however, the British men-of-war had already moved to Anson's Bay, just south of the Bocca Tigris, where their presence elicited a protest from the Chinese and a demand for their removal. On November 19 the Hoppo referred to the pirates as a force "too contemptible to cause a moment's uneasiness" and explained to Captain Page that measures were being taken to destroy them.[50] In the end the warships were allowed to anchor in Anson's Bay, but the Chinese remained firm in their rejection of British aid, and a thoroughly alarmed Emperor now exhorted his own officials to clear the seas so as to spare the empire any further involvement with the foreigners. In his instructions, the Emperor specifically ordered Na-yench'eng to strengthen the local defenses and instill discipline in his troops so that the pirates would voluntarily withdraw and the foreign barbarians would have no further cause for fear.[51]

Eager as Na no doubt was to obey the Emperor, in dealing with the foreign barbarians he had to walk a tightrope. On the one hand, he had the job of convincing them that adequate measures were being undertaken for their safety and that their help was not needed. But on the other hand, he also knew that any intensification of pirate activity or a disruption of trade might precipitate unilateral action. Unfortunately for Na, the situation continued to deteriorate. Not only did the pirates persist in their occupation of the Broadway (as the major passage between Macao and Canton was known) and in interrupting traffic between its major cities, but their incursions deep into the Pearl River began to take place with alarming frequency. During the summer of 1805 they attacked villages in Shun-te, Hsin-hui, P'an-yü, Kuei-shan, and Tung-kuan counties, and raided forts in Hsin-hui and Hai-feng. Passage between Macao and Canton became almost impossible, and in August a chop boat carrying two Americans was captured eight miles from Macao.[52]

Despite the seriousness of the situation Na's defense program moved slowly. At the end of the summer his rice carriers were still not finished. His auxiliary forces of fishermen and salt vessels (*hung-tan yen-ch'uan*) were enjoying some successes against the pirates, but the fishing season was approaching, and they would soon resume their primary occupations. Na's exhortations to form *t'uan-lien* had generated little response, and local defense measures continued in the same sporadic manner as before.[53]

Na's Extermination Campaigns

By late summer Na-yen-ch'eng could not afford to wait any longer. In desperation he undertook the most ambitious offensive of his career: a campaign against the pirates' western headquarters at Kuang-chou Bay (see Map 5, p. 122). Realizing the importance of dislodging the pirates from this stronghold, Na mobilized a fleet of 80 gunboats for an all-out assault.[54] At the head of his expedition were Brigade-general of the Left Flank Lin Kuo-liang, (acting) Colonel of the Hsiang-shan Regiment, Hsü T'ing-kuei, and Lieutenant Colonel Ho Ying of the Hai-k'ou Battalion. Additional forces under the Second Captain of Wu-ch'uan, the magistrate of Hai-k'ang, and the sub-district magistrate of Tung-yang took up positions at the entrance to the bay, while braves from Wu-ch'uan and Sui-ch'i guarded the customs house.

On September 5, as the fleet approached, the pirates opened fire. Soon after, ten additional junks sailed to their aid, and in a battle that raged from dawn until noon, the government forces sank seven pirate junks and captured three. General Lin Kuo-liang pursued some others to Nao-chou Island, where he set their vessels aflame with incendiary weapons and captured four more. By the end of the battle, the pirates had lost 79 men, 26 iron cannon, and an assortment of banners, swords, and guns. Meanwhile, the troops at the entrance of the bay had killed ten others, including Cheng San, the younger brother of the confederation leader Cheng I, and had taken 22 prisoners and a boat, bringing the pirates' total losses for the day to 111 men and 15 junks.

The remaining pirates managed to make their escape, and a typhoon arose to prevent further pursuit. But General Lin Kuo-liang dealt them one last blow. Seeking shelter from the storm, he entered a harbor surrounded by grass shacks, which on closer investigation proved to be the pirates' places for buying rice and selling prizes. These he promptly put to the torch. Nearby, on the sandy bank, were ten empty boats put ashore for repair. Concluding that they too were the property of the pirates, he burned them as well.

The effect of the raid at Kuang-chou Bay was simply to force the pirates to take the offensive. The target they selected was Tien-pai, where 90 loaded salt vessels were awaiting departure. After withstanding heavy fire from the forts onshore, they attacked the salt ships on the morning of September 13.[55] By noon they had reached the harbor of Hsing-p'ing, some three miles away, where a second large fleet was just departing. With the pirates fast approaching and the water forces powerless to act in time, the salt commissioner took matters into his own hands and distributed cannon and fowling pieces to his men. The armed salt crews managed to hold their own against the sampans heading into the harbor, and the pirates were forced to withdraw that night. As they did so, a heavy gale arose, which prevented them from renewing their assault until the following noon. This time their efforts were foiled by a combined force of soldiers, braves, and boatmen, who destroyed several junks, captured 10 pirates, and killed around 100. As night fell, the pirates again withdrew.

The next morning the determined pirates reappeared with 100 vessels for still another try, but the defenders were equally determined. Their cannon scored a direct hit and when a pirate junk burst into flames, its 106 crew members were captured as they made their way to shore.[56] Finally, on September 16, the pirates gave up the attempt to take the harbor and headed for Lien-t'ou, where they remained a few days before being chased back to T'ien-pai. As the government forces converged near Tien-pai, 40 pirate vessels moved farther west to attack Lung-men. The city was saved, but the fort was not. After the pirates cut off the sea approaches, the garrison, isolated on the opposite shore and surrounded by water, surrendered. That night the pirates came ashore, carried off the officers, and burned down the fort.[57]

The final battle in the campaign occurred on September 20, when a group of pirates, still loitering in the vicinity of Hsing-p'ing, again tried to enter the harbor. In a short while, fire from shore forced them to withdraw, but that evening, under cover of darkness, they sailed to Lien-t'ou, where 70 or 80 men went ashore for a new attempt from the land. Before they could complete their mission, however, the

soldiers rallied. The pirates' attack was repulsed and 15 were captured alive.[58]

For Na-yen-ch'eng, the result of the entire campaign was (at the
highest estimate) 600 pirates killed; 18 junks (including the 10 empty
boats undergoing repair) destroyed; and 232 pirates and 8 junks captured. As a major anti-pirate offensive, its results were disappointing:
800 pirates and 26 vessels were no more than a tiny fraction of the
confederation's forces. The pirates were nowhere close to having been
exterminated, and as Na himself later pointed out, they even continued to anchor in Kuang-chou Bay. The Ch'ing navy, despite a good
performance on September 5, faltered thereafter, and most of the
victories were achieved either with the aid of local forces or as the result of onshore action.

The Turn to a Different Policy

After the failure of his offensive, Na found himself in an even more
precarious situation. What else could he do to satisfy an Emperor who
continued to call for sea war? His navy, outnumbered three to one in
both vessels and men, could scarcely be relied on to go to sea, let alone
engage the pirates in combat.[59] For local defense he still had only a few
militia, and as even the Emperor seemed to realize, although Na could
promote the establishment of *t'uan-lien*, he could not organize and
oversee them himself.[60] The Westerners, quiet for the moment, were
increasingly concerned about both the escalation of piracy and the
Chinese government's refusal of their aid. If one of their ships should
be attacked, their demands for retaliation could create havoc for local
administrators.

Persuaded that sea war was now out of the question, Na believed he
had little choice but to adopt a policy of "pardon and pacification." In
theory this policy was to have been employed only when an adversary
was on the verge of defeat, so in applying it to a pirate force reaching
ever new heights of power, Na showed his desperation. In the autumn
of 1805 he issued a proclamation setting out the ground rules for his
new policy. His appeal to surrender was aimed chiefly at those who
had been forced to become pirates against their will. He urged them
to escape from their captors and turn themselves in to the authorities.
If possible, he wanted them also to atone for their past actions by killing their captors or leading Ch'ing officials to their hideouts.[61] As evidence of their sincerity and desire to turn over a new leaf, those who
surrendered were to present the severed heads or ears of their victims
when they came in.

In going this far, Na had already departed significantly from the traditional pardon and pacification policy. But he went even further by allowing all pirates, forced or not, and leaders as well as followers, to surrender. Indeed he even sent out yamen personnel to encourage the leaders to bring their men in. The first to comply was Yüan Ya-ming, who after being summoned by two spies from Hai-feng, persuaded 301 of his followers to surrender themselves and their equipment: 11 large junks, 17 cannon, 27 catties of shot, 55 catties of iron, 36 catties of gunpowder, 180 bamboo spears, 134 short swords, 23 shields, 10 iron chains, and an assortment of sickles, coins, and bullets.[62]

The treatment of Yüan and other early surrendered pirates set the precedent for those who followed. The officials made lists of all who turned themselves in and then presented each former pirate with ten silver taels. Those with no occupation were turned over to the yamen to fill positions as servants (*fu-i*) or military conscripts (*chuang-ting*). Those who wanted to return home were given road passes (*lu-piao*) and released into the custody of their clansmen. Those who were willing to serve in the army were given rations and assigned to battalions. Capable helmsmen were retained by the navy. To make the appeal even more attractive, leaders were rewarded with low military rank and the promise of appointments as sublieutenants or lance sergeants after a certain period of service in the army. Wives and families were settled onshore, where yamen personnel were to keep them under surveillance and file monthly reports on their activities.[63]

The Emperor greeted Na's initiatives unenthusiastically. He believed that the mere pardoning of former pirates was reward enough and disapproved of giving them money or rank. He also frowned on allowing them to enter the army for fear this would encourage even more pirate-soldier collaboration.[64] But the policy was continued despite the Emperor's objections. Between October and December the campaign gained momentum as pirates surrendered by the hundreds. By late October Na was able to report the "return to allegiance" of 1,813 pirates. To each of these, in defiance of imperial orders, he had presented ten silver taels drawn from the provincial treasury's arrest fund (*fan-k'u ch'i-pu-hsiang*). Moreover, he had bestowed military ranks even more generously than before: 10 of the surrendered leaders became lieutenants, and 19 became sublieutenants or sergeants.[65]

Aware of the Emperor's attitude, Na tried to put the best face on his policy by depicting those coming ashore as the starving remnants of a disintegrating confederation. On October 25 he reported to the Emperor that his defense measures had so reduced the pirates' grain supply that they had barely enough for a bowl of congee (gruel) a day. He also reported that hungry pirates were violating their own territorial limits, and that the rank and file were deserting by the score. In Na's description, the pirates were in truly desperate straits:

They are now in a poor and impoverished state at sea. The leaders and followers are both in danger. The sailors they capture are imprisoned in the hold, and it is only when the boats set sail that they are released. The weapons laid up have not been issued to the crew, and they are not allowed to talk with one another in order to prevent mutiny. Each day they have only one meal of congee. Life is hard on board ship (a day seems like a year), so that when the junks come upon sandy or shallow places, many of the pirates jump into the water to escape. . . . Furthermore, the junks of the pirates who have surrendered are in bad shape, with the sails spoiled by damp and mildew. The cannon are not able to fire, and the pirates lack gunpowder and shot.[66]

Na's picture bore little resemblance to the reality of a force that was growing stronger each day, but he continued to cover up the truth by misrepresenting it. In contrast to his predecessors, who had minutely reported the details of each pirate case that came before them, Na's memorials were often little more than long lists of apprehended pirates, robbers, and supply agents.[67] News of major incidents were concealed from the Emperor as long as possible. Not until July did Na report that the Ch'ih-ao fort had been attacked in March; and not until December was the Emperor informed of the pirates' summer raids in Hsiang-shan, Shun-te, and Shui-tung or of their autumn activity in P'an-yü. Other attacks at Sha-chi-yung, Hsiang-shan, and Shun-te went totally unreported; the Emperor learned of them only from a censor.[68] Na also failed to mention that several pirates had escaped while being resettled near Kuei-shan.[69]

But Na's actions finally caught up with him when the provincial governor, Sun Yü-t'ing, alerted the Emperor to what was actually going on. In November Sun sent a memorial to the throne complaining about the bad precedent Na was setting by offering money to pirates who surrendered. Estimating the pirate force at tens of thousands, Sun pointed out that if every pirate accepted the offer and received ten taels, the treasury would soon be exhausted. In fact, he charged, pirates were surrendering only for the money and should there be hard times onshore, they would assuredly turn to piracy again. Meanwhile, public morale had been so badly undermined that many people now thought it more advantageous to be a pirate than to be a "good person." Sun pointed out that the official's failure to investigate the backgrounds of those submitting made it impossible to distinguish between voluntary and involuntary pirates. And how, he asked, could one determine whether the severed heads that the pirates turned in were truly those of pirates? They might easily be heads of captives, refugees, or the miscellaneous dead. Finally, Sun objected to the practice of rewarding with official rank those who had in many cases committed crimes worthy of lingering death and pointed out that soldiers were becoming increasingly resentful of pirates, who so easily obtained ranks superior to their own.[70]

Sun's memorial reached Peking simultaneously with one from Na reporting the surrender of still more pirates. The Emperor replied at once. Stating that Na-yen-ch'eng had been sent to Kwangtung to "exterminate," not "pardon," the pirates, the Emperor criticized his way of handling them point by point. To Na's argument that the pirates were weak and impoverished, the Emperor replied that, on the contrary, it was Na who was weak, and the pirates were taking advantage of that weakness to go ashore, plunder, and cause disturbances. As for rewarding pirates, he had never, under any circumstances, given Na permission to grant them military rank, and he had approved cash grants for only small numbers of people on rare occasions. Since more than 3,000 pirates had surrendered, hardly a small number, Na should not have used the pirate extermination fund to reward them. He had also been wrong in his policy of recruiting surrendered pirates into the army. Soon after this missive was sent, the final break came. On December 12 the Emperor dismissed Na-yen-ch'eng and replaced him with the governor-general of Chihli (Hopei), Wu Hsiung-kuang.[71]

In the short time left to him before his successor's arrival in Kwangtung (January 7, 1806), Na further defied the Emperor by allowing an additional 300 pirates to surrender. Among them were Huang Cheng-sung and Li Chung-yü, two "notorious" leaders who had operated independently of the confederation in eastern Kwangtung. In bringing them to terms, Na exceeded even his own precedent by paying Huang 1,000 taels, allowing him to retain a force of three junks and 180 men to sail with the navy, and commissioning him as a captain. Li Chung-yü was also commissioned as a captain and rewarded with a silver placard. When the Emperor learned of these excesses, he ordered Na brought in custody to the capital where, after a lengthy trial, he was sentenced to military exile and deported to Ili, on the northwestern frontier.[72]

The tragedy of the well-intentioned Na was that of a man left to tackle an enormous task without the right resources. Defeated in his attempts to wage war at sea, Na did not give up, but tried instead to take matters into his own hands. His recourse was to the time-honored expedient of pardon and pacification. But desperation caused him to alter the procedure almost beyond recognition, so that instead of allowing defeated followers to surrender on the eve of their extermination, he was in effect paying off leaders his navy could not touch. In bringing about Na's downfall and exposing the inadequacy of the Emperor's sea-war policy, the pirates demonstrated that they were the dominant military power along the South China coast.

7

Official Policy in Trouble

After Na-yen-ch'eng's fall, the pirates continued to defeat the government forces in a succession of engagements at sea. Most spectacular was their complete rout of Li Ch'ang-keng, the provincial commander-in-chief of Chekiang, in early 1808. For years Li had provided an almost solitary example of a government official resolved to do his duty. As the leading naval officer in both Fukien and Chekiang provinces, he had the special mission of capturing the pirate Ts'ai Ch'ien. This was his goal on January 21, 1808, when he pursued Ts'ai into Kwangtung waters and, in an all-night engagement, destroyed 15 of his junks. At dawn, however, the tide of battle turned and the pirates successfully fended off Li's fire vessels. As Li pulled up for a new attack, a salvo from a pirate cannon struck him squarely in the throat. He died the next day, and all but two or three of his ships were captured.[1]

Li's death was a sobering event that alarmed officials throughout South China. But the most alarmed of all was Wu Hsiung-kuang, the Liang-kuang Governor-general, who grew suddenly apprehensive at this evidence of the pirates' increased audacity and fearful of imperial censure for not having prepared a fleet to cooperate with that from the neighboring province. Li's death compelled officials in Kwangtung to acknowledge the seriousness of the pirate threat and confront the problem in earnest.[2]

Wu's immediate response was to petition the throne for permission to construct a new fleet. Arguing that the rice carriers were incapable of sailing into the rough waters of the outer ocean, he wanted to build 60 "raised-flower" (*teng-hua*) junks instead. These vessels, he pointed out, had already demonstrated their effectiveness against the pirates in eastern Kwangtung. They were approximately 100 feet long, 21 feet wide, and nine feet high, and cost 7,000 taels apiece, excluding arms.[3]

As Wu waited for an official go-ahead, talk of the new fleet reached the supercargoes in Macao. Confident of its potential, Governor-general Wu refused their offers of aid; his new fleet, he told them, would make an official request for English assistance unnecessary.[4] The Emperor, however, did not share Wu's enthusiasm for the new junks, and on July 25 he severely upset the governor-general's plans by ordering him to delay construction until the project could be further investigated. For several months the situation remained in limbo, with neither investigation nor construction being undertaken.[5]

The Invasion of the Pearl River

While officials dallied in Peking, the pirates dealt them another devastating blow by bringing the fight to Canton itself. At this time all the junks allocated for the city's defense were gathered under Lin Kuo-liang, brigade-general of the Bocca Tigris. Early on July 5, 1808, Lin's fleet set sail for a small island not far from Macao, where it encountered a detachment of the Red and Black Flag fleets.[6] Chang Pao, warned in advance of the approaching force, had already determined his strategy. After concealing most of his fleet in a nearby bay, he emerged with only a few junks to confront Lin. Lured by Chang's ruse, Lin promptly responded by sinking seven junks and killing more than 100 pirates. Sparing nothing in his advance, he then sent his 25 ships in pursuit of the pirates. Just as he thought he was on the verge of success, Chang's concealed fleet—more than 100 strong— emerged from hiding, surrounded Lin's ships, and fired on them from all sides. Unable to break out of the encirclement, Lin's men put up a valiant defense. At one point Chang Pao, standing at the bow of his ship, provided a clear target for the struggling general, and Lin, quick to take advantage of this rare opportunity, fired a large cannon directly at him. Chang fell to the deck and was taken for dead. The shot, however, had merely grazed him, and a few seconds later, when the smoke had cleared, the pirate was again standing at his ship's bow.

Soon after, some well-aimed fire disabled Lin's junk and allowed Chang Pao's vanguard to board. Once on deck, the pirates beheaded the helmsman and took command of the ship. But Lin's men put up a stiff fight; bloody clashes throughout the day yielded an accumulation of corpses in the hold. The tide of battle turned when the septuagenarian Lin, vowing that he would die fighting, was stabbed by one of Chang's subordinates. At that point the pirates were able to sink three imperial junks and capture 15 soldiers. In the end fewer than seven of Lin's junks remained intact.[7]

These losses did not deter the Emperor, who continued to call for sea war. The man he chose as Lin's successor was the former provincial commander-in-chief, Sun Ch'üan-mou, who, after being dismissed for his defeat in 1803, had worked his way back up through the ranks of the bureaucracy.[8]

Meanwhile, Wu Hsiung-kuang, like Na-yen-ch'eng, had been forced to hire salt vessels and fishing junks to round out his navy.[9] This rag-tag fleet, under its acting commander, Lieutenant Colonel Lin Fa, was humiliated in its first encounter with the pirates in late September. Indeed, Lin had sought to avoid the encounter to begin with. Accidentally discovering the pirates in a bay, he turned tail and fled. When Lin, after being pursued to a small island south of Hong Kong, at last stood and fought, the astonished pirates temporarily retreated. But a sudden change in the weather allowed them to advance and deliver a barrage that cost Lin six junks and 24 men.[10]

In defeating Lin Fa, Chang Pao eliminated the major impediment to his entrance into the Pearl River. Thereafter, pirates swarmed into the tributaries of the interior, and official policy was in trouble. The governor-general's attempt to confront the pirates at sea had failed. The provincial fleet had been reduced by half. More junks awaited repair in the dockyards than sailed the sea, and Canton was left with little protection. Provincial resources were at an all-time low.[11]

In 1809, with the situation becoming more critical every day, the Emperor replaced Wu Hsiung-kuang with the Chinese bannerman Pai Ling. During his earlier stint as governor of Kwangtung, in 1805, Pai Ling had won universal acclaim as a zealous and capable administrator.[12] Eager to live up to his reputation, he set to work on the pirate problem soon after his arrival in April. He first sought to strengthen the navy with a request for 40 new rice carriers in place of the 20 raised-flower junks Wu Hsiung-kuang had asked for (on which no construction had begun). A few weeks later, after a new assessment of the situation, Pai revised his request; now he thought 100 rice carriers would have to be built if the navy was to have any hope of defeating the pirates at all.[13]

As Pai himself acknowledged, the construction of so large a fleet would require time, and the province was in immediate need of vessels. So for the short term Pai, like his predecessors Na-yen-ch'eng and Wu Hsiung-kuang, resorted to the expedient of hiring private craft. If the Emperor permitted, he would hire 90 of the largest salt

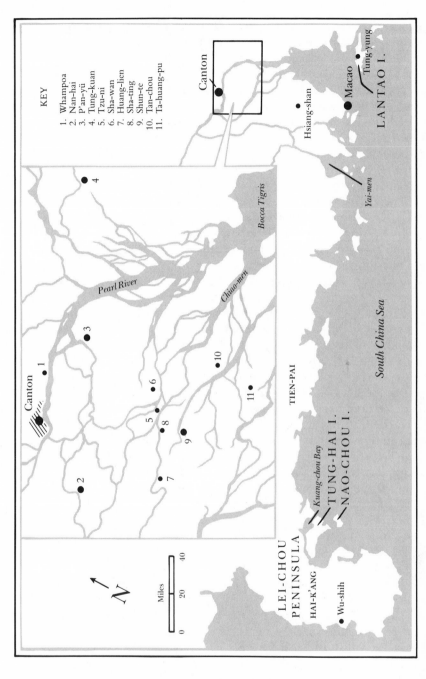

KEY
1. Whampoa
2. Nan-hai
3. P'an-yü
4. Tung-kuan
5. Tzu-ni
6. Sha-wan
7. Huang-lien
8. Sha-ting
9. Shun-te
10. Tan-chou
11. Ta-huang-pu

Canton

Pearl River

Bocca Tigris

Chiao-men

Canton

1

3

6

5

8

9

7

2

4

10

11

TIEN-PAI

LEI-CHOU PENINSULA

HAI-K'ANG

Kuang-chou Bay

TUNG-HAI I.

NAO-CHOU I.

Wu-shih

Hsiang-shan

Macao

Yai-men

LANTAO I.

Tung-yung

South China Sea

N

Miles

0   20   40

Map 5   Sites of pirate activity in Kwangtung. The Bocca Tigris (inset) was also known variously as the Bogue and Hu-men.

and fishing junks available, and then, as each new rice carrier emerged from the dockyard, one of the hired vessels would be retired. Pai also wanted to hire a fleet of red-, green- and white-hulled cargo junks to station at strategic points, such as Yai-men, Wei-chia-men, Hu-t'iao, Mo-tao, Hu-men, and Ma-ch'i, and to fit out 150 of the province's smaller craft, man them with volunteers (*chuang-yung*), and send them out to work with the navy's river patrols. As a further measure of protection for the center of the province, he wanted to transfer the 50-junk fleet of the Chieh-shih Brigade, under General Huang Fei-p'eng, to the mouth of the Pearl River.[14]

While these requests were being considered, Pai Ling took measures to starve out the pirates from the shore. Convinced that it was only because of supplies reaching them from the interior that they survived, Pai decided to sever their supply lines by forcing salt to travel overland instead of over the sea, and by imposing a coastal embargo that would prevent all junks from leaving port.[15] In this policy Pai Ling differed little from his predecessors, for both Na-yen-ch'eng and Wu Hsiung-kuang had also tried to disrupt the pirates' sources of supply. But Pai had more success in implementing it. Now that the pirates could no longer be ignored, the public was more willing to respond to his promulgations. Ships that had already left port were called back. Coastal inhabitants were severely admonished to stop aiding pirates and paying them blackmail. The garrisons along the coast were beefed up, and special personnel were sent to implement the embargo.[16]

Pai's plan quickly bore fruit as the pirates began to experience difficulty procuring food. What Pai had not foreseen, however, was that hungry pirates, instead of loitering on the ocean awaiting government extermination, would simply go ashore and help themselves to the harvest. They made their first onshore foray for food on June 10, when Wu-shih Erh and his Blue Flag Fleet sailed into a harbor not far from Tien-pai and went on land to raid; a few days later they destroyed the fort at Ch'ih-shui.[17] Closer to Canton, the Red Flag Fleet was also searching for food. After an inconclusive battle with the forces of the provincial commander-in-chief, the pirates moved inland, sailing through the narrows at Yai-men and Wei-chia-men, which gave them easy access to the markets of Nan-hai, Hsin-hui, K'ai-p'ing, and Shun-te counties.[18]

With pirates threatening the interior, Ch'ing officials had to act. Sun Ch'üan-mou (who on June 11 had replaced the ailing Ch'ien Meng-hu as the provincial commander-in-chief) left the Bocca Tigris to confer with the governor-general in Canton. By this time 35 of the rice carriers under repair were ready for service and were turned over to Hsü T'ing-kuei, the brigade-general of the Bocca Tigris, who already had 53 salt junks deployed on the rivers.[19]

On July 20 (1809) Hsü T'ing-kuei anchored at Wei-chia-men, seeking shelter from the weather. There he was spotted by Chang Pao, who despite the heavy rain had sent out a reconnaissance party. The next morning Hsü found himself surrounded by the White Flag Fleet. Though they were caught with their sails down and their ships at anchor, Hsü's men put up a good fight, and in the end virtually destroyed the White Fleet. Among the pirates' casualties were the White Fleet's leader, Tsung-ping Pao, and the father of the Black Fleet's leader, Kuo P'o-tai.[20]

Just as panic was breaking out among the pirates, Chang Pao appeared with 300 vessels. A sudden wind prevented Hsü's ships from maneuvering into position to fire their cannon, but enabled the pirates to sail close enough to launch a barrage of fire balls. Five of Hsü's junks were instantly destroyed. About noon Chang Pao pressed close to his enemy's flagship and set fire to its stern. As the junk burned, the pirates boarded. Liang P'o-pao was first to cross, followed by Chang Pao and a host of others. In the fighting that followed, Hsü was killed, and his lifeless body fell overboard into the water. Strong winds prevented Hsü's forces from renewing the charge. One major managed to down an enemy, but it cost him his life: the pirates boarded his vessel and threw him overboard. The government's losses for the day were devastating. Only ten of Hsü's 35 rice carriers returned to port.[21]

In routing Hsü-T'ing-kuei, the pirates proved themselves capable of destroying war junks faster than the government dockyards could produce them. In the year since General Lin Kuo-liang's defeat, the provincial navy had lost 63 rice carriers or nearly half of its theoretical 135-ship allotment, which left only 19 to defend the entire middle district. Most of the auxiliary salt and fishing vessels were now out of commission as well. At this point, even the Emperor acknowledged the futility of continued sea war, and the policy was abandoned while the navy rebuilt. A hundred rice carriers and 1,000 cannon were slated for construction.[22]

T'uan-Lien and Local Defenses

With the Ch'ing navy out of the picture and the embargo seeming only to drive the pirates farther inland, Pai Ling turned to the local elite in the hope that they might be able to hold the pirates at bay. Convinced that the pirates could be stopped only by allowing villagers to defend themselves, he exhorted the gentry to form local militia (*t'uan-lien ting-yung*). At the same time he authorized villagers to cast their own cannon and called for a rigorous enforcement of the *pao-chia* and *ao-chia* laws already on the books.[23] Unlike Na-yen-ch'eng's proposals a few years earlier, Pai's initiated a flurry of local military activity.

In Hsiang-shan county Magistrate P'eng Chao-lin established a public office near the county seat, where he consulted with the local gentry and hired junks to defend the city. Trained stalwarts and villagers were stationed along the rivers. Watchtowers and stockades equipped with gongs for spreading alarms were established at strategic points. The *chin-shih* Cheng Ying-yüan mobilized a force of braves, and assigned villagers to drive stakes and construct barricades in the river. Elsewhere in the county Li Tso-yüan revived the *pao-chia* registers and formed a genuine militia.[24]

In Nan-hai county a scholar (*chü-jen*) from Li-yung recruited braves and saw that they were regularly drilled. In Ta-lan another scholar induced four villages to join in a program to protect the "good people" (*liang-min*) and root out the "bad."[25] Activities also got under way in Shun-te, where several villages formed *t'uan-lien*. Some 200 braves were brought to the county seat to be personally led by the Expectant Magistrate. Other militias were organized by Licentiates Kan T'ien-ch'iu and Lo Ch'i-ch'ien, who obtained cannon and persuaded their clansmen to contribute funds.[26]

In the more populous parts of the Pearl River Delta, local defense measures often sufficed to repel the pirates. On a foray into Shun-te the Black Fleet leader Kuo P'o-tai decided to bypass the county when he learned of the elite's preparations and moved farther upriver instead. But there, too, news of the local defense forces deterred his advance. At Pan-sha-wei the local elite had contributed 300 silver taels for a force of stalwarts and the construction of a new fort.[27]

Chang Pao's Red Fleet experienced similar setbacks. On August 18 they were badly beaten when they struck at the village of Pao-t'ang-hsia, in Tung-kuan county. Buoyed by a prophecy of success from their gods, the residents rained down tiles and stones on the pirates, who were soon immobilized when their guns failed to fire. As reinforcements from a neighboring village arrived, 100 pirates were killed and seven of their leaders were captured. The villagers also recovered a large official seal, which, along with the captured boats and weapons, was turned over to the authorities.[28]

Several days later, on August 26, Chang Pao attacked Lao-ts'un (also in Tung-kuan county), where he was once more defeated. Knowing beforehand that the pirates would come, the villagers positioned large cannon in strategic spots and cut trees and wood to erect palisades. Behind the palisades they concealed a few soldiers to await the pirates' advance. The pirate leaders, perceiving only slight opposition, rushed ashore. The gunpowder blazed but the villagers' cannon failed to sound. The pirates, suspecting an ambush, signaled for reinforcements to come ashore. Retreating villagers led them straight to the ambush, whereupon the concealed soldiers sprang forth and butchered the invaders, who lost three vessels and approximately 100 men.[29]

As one might expect, clever stratagems were often employed by the other side in this game of wits. In some instances pirates passing themselves off as gentry actually obtained cannon from the local authorities. In others, they lulled areas into a false sense of security by seizing official craft and pretending to carry out village patrols; after the reassured villagers let down their guard, entry was easily made. On one occasion some pirates who had disguised themselves as itinerant merchants and magicians in order to spy on the village market tried to trick the villagers into attacking a party of soldiers coming ashore by insisting that they were pirates.[30] (This bold entry into market towns in disguise was a common ploy.)

When it came to a show of arms, the pirates often prevailed. The defeat of Hsü T'ing-kuei opened the way for them to penetrate the inland waterways farther than ever before. The Black Fleet leader Kuo P'o-tai promptly embarked on a six-weeks-long campaign in the Pearl River that resulted in the death of approximately 10,000 people.[31] On the very day of Hsü's defeat (July 21), 100 junks of the Black Flag Fleet proceeded up the river to Hsiang-shan and threatened to destroy the county seat unless considerable supplies of commodities and money were guaranteed them. In the course of this raid the pirates completely destroyed the preparations for a new fort that the governor-general had ordered built near the entrance of the river and did damage to a newly built fort farther upstream. At Heng-tang, a village in Hsiang-shan county, the pirates went ashore and killed 66 villagers who tried to stop them. On August 11 their advance reached alarming proportions when, just 16 miles from Canton, they burned the customs house at Tzu-ni, set up a blockade within the vicinity of Canton, and dispatched messengers to demand payments from all the nearby settlements.[32]

In what would prove to be a tragic decision, the villagers of San-shan chose not to pay and began preparing for an attack. They built a palisade, hurriedly drilled men, and cast weapons; all males between

16 and 60 were assigned to stand guard on the shore. Kuo-P'o-tai, on learning that his request for money had been spurned, stormed the village by night. But the palisade held and absorbed the brunt of his fire, and the villagers overpowered his vanguard. Enraged, he regrouped his men and inspiring them to a second try with the promise of ten *chin* for each head taken, he gave the order to raze the palisade.[33] Though the villagers, led by Liang K'o stopped one group of invaders, another group caught them from the rear and quickly did away with the unfortunate Liang. Worse was still to come. The villagers' cannon burst, and the pirates were able to make quick work of their weaponless opponents. In a last-ditch effort, one of the villagers jumped onto a roof and showered the pirates with buckets of lime and dust; the pirates soon downed him with spears and then descended on the village. For three days they plundered and looted, and when there was nothing more to take, they burned the village to the ground. As they departed, they suspended the heads of 80 villagers killed in the combat from the limbs of a banyan tree near the shore; the women and children found locked in a village temple they carried off to their ships.[34]

From here the pirates moved on to attack Ma-chou (August 13), San-shan (a second village by that name but written with different characters, farther upriver than the first; August 16), and P'ing-chou, all in Shun-te county, where they again overcame the local resistance and helped themselves to the property of fleeing villagers. On August 18 they reached Sha-wan. Unable to take it, they then crossed back into Shun-te county two days later. There they ran into the strongest resistance yet, at Huang-lien, a village located at a critical junction of communication on the border between Nan-hai and Shun-te counties.[35] For six days braves led by the scholar Wen Ju-neng withstood Kuo's assault and forced the pirates to retreat. But at last they returned and, in a new assault, surrounded the town. Huang-lien was saved only after eight neighboring villages sent in reinforcements and Lieutenant Ho Ting-ao arrived with 45 fishing vessels and a force of 1,440 men.[36]

Meantime, as Kuo P'o-tai had been working his way through the Inner Passage, Chang Pao had been operating in the main channel of the Pearl River. Flushed with success over his defeat of Hsü T'ing-kuei, he had swept into the river and left in ruins a new fort being constructed near its mouth. He nearly destroyed a second fort just below Hsiang-shan. His advance reached alarming proportions when, at the second bar (in Tung-kuan county, halfway between Whampoa and the Bogue), he overtook a fleet of provincial war junks and sent them fleeing for cover. Commenting on the pirates' raid, the supercargoes of the British East India Company wrote, "tho' they have now been some weeks in the river, they seem to have met with no opposition from any but the people of the towns and villages they have attacked."[37]

On September 8 Chang Pao surrounded two islands located at the second bar. At the first of these, Tao-chiao, he was stalemated for several days, at a cost of a dozen islanders wounded or killed. But finally the pirates were able to charge ashore, to capture 20 women and kill 1,000 residents.[38] At the second island, Ta-fen, weirs in the harbor and soldiers onshore held back the pirates' advance. But the attack gave rise to a new wave of panic that sent people flocking to Canton and prompted city officials to declare martial law.[39]

Moving on, Chang Pao destroyed a large town not far from the Bocca Tigris and killed 2,000 inhabitants.[40] On September 14 he advanced on Hsin-tsao in P'an-yü county, where the villagers, seeing his approach, prepared their defenses and hid their wives and families. The next morning the pirates attacked. One company was halted when they set out to destroy a water gate. As they passed by a condiment shop that stood at its entrance, the shop's staff hurled crocks of sauce at them from the roof. Slipping and sliding, many of the pirates were killed as they fell. Some of them then tried to attack the shop from the rear, but two villagers headed them off. A second pirate company, trying to enter at Yung-wei-she, was twice put to flight by the villagers there. Forced to withdraw, the angry pirates burned the village's bamboo palisade as they fled.[41]

Chang Pao's setback was only temporary, however. On September 25 he met up with Cheng I Sao at Lantao and was ordered to proceed upriver on another fee-collecting cruise. He promptly set out for Sha-ting, located west of the Bogue not far from Tzu-ni, and at midnight he anchored his 300 vessels close to a town surrounded by water and orange groves. In preparation for the attack, the pirates burned the customs house at Tzu-ni, destroyed a number of houses, and captured 400 prisoners. (This was the incident that Glasspoole witnessed, in which the townspeople, after some hard bargaining, got the pirates to settle for a sum of 600 dollars, to be paid on their return downstream.)[42]

By October 1 Chang Pao was at Kan-chiao, but unable to take it, he continued upstream during the night and anchored quietly in front of Ch'en village. Early the next morning the pirates sailed in on their sampans, swords in hand. The residents had taken measures to protect themselves, but their 3,000 stalwarts proved no match for 500 pirates. They simply ducked the defenders' initial fire and came at them spread out in a wall-like formation. During a short and bloody battle, the defense crumbled. Many of the villagers fled to the nearby hills, and others escaped to an old market site. Women in tears, babes in arms, pleaded for mercy; the elderly and infirm, unable to run, were captured or killed. Finally, balked from further pursuit by a wide ditch, the pirates amused themselves by burning 20 homes.[43]

The next morning a large company of pirates renewed the assault. The attempts at resistance were again overcome, and the village lay open for plunder. Pirate sampans laden with goods came and went in quick succession. In the course of the day 250 women and several children were captured. Stripped of everything valuable, Ch'en village was reduced to ashes. The pirates remained in the vicinity for three days arranging the ransom of the prisoners. During this period the inhabitants never ventured from the hills, although there were seldom more than 100 pirates onshore at any given time.[44]

Finally, after the arrival of 1,000 braves from a nearby settlement, the pirates sailed on to Lan-shih, a strategically important port and garrison in Nan-hai county whose inhabitants had long since taken steps to defend it. Cannon obtained from the local garrison guarded its gates. Mutual-surveillance organizations had drilled and established regular patrols.[45] When the pirates struck on October 5, order should have prevailed. But as soon as they set fire to the garrison, the soldiers fled in terror. The pirates then seized the garrison's abandoned junks and attacked the city. The *pao-cheng* Huo Shao-yüan led his militiamen to intercept them, but at their first taste of combat, they too took flight. Left on his own, Huo then exhorted the townspeople to make a stand. Those armed with iron spears were escorted to the front. The pirates, angered to find cannon fire ripping through their junks, pressed in harder still, until all resistance collapsed. The pirates then marched onshore and took their revenge by burning 400 homes and killing a dozen residents, including the *pao-chia* leader himself.[46]

The pirates remained in the vicinity for several days, destroying nearby towns. During this period they had a near brush with the provincial navy, which had been on the hunt for them. On October 6 a fleet of 40 junks reached Chin-kang, a port located not far from Sha-wan. Since it was already evening, the commander, Major Lin Sun, ordered his junks to anchor at Tzu-ni, and Chang Pao took his fleet to Sha-ting. The next morning the pirates, eager for an encounter, sailed to Tzu-ni, intending to take Major Lin by surprise. But Lin, realizing that the pirates had gathered and that he was outnumbered, had already escaped. Unable to find him, Chang was forced to return to Sha-ting.[47]

On October 8 the pirates again tried to take Kan-chiao with a fleet of small boats. The villagers responded with a salvo of cannon fire that kept them at bay and wounded two of their party. The pirates then approached with their large junks and tried to gain the shore from the front. The villagers again impeded their advance and forced them to spread out in several directions at once. Finally they broke through at a weir and stormed ashore with their banners unfurled.

Nearby, at Lin-t'ou, a fierce battle took place in which villagers led by a boxing master managed to wound a dozen pirates and force the whole company's retreat. Chang Pao, however, rallied his men, and this time the villagers were unable to stop him. When the boxing master fell, his daughter took up the cause by grabbing a knife and cutting her way to the center of the battle. She, too, was killed.

The pirates were temporarily halted as retreating residents cut the bridge and tried to flee. The pirates, however, swam the river, opened fire, and set off looting in all directions. Among their prizes were large quantities of clothes, money, and silk. They also carried off 1,140 prisoners and set fires to scores of dwellings.[48]

By late October the provincial navy was back to strength and ready for action. The 80 rice carriers ordered after Hsü T'ing-kuei's defeat emerged from the dockyards, and set out for Sha-wan, under the command of Sun Ch'üan-mou. On the evening of October 21 one of Chang Pao's rowboats informed him of the approaching fleet. Always eager for an encounter, Chang seized a flag and signaled 50 junks to sail out and intercept it. The fighting began during the night but stopped briefly at dawn, giving Chang a chance to send for the rest of his boats. Reinforcements proved unnecessary, however, for within an hour Sun had been soundly defeated. Unwilling to submit, one of his captains declared that no pirate's knife was going to kill him, and set fire to the powder magazine of his ship, blowing himself to bits as his enemies boarded. Sun Ch'üan-mou himself escaped only by leaving the fleet in charge of his brother and heading for Lantao. After sinking two rice carriers, Chang Pao returned to Sha-ting with three others in tow.[49] Sun's defeat at Sha-wan demonstrated that little had changed in the Ch'ing camp. Despite their new vessels, the provincial forces remained as incapable of suppressing the pirates as ever. By contrast, the pirates' military power was now at its zenith. With little to challenge them, they made their way upriver and boldly attacked Ta Huang-pu.

On the evening of November 1, 300 of Chang Pao's vessels anchored near the city, which was guarded by a small fort and 20 war junks lying at anchor. Early the next morning some 3,000 to 4,000 pirates assembled on sampans, with their largest junks hauled in close to cover the landing. Turning first to the fort, they fired at it steadily for about an hour, until the walls gave way and the soldiers retreated in confusion. Once past the fort, the landing parties found themselves cut off by the junks of Ho Ting-ao, who earlier in the year had aided in the defense of Huang-lien. Some 300 pirates then swam ashore, ran along the bank until they came abreast of Ho's junks, and plunged back in the water to board them. Now surrounded, Ho and his men jumped overboard and tried to reach land. The pirates followed and cut most of them to pieces. Ho himself was severely wounded and died after exhorting those who were left to continue to resist. But there was no fight left in them. The pirates captured all of Ho's junks, towed them out of the harbor, and attacked the town with fury. At one of the entrances residents, entrenched behind a palisade, held them back for a quarter of an hour. Chang Pao broke through, however, by ordering Kuo P'o-tai and Liang P'o-pao to attack from the rear. The palisade gave way, and with great butchery, the pirates drove the inhabitants into the hills.

As the pirates were leaving the residents rallied, retook the settlement, and killed almost 200 men. Their appetites whetted for revenge, the pirates regrouped, landed a second time, and set fire to everything in sight. To inspire enthusiasm for the second assault, pirate leaders promised their men ten dollars for every head they cut off. Glasspoole, who witnessed the battle at Ta Huang-pu, recalled seeing a pirate with two heads tied to his neck by their queues who appeared to be eagerly in search of a third.[50]

The Ch'ing Alliance with the Foreigners

As early as August it was clear that the pirate threat had become too great to be contained by local defense forces. By then pirate cannon could be heard daily in Canton, and the city was in a state of panic. Chang Pao, at the height of his daring, posted a notice of his intention to attack and demanded that Governor-general Pai Ling come up with a ransom of money and provisions. Throughout the city large numbers of people openly boasted of their association with the pirates.[51] Chinese merchants and officials, who just a few years before had deemed the pirates "too contemptible to cause a moment's uneasiness," were now in "great alarm."[52] Pai Ling, heralded on his arrival in Kwangtung as a savior, was now scorned for having demonstrated so little of the ability for which he was extolled.[53]

As the state of the river worsened, the British saw the bottom drop out of the foreign market. "We are sorry to state," the supercargoes reported, "that the trade in opium and every other article is likely to suffer more seriously from the increased force of the ladrones, who have during the last three or four months been carrying on the depredations with much greater force and audacity than we have hitherto witnessed."[54] The consulate's report was equally grim: "Country ships trade as usual but the markets are miserable for all imports . . . owing to the fleet of pirate junks infesting the rivers."[55]

On September 5 the situation became even more critical when the pirates moved in on Macao. There they detained three large junks of a Siamese tribute mission and drove five American ships to safety under the settlement's guns. To cap off their activities, they captured the brig of Antonio Botelho Homen, the Portuguese governor of Timor.[56]

In desperation, Chinese officials looked with renewed interest at the West and solicited each "barbarian" in turn, hoping to obtain aid in the least embarrassing way. Turning first to the Portuguese, who had the most to complain about, they sent a letter to the governor of Macao on September 9, asking for an armed cruiser to drive the pirates from the river. The Portuguese were only too eager to comply, for the spectacle of their brig being towed by the pirates in front of the city with its flag trailing in the water had readied them for revenge. They quickly placed the two vessels then in port under the command of José Pinto Alcoforado de Azevedo e Souza, and on September 12 he set sail.[57] On September 15 he caught up with Chang Pao near Whampoa, where according to a Portuguese source, "the muddy waters of the river ran red with blood."[58] The Portuguese in fact fared poorly in this encounter. As soon as one pirate junk withdrew, another appeared to take its place. When one of the Portuguese ships, the *Belisario,* was split by a barrage and retreated, it was followed in quick order by its sister ship, the *Princesa Carlota.*[59]

In the meantime the Chinese took other steps to remedy the situation in Macao. In early September provincial officials made overtures to the British about the possibility of hiring the country ship *Mercury* to free the Siamese tribute vessels. The British agreed, but demanded that the request be put in writing by the governor-general. When the governor-general refused, the British withheld the ship, and the Chinese then turned to the Americans for help. The U.S. consul was sympathetic, but informed them that insurance stipulations made it impossible to send ships under the U.S. flag.[60]

This left the Chinese with little alternative but to reopen their negotiations with the British. On September 13 the governor-general instructed the Hong Merchants to invite the *Mercury* to sail with Chinese war junks.[61] The supercargoes gave their reluctant consent, and on September 15 the *Mercury* set sail, carrying 20 cannon and 50 American volunteers. It was joined by 60 provincial war junks and three officers of rank.[62]

Success was almost immediate. The *Mercury* cleared the decks of all who approached with grape shot, and no pirate ship was able to withstand its fire after the first day. By the end of the month the pirates had been driven from the Inner Passage and bottled up between Lantao and Lintin. Captain John Williams, confident that they could be quickly destroyed, asked the governor of Macao to send in his cruisers and a couple of launches for boarding. But the appeal was ignored, and the pirates escaped.[63]

Throughout October negotiations between the British and the Chinese faltered over British insistence on a written application from the Chinese as a condition for further aid. But Sun Ch'üan-mou's defeat at Sha-wan on October 22 lent new urgency to the situation and compelled the Chinese officials to intensify their efforts to reach an accord; three days later the Hong Merchants appeared before the supercargoes to impress on them the need for action.[64]

An interview between Governor-general Pai Ling and Captain Austin, commander of the HMS *St. Albans*, was arranged for November 2. But before the meeting could take place, the Portuguese, anxious to prevent such an alliance, acted quickly to forestall it by offering to lease six warships to the Chinese. This offer accomplished its goal: the Sino-British negotiations were cut off. In response to the Portuguese offer, Pai Ling dispatched three emissaries to Macao. The result was an agreement, signed on November 23, that called for six Portuguese ships to join the Chinese navy on patrol between the Bocca Tigris and Macao for six months. The agreement further provided for the equal division of prizes taken through joint action, a payment of 80,000 taels to the Portuguese for the use of their craft, and the restoration of the "ancient privileges," or demands of sovereignty and rights claimed by the Portuguese, at the end of the mission. The Portuguese quickly fitted out an expedition of six ships, 730 men, and 118 cannon.[65]

In actuality, the agreement may have done little more than sanction existing practices, for by November 23 the Portuguese and the Chinese had already been cooperating in an anti-pirate campaign since at least early November, when Cheng I Sao suddenly left the Pearl River and, with only a few vessels, anchored in the bay north of Lantao Island. Ch'ing officials now had a surefire way to clear the river: a surprise attack would force Mrs. Cheng to call out the pirate fleets to her aid. The problem was, the Chinese officials did not have the means. The new provincial fleet was not yet assembled, and the 35-junk auxiliary force of Magistrate P'eng Chao-lin could not be mobilized in time. Unwilling to miss this opportunity, the Chinese asked the Portuguese to keep Cheng I Sao's forces occupied until P'eng's junks could join them.

On November 4 the plan bore fruit, as Cheng I Sao, "harassed by three Portuguese ships and a brig," sent out her summons.[66] In the next three days the vessels of the Red Flag Fleet, under Chang Pao, Hsiang-shan Erh, and Cheng Pao-yang, sailed out to join Mrs. Cheng at Lantao. By the third day Magistrate P'eng Chao-lin's fleet of fishing junks had arrived on the scene as well. The first confrontation took place on November 8, when, according to Glasspoole,

the Ladrones had only seven junks in a fit state for action; these they hauled outside, and moored them head and stern across the bay; and manned all the boats belonging to the repairing vessels ready for boarding.

The Portuguese, observing these manoeuvres, hove to, and communicated by boats. Soon afterwards they made sail, each ship firing her broadside as she passed, but without effect, the shot falling far short. The Ladrones did not return a single shot, but waved their colours, and threw up rockets, to induce them to come further in.[67]

The contest ended inconclusively, with the provincial forces able neither to enter the bay nor to attack. In the meantime, the pirates took advantage of the respite to finish their repairs.

Action began in earnest on November 19, when the pirates awoke to find themselves surrounded by an even larger fleet. During the night P'eng Chao-lin's 35 fishing boats had been joined by 60 junks, with 1,200 cannon and 18,000 men, under the joint command of Sun Ch'üan-mou, Huang Fei-p'eng, and Wang Kuo-pao. With Sun stationed in the east and P'eng in the west, the pirates' exits were blocked. On nearing the pirates, the government vessels "formed a line, and stood close in; each vessel as she discharged her guns, tacked to join the rear and reload."[68] The barrage continued for two hours, until a firebrand thrown by the pirates exploded one of the largest enemy junks. Thereafter the government forces maintained a more respectful distance but kept up the fire until the wind fell on the evening of November 21.

That night the pirates, eager to go on the offensive, towed out their seven large junks, accompanied by 200 rowboats, in preparation for an attack. But a sudden breeze threw their plans into disarray. Their adversaries escaped, leaving them with no choice but to return to the bay.

The government war junks soon returned, and the firing continued for two more days. When it again fell calm on November 23, Chang Pao hoisted his mainsail as a signal to move. Hoping for an assault on the Lantao garrison, the pirates towed out 15 junks and readied a landing party of 2,000. A sudden gale thwarted this endeavor, too, and the pirates were forced to abandon the idea after taking only one enemy junk.[69] A constant barrage of Chinese and Portuguese gunfire followed them as they retreated to the bay. The next evening 100 of their smaller vessels stole out of the bay and escaped to the east. Portuguese pursuit proved of little avail.

With the remaining pirates anchored close together in the surrounded bay, Sun Ch'üan-mou hit upon a new stratagem. He had the holds of 43 junks filled with straw and their decks piled high with explosives. Taking no chances, he then sank old, rotten cargo carriers at both entrances to the harbor and transferred 1,000 soldiers to the Lantao garrison.

With the pirates now boxed in on both sides, their defeat seemed inevitable. Reports flew back to Canton, and rumors of their imminent destruction spread far and wide. Pai Ling came from Canton to watch the spectacle, while Sun waited impatiently for the correct winds and tide. Finally, on November 28, Sun had all the conditions he needed: a strong breeze, a tide leading directly into the bay, and pirate boats lying so close together that it would be impossible to miss them. With great anticipation, the fire ships were launched.

From his vantage point amid the pirates, Glasspoole followed the action closely:

[The fireboats] came very regularly into the centre of the fleet, two and two, burning furiously; one of them came alongside of the vessel I was in, but they succeeded in booming her off. She appeared to be a vessel of about thirty tons; her hold was filled with straw and wood, and there were a few small boxes of combustibles on her deck, which exploded alongside of us without doing any damage. The Ladrones, however, towed them all on shore, extinguished the fire, and broke them up for fire-wood.[70]

Unfortunately for Sun, at that point the wind changed, and two of the fireboats were blown back whence they had come. The grand show Pai Ling had anticipated concluded with the fireboats igniting two of the junks that had launched them.[71]

The next day the pirates managed to tow out their large vessels, hoist the sails, and escape to the outer ocean. From the Ch'ing point of view, the episode was an unmitigated disaster. Westerners as well as Chinese had proved unable to destroy the pirates. A search for excuses followed. In the most extravagant of these, the pirates' escape was attributed to Commander Sun's defection to the Ladrones.[72] There is no evidence to substantiate that allegation, but a few days after the battle Sun was dismissed from office for the second time in six years. Pai Ling quietly returned to his yamen in Canton and tried to downplay the incident by reporting heavy pirate losses to the Emperor. By Pai's reckoning, the pirates' toll for the nine-day period between November 19 and November 28 was 20 junks sunk, six junks captured, and 1,400 men killed. Adding still further to his accomplishments, he reported that 34 of the casualties were *t'ou-mu*, including Chang Pao's brother Chang Sheng-tzu.[73] The Portuguese, who had taken credit for constructing the fire vessels, also tried to hide their embarrassment by exaggerating the outcome, reporting that at least a third of the pirate vessels had been destroyed.[74]

Glasspoole, however, told a far different story. According to him, the blockade amounted to little more than a respite during which the pirates "completed all their repairs" and lost "not a single . . . vessel."[75] Instead of Pai's 1,400 pirates killed, he reported just 40.

In sailing away from Lantao largely unscathed, the victorious pirates had not only held their own, but also proved themselves the military masters of the water world. In totally routing the provincial fleets, they had forced government officials to swallow their pride and accept aid from the "barbarians." Now, in standing up to the West, they appeared unstoppable.

At this time, Chang Pao, heady with success, proudly boasted to the Portuguese:

At the present time I have many ships and provisions and all that is necessary for ordinary use; nothing is lacking to me; all that I have is enough for a long time. . . . At this time I beg of you to give me four of the armed vessels that are under your control, to make use of them as I wish, for with their help I will be able to restore the lands of the empire. Be assured that when I have restored them and possess all the lands of the empire under my power, I will . . . give to you, my brothers . . . two or three provinces [of your choice].[76]

8

The End of
the Confederation

By late 1809 tensions that had been previously masked for the good of the confederation were emerging into the open. After warding off the most powerful attack ever launched against them, the pirates stopped fighting the Ch'ing and started quarreling with one another.

Sheer magnitude may have subjected the confederation to tension from below, but success seems to have precipitated conflict from above. For years the Black Fleet leader Kuo P'o-tai had been deeply jealous of Chang Pao. Kuo, a longtime colleague of the confederation's founder Cheng I, resented the rise of a man whose rank had once been inferior to his own, and the more so because Chang's Red Flag Fleet was larger than his. But most of all he was jealous of Chang's success in winning the affection of Cheng I Sao, of whom he too was deeply enamoured.[1]

Even before Chang Pao's encirclement at Lantao, Kuo P'o-tai, the confederation's most reflective and dissatisfied leader, was pondering the uncertainty of a pirate fate. As the first to have perceived that piracy may have reached its peak, he began brooding about how its gains might be best preserved: "For a long time I had wanted to surrender, but fearful that the officials would punish me for my crimes, I delayed."[2] Kuo's fear was justified, because ever since the time of Na-yen-ch'eng, sea war had been the accepted means of countering pirates. By late 1809, however, provincial administrators were so desperate that they were willing to let even fleet leaders surrender, provided that they demonstrated sufficient "merit" or "sincerity." Governor-General Pai Ling posted placards in all the ports exhorting pirates to "return to allegiance" and on several occasions even dispatched emissaries to appeal to them in person.[3]

In the case of Kuo P'o-tai, these pleas had fallen on receptive ears, and the action at Lantao, in which he was not directly involved, gave him an opportunity to demonstrate his "sincerity." At the end of the siege, as Chang Pao was preparing to escape, he discovered that his junks were so heavy that he could not use the tide to escape and sent a messenger to Kuo asking for aid. Kuo, unwilling to jeopardize any chance to surrender, refused.[4] Chang vowed to have his revenge, and in doing so made conflict between the two men inevitable.

The showdown was not long in coming. On December 11 Chang entered the inner rivers (*nei-ho*) from Chi-shui-men in Hsin-an. There he encountered the fleet of Sun Ch'üan-mou and Huang Fei-p'eng in an engagement that cost him at least three junks, along with 600 men and 20 leaders, including two squadron commanders, Li Ch'ang-tzu and Lao Chün-shih, and a nephew of Cheng I Sao's. (He may have lost as many as 18 junks, if the Portuguese claims of participation in this battle are to be believed.) Seeing that victory was not possible, Chang escaped to the outer ocean, where the two sides clashed again the next day. With his provisions running low, Chang intended to reenter the inner rivers and seize food near the Bocca Tigris, so he anchored to wait for favorable winds. At this point Kuo P'o-tai's Black Fleet appeared, and Chang sent his own fleet to attack it. They met in the outer ocean not far from the Bocca Tigris, and after the smoke cleared, it was Kuo P'o-tai who emerged as the winner. He in fact routed the already weakened Red Flag Fleet, which suffered 1,000 casualties and saw 16 of its junks and 321 men captured.[5]

In anticipation of the conflict, Kuo had already paved the way for his surrender by sending his mother, his wife, his brothers, and 50 other family members ashore at Hai-k'ang to inform the officials of his intentions. He had also ordered 43 pirates under Feng Yung-fa to initiate the surrender process in Hsin-an and 79 under Chang Jih-kao and Kuo Chiu-shan to follow suit in Yang-chiang.[6] Thus, once he defeated Chang Pao, he was in a good position to negotiate the terms of his surrender, for he now had captives to turn over as evidence of his "sincerity." But mindful of what the surrender of a force as strong as his Black Flag Fleet meant to the Chinese officials, Kuo had no intention of selling himself short or exposing himself to government duplicity. Accordingly, he insisted that Miguel de Arriaga, the *ouvidor* (judge and auditor) of Macao, act as mediator in the surrender procedure. With Arriaga's assistance the negotiations proceeded smoothly, and the two parties reached an accord only a little more than a month after Kuo's battle with Chang.

The Black Flag Fleet's return to allegiance took place on January 13,

1810. Governor-general Pai Ling left Canton and made his way to Kuei-shan county, where he received Kuo and an important *t'ou-mu*, Feng Ch'ao-ch'ün, from the Yellow Flag Fleet. The two pirate leaders handed over 5,578 men, 800 women and children, 113 junks, 500 cannon (87 of which had come from Cheng I), and 5,000 assorted weapons.[7] At this point Kuo turned in the 321 Red Fleet members he had taken captive. As a return gesture of good faith, the governor-general allowed him to change his name to Kuo Hsüeh-hsien (which appears to have been his original name) and rewarded him with the rank of sublieutenant.

Immediately thereafter, Sublieutenant Kuo P'o-tai joined the Ch'ing navy in its expeditions against the pirates. News of his participation in a campaign in which eight junks were destroyed and 14 damaged so pleased the Emperor that he rewarded Governor-general Pai Ling with a peacock feather and rescinded his order to arrest Sun Ch'üan-mou, who had been cashiered after his disgrace at Lantao.[8]

Kuo P'o-tai's surrender was followed by a spate of others, including almost 300 pirates from Chang's Red Fleet. Within three weeks the number of surrendered pirates exceeded 9,000 (see the accompanying table for their affiliations and other data).[9]

Surrendered Pirate Leaders and Their Followers, Early 1810

Leaders	Fleet(s)	Date of surrender	Number of followers[a]	Place of surrender (county)
Kuo P'o-tai, Feng Ch'ao-ch'ün	Black, Yellow	Jan. 13	6,378	Kuei-shan
Feng Yung-fa, Chang Jih-kao, Kuo Chiu-shan	Black	Jan. 14	500	Yang-chiang, Kuei-shan
Li T'u-hsing[b]	Black	Jan. 14	29	Tien-pai
Chan Ya-szu[b]	Red	Jan. 18	19	Hai-k'ang, Sui-ch'i
Kao Ya-hua[b]	Red	Jan. 18	12	Hsiang-shan
—	Black	Jan. 20	28	Hsin-ning
Lin A-mu,[b] T'an Ya-jui, Liang Kuang-mao	Red	Feb. 1	286	Yung-an, Hai-feng, Kuei-shan
Ch'en A-tsung,[b] Chen A-yu[b]	Blue	Feb. 7	723	—
Ch'en Sheng, Hang Chung, Ch'en Yao	Yellow	—	1,200	—

SOURCES: CP 1120/10, CC15 i 22; KTHF 42: 39, n.d.
[a] Includes women and children; excludes captives turned in.
[b] *T'ou-mu.* Others may have been *t'ou-mu* but are not so identified in the records.

The Surrender of Chang Pao and
the Other Fleet Leaders

On hearing of Kuo's surrender, Chang Pao, vowing that he would never follow suit, launched a major campaign in the Pearl River Delta. In mid-January he defeated the Sino-Portuguese fleet guarding the Inner Passage and entered the river with a force of between 200 and 300 junks. He anchored at Tzu-ni, and from there continued to harass the Inner Passage fleet by sending out small divisions to engage it in combat. Then, on January 29, he attacked a boat belonging to the country ship *Sir Edward Pellow*, killed the officers, and escaped with three chests of silver valued at 13,500 Spanish dollars. Finally, after celebrating the lunar New Year with such verve that his gong-beating and fire crackers resounded for miles, he stationed himself at T'an-chou and sent out expeditions to attack nearby villages in Shun-te and Hsiang-shan counties.[10]

Yet for all Chang's success, Kuo P'o-tai's surrender had already influenced some members of the Red Fleet to surrender and had given others food for thought. Noting how Kuo flourished under government protection, they wondered whether they, too, might not be accorded such privileges. Gradually even Chang Pao warmed to the idea of surrender, but only if it could be on his own terms. To test the procedure, he first ordered his *t'ou-mu* Cheng Tsung-fu to seek permission for the entire Red Fleet—14,000 men and 150 *t'ou-mu*, 260 junks, and 1,000 cannon—to surrender.[11]

Governor-general Pai Ling, though well aware that Chang's surrender with amnesty would meet with little approval from either the Emperor or the coastal inhabitants, was persuaded that with this move the rest of the pirates could be easily brought to terms.[12] As a result he posted additional notices encouraging surrender in all the ports, and by late February the negotiations for Chang's return to allegiance were under way.

For a go-between, the state chose Chou Fei-hsiung, a doctor, conjurer, and opium addict from Macao, who was a longtime acquaintance of the pirates and could be expected to win Chang's confidence. At the end of their meeting, Chang and his colleagues agreed to assemble their fleet outside the Bocca Tigris at Sha-chiao in order to finalize the details of their surrender.[13]

Like Kuo P'o-tai before him, Chang was anxious to protect himself from possible treachery on the part of the government, and thus he too insisted that he would return to allegiance only in the presence of Ouvidor Arriaga.[14] The Chinese acceded to this request, and two of their officials, the Mandarin of Casa Branca and the magistrate of Hsiang-shan, sat in on Arriaga's first meeting with Chang. With their approval it was agreed that the pirates would meet with the governor-general near the Bocca Tigris.[15] On February 21 the 260 vessels of the Red Flag Fleet entered the Pearl River and anchored near Chuenpi to await the arrival of the negotiators. Pai Ling, accompanied by the sub-district magistrate of Tzu-ni, Chang Yü-chih, and P'eng Chao-lin, left Canton the same day, and Arriaga set out from Macao.[16]

When the pirates saw the governor-general's boat approaching, they hoisted their banners and saluted him with cannon fire. Pai Ling was somewhat taken aback by this display, but his fears were soon dispelled when he saw the pirates' dragon boats approaching. He beckoned the pirates aboard and informed Chang Pao that he would grant him three days to draw up a list of the junks and weapons to be presented. Chang agreed, and the conference adjourned on a note of optimism.[17]

After this auspicious beginning, however, the negotiations quickly broke down, and the pirates withdrew from the river. Chinese officials blamed the breakdown on the coincidental departure of ten Indiamen, which sailed by the conference headquarters and alarmed the pirates, who suspected some sort of Sino-European collusion.[18] The real problem, however, seems to have been one of the conditions the governor-general set for the pirates' surrender, namely, that they would have to hand over all of their junks and settle onshore. Cheng I Sao and Chang Pao found those terms unacceptable and demanded that they be allowed to retain 80 vessels and 5,000 subordinates to join in the anti-pirate campaign in western Kwangtung.[19]

On this issue compromise seemed impossible, for the Emperor was adamantly opposed to such a settlement:

If indeed the said pirates sincerely come to surrender, then they must turn in all of their junks and weapons. How can they ask to retain several tens of junks? If their purpose is to accompany the army in going out to sea to attack and arrest pirates in atonement for their crimes and to show merit after their surrender, why can they not be apportioned among the various vessels already in the navy?[20]

In the meantime Chang Pao had used his time in the river wisely. Even as he had been talking with the Chinese officials, he had approached the British, hoping to win them over or at least neutralize them in the event that his negotiations with the state failed. On one occasion he even played host to Captain Austin of the HMS *St. Albans*, the senior British naval officer in China, and Captain Campbell of the

Indiaman *Nottingham*. Chang Pao received his guests politely. Expressing his respect for the British nation, he made several inquiries concerning their men-of-war, indicated his willingness to refrain from further molesting English property, and, as an act of good faith, released into their care a Dutch boy captured from the American schooner *Pilgrim* a year and a half earlier. Before they departed, Chang also presented the captains with chops granting safe passage to English ships.[21]

On March 16 the supercargoes of the East India Company decided to acknowledge Chang's overtures with a few small presents and a letter from their president. A few days later he responded by granting another set of passes allowing vessels with British goods to proceed from Hsiang-shan to Macao. Chang's strategy paid off, just as he had hoped it would. After the pirates returned to the Inner Passage, the commander of the cruiser *Antelope* met with them at Mo-tao, near Hsiang-shang, to inform them that the English would not interfere with them in the future if British property was not directly attacked.[22]

After this satisfying conclusion to the discussions with the British, some of the Red Flag Fleet resumed its activities with a vengeance. Particularly hard hit was Ch'ang-sha, where one contingent fought its way in on March 14 and burned 62 residences and more than 200 shops and buildings.[23] From there the group proceeded on to raid coastal villages in the vicinity of Hsin-hui and were driven back only at San-ta, when the local braves were joined by others from nearby villages.[24]

In bringing their force to bear once more, the pirates made it clear that if Pai Ling wanted to be rid of them, he would have to compromise. Yet Chang himself, still eager to surrender, was ambivalent about the resumption of activities. Fearing that his own chances would be jeopardized by the raid at Ch'ang-sha, he turned on those who had conducted it. As a further demonstration of "good faith," he stopped accepting protection money from merchants. He also continued sending his agents ashore to surrender, including Wu Lien, with 22 men, a junk, and 37 cannon (at Hsin-an); Hsü Ya-san, with 34 men, a junk, and 50 cannon (at the Bogue); and Huang Ya-ch'eng, with 42 men, 2 junks, and 67 cannon (at Macao).[25]

But for Chang Pao and the bulk of the pirates, the impasse remained. The deadlock was finally broken by Cheng I Sao, who resolved to go unarmed to the governor-general in Canton. Over the objections of her subordinates, she presented herself to Pai Ling on April 17, leading a delegation of 17 women and children, including the wives of five of Chang Pao's closest associates: his third cousin Chang Kuang-ch'i, his *t'ou mu* Mo Jo-k'uei and Fang Wei-fu, his son Chang Pao-tzu, and his major second in command, Hsiang-shan Erh.[26] On receiving them, the governor-general began by professing his desire to pardon the pirates. But the same old obstacles soon emerged. Cheng I Sao, a tough bargainer, still insisted that Chang Pao be allowed to retain a company of junks for use in the salt trade. Secure in the knowledge that time was on her side, and that threats to return to her former activities gave her the ultimate advantage over the governor-general, she remained indifferent to all proposals until at last Pai Ling yielded to her demands.[27]

Thanks to Cheng I Sao's initiative, Pai Ling left Macao on April 14 for a new conference with the pirates. The most important leaders— Chang Pao, Cheng Pao-yang, Hsiang-shan Erh, and Liang Ya-k'ang, the adopted son of Tsung-ping Pao—who had been anchored near Fu-yung-sha in Hsiang-shan county for several days, also quickly went there.[28] The conference, which was also attended by Arriaga, took place in a small pagoda on the outskirts of Macao. The first meeting proceeded smoothly. The pirates respectfully kowtowed and apologized for having fled during their last meeting. Chang Pao accounted for his activities during the interim and was again instructed to draw up a list of his junks, weapons, and subordinates.[29]

The actual surrender occurred on April 20, 1810, when 17,318 pirates, along with 226 junks, 1,315 cannon, and 2,798 weapons, were presented to the authorities. Of these, Chang Pao handed over 105 junks and 9,344 pirates, Cheng I Sao 24 junks and 1,433 pirates, Cheng Pao-yang 27 junks and 1,686 pirates, Hsiang-shan Erh 59 junks and 4,163 pirates, and Liang Ya-k'ang 10 junks and 667 pirates. (The fleet affiliation of one junk and 25 pirates is unknown.) Thirty-three of the surrendered vessels were either rice carriers or war junks captured during the encounters with Lin Kuo-liang and Hsü T'ing-kuei. Besides the thousands of pirates from Kwangtung, the Red Flag Fleet included 220 men from Fukien, 13 from Chekiang, 7 from Kwangsi, one each from Kiangnan, Hunan, and Szechwan, and 43 from Vietnam.[30] Not all of these pirates came in voluntarily, however. As a demonstration of his "sincerity," Chang presented the leaders responsible for the raid at Ch'ang-sha, whom he had been holding in custody.

Although the details of the settlement were kept secret, there is no question that Chang was liberally rewarded. He was given the rank of lieutenant, was allowed to retain a private fleet of 20 or 30 junks, and was paid a large sum of money with which to establish his followers onshore.* Cheng I Sao was given permission to marry Chang Pao, and the rank-and-file pirates who so desired were allowed to join the army.[31]

In the end some 350 of the worst offenders were excluded from the amnesty. Of those, 60 were banished for two years, 151 were sent into perpetual exile, and 126 were killed by strangulation or decapitation. Fourteen were executed outside the gate of Macao, where their heads were displayed on a pike and left to rot.[32]

But for Chang Pao still greater triumphs lay ahead. On May 24 he was received as a visitor of state in Macao, where he supposedly met the commanders of the cruisers that had blockaded him at Lantao, as well as the city's leading residents.[33] Later that day he and Kuo P'o-tai set out as part of an expedition to exterminate the Blue, Yellow, and Green Flag fleets of their former associates Wu-shih Erh and Tung-hai Pa, who were still operating with more than 100 junks and several thousand men in the Lei-chou region of western Kwangtung.[34]

Before launching the expedition, the Chinese sent a letter to the Vietnamese Emperor explaining its purpose and requesting troop re-inforcements at the border. The force was a substantial one, com-posed of 130 junks, 7,000 soldiers, and 3,000 stalwarts (*chuang-yung*) divided into three companies. The first company was headed by the provincial commander-in-chief, T'ung Chen-sheng, the second by Sun Ch'üan-mou, assisted by Kuo P'o-tai, and the third by the colonel of the Hsiang-shan Regiment, Hung Ao, assisted by Chang Pao.[35]

The expedition was a great success. After its first encounter with the pirates, the leaders Ch'en Yü-pao and Ts'ao Ya-wan promptly sur-rendered. Next the right-hand man of the Yellow Fleet leader, Tung-hai Pa, and 390 of his men were captured by Chang Pao at Ch'i-hsing. Then several vessels from the Green Fleet were destroyed at Fang-chi, just outside of Tien-pai. As the pirates retreated, the government ships opened fire and captured Chu Ya-pao and 278 of his followers.[36]

On May 29 Wu-shih Erh sent one of his captains, Chang Ya-an, to Nao-chou to beg Chang Pao's permission to surrender. But when Chang Pao arrested the emissary, Wu and his brother, fearing treach-ery, fled with their fleets to Hainan. Pursuing them there, Chang Pao urged them to surrender, but the now wary Wu rallied his men for a showdown. It came on June 13 and 14. In a decisive battle at T'an-chou, Wu lost more than a dozen junks. Foreseeing defeat, Wu pre-

*Following the precedent set for Kuo P'o-tai, the Ch'ing officials allowed him to change his name. In place of the character *pao* meaning "to protect," he now took the character meaning "treasure."

pared to flee and go into hiding, but before he could escape, Chang Pao boarded his vessel and seized him.[37] Within a few minutes his brothers Wu-shih Ta and Wu-shih San, along with other family members and his *t'ou-mu*, were also captured. The Blue Flag Fleet formally ceased to exist.

By this time Governor-general Pai Ling had arrived on the scene to take charge of the operations against Wu. His first act was to call a rendezvous at Lei-chou, where the three companies handed over their haul: 86 junks, 291 cannon, 1,372 weapons, and 490 prisoners, including 128 women who had been captured, imprisoned, and raped. He then proceeded to Hai-k'ang, where he had the squadron leader Wu-shih Erh and seven of his *t'ou-mu* beheaded at the north gate. Their fate was soon shared by Huang Ho, the squadron's clerk and strategist, and 110 others.[38]

Finding himself isolated, Tung-hai Pa, the leader of the last of the fleets, the Yellow Flag Fleet, quickly asked to surrender. Accompanied by 12 *t'ou-mu* and accountants and 3,400 members of both his own fleet and the Green Flag Fleet, he made his way to Hai-k'ang, where he was imprisoned while his fate was deliberated.[39] Although it appears that Pai Ling was initially willing to pardon him and had actually memorialized the Emperor requesting permission to remit the death sentence and banish him instead to Hei-lung-chiang as a slave, the inhabitants of the region protested so vigorously that the governor-general was at last forced to order Tung-hai Pa's execution. Before the sentence could be carried out, however, the Emperor's response to Pai Ling's petition arrived: not only did he lift the pirate leader's death sentence, but on the grounds that Pa had long harbored the intention of surrendering but had been unable to do so owing to pressure from Wu-shih Erh, the Emperor overruled the idea of exiling him and allowed him to return home.[40]

The Motivations for Surrender

The surrender of Tung-hai Pa brought to an end the heyday of piracy in South China. The navy soon dealt with the remaining small groups still operating at Hai-k'ang, Hainan, Sui-ch'i, Hsü-wen, Chang-hua, Wu-ch'uan, Ch'in Chou, and Tan-chou. In this final sweep 228 pirates were killed and 71 captured; 1,000 diehards finally surrendered.[41]

The reasons for the pirates' sudden turnabout from success to surrender have been the subject of wide-ranging speculation ever since. At the time the Portuguese attributed Chang Pao's decision to their own valor and military might. Chang Pao supposedly entered the pagoda in Macao where the surrender agreement was reached, turned to Arriaga, and said:

Great motives have made me surrender and negotiate with you my capitulation to enter into the class of officials as promised by the Emperor. But I confess to you that the principal one was knowing my own weakness in comparison with your [Portuguese] power. I have seen you and I am satisfied. I owe much to nature and to my own hard work, but in all I have found myself conquered by you.

Then, turning to the Chinese, he allegedly reiterated: "For fourteen years you have experienced the power and vigilance of my scepter. You now know from my own mouth that the Portuguese valor was what destroyed it."[42]

Ch'ing officials, for their part, preferred to believe that Pai Ling's embargo had left the pirates "poor" and "contracted," and hence eligible for "pardon and pacification."[43] More recently, one scholar interested in social dissidence and the development of regionalism after the Opium War has argued that the "virtual exclusion [of piracy] from the inner waters [in late 1809] was largely a tribute to *t'uan-lien* in existence thirty years before the Opium War."[44]

In fact all of these elements were working against the pirates by 1810. The Portuguese, despite their defeat at Lantao, remained as intent as ever on exterminating them and continued to harass them. According to a Portuguese source, they had an encounter with Chang Pao's fleet as late as January 21, in which they destroyed his floating pagoda.[45] It is also true that Pai Ling's trade embargo was making food dear along the coast, and that as prices skyrocketed villagers bent on protecting their larders took more concern in their own defense.[46]

But none of these elements alone accounts for the pirates' decision to surrender. Apart from their success on January 21, the Portuguese did not make any single-handed breakthrough against the pirates; indeed, they usually fared poorly against them. As a result their claims, which are often nationalistic to the point of chauvinism, must be viewed with considerable skepticism. On the Chinese side, it is unlikely that by January 1810 difficulties of supply had reduced the pirates to the straits depicted by Ch'ing officials. At the very moment Pa Ling was describing them as lacking the resources and vigor for further resistance, Chang Pao was boasting to the Portuguese that he had "enough [stores] for a long time."[47] As for the argument that *t'uan-lien* and other local defense forces brought the pirates down, to say that they were largely responsible for the "virtual exclusion" of piracy from the inner waters is an exaggeration. Though they often inflicted severe damage on pirates who came ashore, the pirates cannot be said to have been at their mercy. Moreover, *t'uan-lien* neither functioned nor had the potential to function as offensive units capable of totally destroying the pirates. Local militia made no attempt to meet the pirates head-on by going after their bases. At best their capabilities were defensive and confined to repelling invasions or keeping pirate boats at bay. In fact, as we have seen, at the time of the pirates' last great campaign in 1809, they were not driven from the Pearl River by *t'uan-lien* or anyone else. They withdrew of their own accord to help Cheng I Sao. Far from having been "excluded" from the river, they virtually controlled it.

Each of these as explanations has the same weakness. In looking to events that were taking place outside the confederation, they overlook the most fundamental causes of all: what was going on among the pirates themselves.

In considering this question, one cannot but be struck by the similarity between the confederation and other patron-client organizations, where the possibilities for cleavage are often increased by success. Victory over a common enemy can open the door for divisive struggles over the fruits of that victory or cause some within the group to go their own way.[48] At this critical juncture, support for the movement may fade, and new leaders may arise to challenge the old ones.[49] In this instance the pirates' confederation seems to have been strong enough to prevent new bids for leadership at the top, but not strong enough to prevent individual fleets from dropping out. In this respect Kuo P'o-tai's defection set a negative example for personal interests taking precedence over those of the group. Yet, as Kuo himself almost certainly realized, the strength of the confederation was still such that he (and others of the same mind) could not have pursued piracy on their own, with the prospect of facing opposition from former allies as well as government forces. Thus his only real choice was to surrender to the state when he no longer desired to be a part of the confederation.

Success can contribute to the disintegration of patron-client organizations in yet another way, for the larger they become, the more they tend to acquire subordinate leaders far removed from the top, a development that increases the chances for internal cleavage. The likelihood of information becoming distorted as it flows through more and more levels is also increased. As a result there are limits to the number of levels through which organizations of this sort can extend their reach and on the degree to which each of these levels can work together in finely coordinated activities.[50]

Since the confederation was held together solely by the charisma of its leaders, there were limits on how far it might widen its base. Although the leaders succeeded in bringing most of the south coast's petty pirates under their sway, they were never able to extend their influence very far east of the Pearl River Delta or to link up with Ts'ai Ch'ien and Chu Fen, the pirate leaders of Fukien. There also seem to have been limits on how far down authority could be extended before the ties binding leader and follower dissolved. The confederation's tendency to add increasing numbers of commanders at the lower levels who were not personally selected by the co-founders themselves, but instead commissioned by their lieutenants, must have weakened bonds of loyalty. Some of these leaders seem to have paid more attention to the interests of their own vessels than to the obligations owed to fleet leaders, and thereby given rise to squabbles over spoils and privileges. In 1809 the pirates, at the height of victory, turned inward against themselves.

Of the pirates' later history, little is known. For Chang Pao, however, the dismantling of the confederation opened the way to a new and even more successful career, for he paralleled his meteoric rise through the pirate hierarchy with an equally spectacular rise through the ranks of the military bureaucracy. As the western expedition drew to a close, the former pirate was rewarded with a peacock feather, promoted over others to the rank of second captain, and appointed to a post in the Shun-te Regiment. For a time he lived in Canton, under the protection of Pai Ling, but the people of the region protested so vigorously that in November 1810 the Emperor recommended his transfer to another province. At length Chang Pao was moved to Fukien, where he became a lieutenant-colonel in the Min-an Regiment.[51]

There, in 1813, he and Cheng I Sao became the parents of a son, Cheng Yü-lin. Even with his new position on land, Chang Pao apparently did not completely forget his past activities, for in 1815 he was instrumental in the apprehension, in Canton, of six of the principal Chinese opium dealers in Macao. As the report had it, Chang, "fully informed of the opium trade from his days as a pirate," had seized some opium vessels in Fukien, learned from their crews that their sources of supply were the Macao dealers, and notified the governor general of Fukien, who in turn notified his counterpart in Canton to arrest them.[52]

After rising to the rank of colonel, Chang Pao was appointed to a important position in the Pescadores, where, as the head of the P'eng-hu Regiment, he was in command of two battalions and in sole charge of the islands' defense. Here he came to the attention of Lin Tse-hsü, the salt inspector of the Kiangnan Circuit, who later achieved fame as an imperial commissioner during the Opium War. Lin was so angered at finding that a surrendered criminal, especially one with a reputation like Chang's, had risen to the post of colonel in less than a decade, he sent a memorial to the Emperor recommending that limits be put on the rank to which such offenders could aspire. Stating that Chang Pao was an opium smoker and a man with no knowledge of etiquette, Lin wanted to bar him from rising still further, to the rank of brigade-general, and to prevent others like him from taking over the army.[53] Nothing came of Lin's proposal, however, and two years later, in 1822, Chang Pao, aged 36, died (presumably of natural causes) at his post in the Pescadores.[54] Thus ended the spectacular rise of this illiterate fisherman's son, who reached the second level of the Chinese military bureaucracy at an age when the majority of his most successful contemporaries would have just finished passing their Metropolitan Examination and would have been fortunate to have received their first low-ranking positions.

In 1824 Cheng I Sao, now widowed for the second time, returned to Kwangtung with her 11-year-old son. After lodging temporarily at the home of a former pirate, the still wealthy woman settled near Canton, where she did not hesitate to recall for her son the exploits of his father. At the same time she insisted that he learn to shoot and hunt so that he could surpass his father as a military official. Twice each day she took him to the family's shrine to honor the memory of Governor-general Pai Ling, whose picture was kept there. Gradually, however, Cheng I Sao's hopes for an illustrious heir vanished, for although her son was nominally a lieutenant in the army, he never served, and in 1840, at the age of 27, he was arrested for gambling. He became ill and died shortly after.[55]

Quiescence did not suit Cheng I Sao. In 1840 the 65-year-old dragon lady, still going strong, filed charges against the official Wu Yao-nan for having embezzled 28,000 taels of silver that Chang Pao had handed over to him in 1810 for the purchase of an estate. Submitted along with the charge was a letter of receipt as proof. The disposition of the case fell to the new Liang-kuang Governor-general—none other than her husband's adversary, Lin Tse-hsü. Lin was puzzled by the timing. If Chang Pao had turned the money over to Wu Yao-nan in 1810, why had Cheng I Sao waited 30 years to make her complaint? Because the magistrate of Nan-hai county had not found a witness to the transac-

tion, and the handwriting on the receipt bore little resemblance to
Wu's, the governor-general concluded that Cheng I Sao had leveled a
false accusation, and closed the case. But the suspicious Lin pursued
another matter that came up in the proceedings. Cheng I Sao had created further trouble for herself by identifying herself in writing as a
ming-sao, or wife of an official. On investigation Lin discovered that in
1821 the plaintiff had petitioned to have the title of her second husband, Chang Pao, extended to her as well. Since such an extension
was illegal in the case of wives who had remarried, to say nothing of
those whose husbands were former outlaws, Lin Tse-hsü proposed to
his superiors in Peking that the title be retracted.[56]

After this brush with the authorities, Cheng I Sao appears to have
spent her last days quietly in Canton, "leading a peaceful life so far as
[was] consistent with the keeping of an infamous gambling house."[57]
She died in 1844 at the age of 69.

In a much less flamboyant way than either Chang Pao or Cheng I
Sao, Kuo P'o-tai also enjoyed success in his retirement. Choosing to
live in Yang-ch'eng, he refused a military promotion after Chang Pao's
surrender. There he hired a tutor for his son and took him each year
to sweep his mother's tomb at the foot of the White Cloud Mountains,
just north of Canton. After years of living the kind of quiet life he had
always desired, Kuo P'o-tai, the scholar-pirate, died of natural causes
at home.[58]

Conclusion

As this excursion into maritime history has shown, the rise of piracy within the Cantonese water world during the late eighteenth century was not monocausal. None of the approaches presented in the Introduction, neither ecological conditions, outside intervention, nor internal developments within pirate gangs themselves, fully accounts for its escalation.

Ecological conditions within the water world help to explain why piracy persisted over the centuries as a temporary survival strategy of impoverished fishermen. By the late eighteenth century overpopulation, land shortage, increased trade, and Kwangtung's need for Vietnamese rice had clearly led to the intensification of piracy throughout the water world. Yet in this instance intensification meant simply an increase in the frequency of its occurrence, for small, part-time gangs seem to have been unable to cross the threshold from petty to large-scale piracy.

Unable to expand from within, the pirates' impetus for growth had to come from without. As was often the case in Western history, outside support and patronage enabled piracy in the Cantonese water world to expand. Without Tay-son sponsorship piracy in the South China Sea would probably not have escalated to the extent that it did, but piracy under the Tay-son was not yet at its zenith. Pirates did not yet constitute a well-organized confederation of Six Fleets. Thus, outside patronage was but an intermediate step on the pirates' road to the big time.

In contrast to pirates elsewhere, who reached their apogee under external sanction, the pirates studied here attained their maximum strength after formal patronage had ceased. Upon their return to the Middle Kingdom after the Tay-son defeat in 1802, erstwhile pri-

vateers reached their height while functioning in open hostility to the
governments of China and Vietnam alike. So, although external support was an important element in the pirates' rise, it does not fully
explain it either.

The Tay-son demise confronted the pirates with a devastating
setback. Their survival during this period of turmoil and their re-
emergence as powerholders along the China coast can only be attributed to internal developments. Foremost among these was the
emergence of farsighted leaders who were able to effect among remnant bands an organizational stability that enabled them to endure.
What was unusual about these leaders was that they were the heirs to a
tradition of piracy dating from the sixteenth century. Although certain other areas of the world, such as the Persian Gulf and the Mediterranean, have been the sites of recurrent piracy, none appears to
have produced a veritable dynasty like that of the Chengs, in which
family members followed one another in piracy for generations.[1]
Foremost among the family's leaders of the late eighteenth century
was Cheng Ch'i, one of the most enterprising pirates of Chiang-p'ing,
who was an early recruit of the Tay-son. After his death in 1802 his
cousin Cheng I emerged as the pirates' leading unifier and confederation builder. Cheng I's sudden death a few years later saw the over-
lordship of the pirates pass, not into the hands of a male descendant
of the family, but into those of a woman, Cheng I Sao, who had married into it.

Throughout most of the world piracy has been a male occupation
that has tended to exclude women, let alone give them leadership.
A widely held myth that women on board portended bad luck for the
fate of a ship may have contributed to their status as persona non
grata on Western vessels and caused pirate leaders to bar them from
their bands. As a result the appearance of women in Western pirate
gangs was so rare that their mere presence on board ship usually
sufficed to earn for them the title "heroine."[2]

Given the way in which Confucian attitudes militated against public
roles for women in imperial China, one might expect the presence of
Chinese women at sea, let alone their participation in pirate gangs, to
have been even more circumscribed than in the West. The phenomenon, however, is perhaps less surprising in the Chinese context that
one might at first expect. In the water world from which they sprang
women participated fully in all aspects of life at sea. Not only did the
work and reside alongside their husbands on board ship, but the
were also responsible for much of the skulling and handling of cra
of various types. Thus their presence on pirate ships was merely a

extension of everyday practice. Moreover, by the eighteenth century the precedent for women as leaders of both religious sects and anti-dynastic rebellion had been firmly established, and romantic literature boasted an entire genre of women warriors whose heroines were known throughout China.[3] Finally, Cheng I Sao's ascent was very much in keeping with the tradition of Chinese women rising to power through marriage. Marrying well and then assuming the mantle of power on the death of the husband was the most expedient avenue of female mobility in nearly every social circle in China. Among the elites and the socially well connected, this was the path to power of such "notorious" femmes fatales as Wu Tze-hsien, Yang Kuei-fei, Tzu-hsi, and more recently, Chiang Ch'ing. The practice of widows coming into power prevailed within the bandit and secret society groups of the south as well.[4]

Nevertheless, Cheng I Sao wielded authority in ways that made her unusual even by Chinese standards. Throughout her career she acted in open defiance of Confucian behavioral norms. As Cheng I's wife she was anything but a docile, submissive homebody. As his widow she not only failed to remain chaste but even married her adopted son. Despite such conduct she was able to win so much support that the pirates openly acclaimed her as the one person capable of holding the confederation together. As its leader she demonstrated her ability to take command by issuing orders, planning military campaigns, and proving that there were profits to be made in piracy. When the time came to dismantle the confederation, it was her negotiating skills above all that allowed her followers to cross the bridge from outlawry to officialdom.

Although leadership was crucial to the overall success of the pirate enterprise, apart from the extraordinary skills of specific individuals, there seems to have been little in the way of ideological motivation that accounts for the pirates' rise. Among Chinese scholars of the last few decades there has been a marked tendency to view nearly all domestic disorder as "righteous peasant uprisings" and the real motive force of a protorevolutionary tradition that led to the Communist victory in 1949. This practice has led to a tendency to overdramatize the political aspects of unrest and to see in even the most rudimentary forms of disorder an incipient rebelliousness that manifested itself in varying degrees of conscious resistance against the Ch'ing.[5] As a result those accounts have exaggerated the political self-consciousness and hence ideological inspiration of popular movements.[6]

Scholars in the West have also tended to regard rebellion as the natural and almost inevitable outcome of large-scale collective violence sustained for any length of time. In describing the growth of popular movements, they tend to speak of insurrection as "transforming" or "converting," either successfully or unsuccessfully, into rebellion.[7]

But there is little evidence to support the view of the pirates as rebels against an oppressive state. Visions of themselves as Emperors occupying the heavenly throne may have fired the imaginations of leaders like Cheng I or Chang Pao, and the prospect of holding rank or titles may have appealed to recruits during both the Tay-son and the subsequent confederation era, but political ideology alone would not have sufficed to hold the pirates together. Their primary preoccupation was making money, a goal that seems to have taken precedence over all other forms of activity, including both social protest and political rebellion. Negative evidence for this interpretation can be found in the articles signed by the seven pirate leaders in 1805; the agreement provides no reason other than economic gain for the founding of the confederation.

Furthermore, the dismantling of the confederation almost at the moment of its greatest triumph is incomprehensible if the leaders' rhetoric of rebellion is taken at face value. This is not to deny that pirates found themselves in an antistate position as they locked in combat with the dynasty, but only to suggest that the nature of their confrontation was more an economic competition over scarce resources (and rights to command the proceeds of trade) than a political contest for administrative authority. Indeed, in order for their operations to succeed, the pirates really needed the state more as an instrument to prey on and profit from than as an enemy to overthrow. Consequently, from their point of view, the Ch'ing as a state strong enough to provide sufficient order for the flourishing of commerce and yet weak enough to preclude close administrative control along every inch of the coast may have afforded an ideal backdrop to their activities.

Additional evidence for regarding pirates as something less than rebels is seen in their interest in collaborating with the state whenever possible. By throwing in their lot with the Tay-son, the pirates manifested their first tendency toward such cooperation, for at the time of their most extensive pirate patronage, the Tay-son were the recognized sovereigns of Vietnam. Later on, the pirates repeatedly engaged in negotiations with yamen personnel and at times even drew them actively into their service.

In selling protection and escort services to the salt fleets, fishing vessels, and riverine villages in China, the pirates again demonstrate their interest in treading on certain official prerogatives without an apparent desire to overthrow the state in the process. From this perspective, their ultimate return to allegiance should probably be regarded more as evidence of willingness to profit from still another opportunity for advancement than as capitulation. In short, as a group primarily concerned with financial gain, the pirates must call into question the assumption that the primary motivation for large-scale collective violence is necessarily ideological, and that its ultimate goal is inevitably rebellion.

If the pirates were not rebels, were they only Chinese bandits in another guise? Well, yes and no. From one perspective it is true that the pirates bore a remarkable resemblance to Chinese troublemakers on land (something that is implicitly recognized in the Chinese terms *hai-tao* and *hai-tsei*, which can be literally translated as "sea bandit"). Their nearest parallel is the Nien. Like the petty pirates of Chiang-p'ing, the Nien until 1853 consisted of small and independent gangs that roamed the border region between Shantung, Honan, and Anhui provinces during the late eighteenth and early nineteenth centuries, raiding settlements, ransoming captives, and collecting tribute in the form of protection money. They too were initially drawn from the misfits and marginal groups of society. And like the petty pirates they began as a loosely organized group with no fixed membership.[8]

In their early stages both the pirates and the Nien practiced a kind of guerrilla warfare in which survival depended on the ability to range unencumbered through widely scattered territory and to melt away upon contact with a superior force.[9] Later, both transformed their enterprises beyond petty undertakings through alliances with more powerful groups, the Tay-son in the one case, and the Taiping in the other.[10] In neither case did the organizations that developed function predominantly as religious associations. Religion certainly did not constitute the major reason for the pirates' existence, and although the influence of White Lotus ideology on the Nien has been a topic of controversy during the last decade, current scholarship tends to minimize its impact. One scholar who has characterized the Nien as bandits "interested in plunder rather than proselytizing" contends that they gave rise to the only large-scale nineteenth-century rebellion in China not fueled by religious belief.[11]

As their enterprises grew and their ambitions broadened, both the pirates and the Nien found it necessary to develop powerful military organizations and to transform into more formal structures the patron-client relationships that had characterized their early movements. In their subsequent adoption of identifying banners, the two groups again resembled one another, for just as the pirates used colored flags to identify their six fleets, the Nien used such flags to designate their major armies.[12]

Finally, in the end both the pirates and the Nien readily abandoned their missions when presented with better offers by the state. Although the Nien had progressed considerably farther on the road to rebellion than the pirates, neither group was inherently rebellious. As others have already pointed out, the weaknesses of bandit organization (the patron-client bases on which they were founded, the looseness and informality of both intra- and intergang cooperation, and the inability of such associations to survive their leaders), along with the tendency of such gangs to pattern their military hierarchies on those of the "orthodox" elements of society, frequently gave rise to groups that could be readily co-opted by the state through the prospect of greater gain.[13]

Yet for all that they shared in common there were significant differences between the two groups. For the Nien, grounded as they were on the continent, secure bases and territorial headquarters were crucial. In order to obtain them, they had to convert village elders, elites in charge of local defense, and the communities under their authority to their cause. By using self-defense forces, with their strong ties of kinship, the Nien were able to infiltrate walled communities and win over entire clans of gentry and commoners alike. Moreover, they deliberately set out to amass peasant support by adopting such Robin Hood–like slogans as "Carry out the will of Heaven; kill the rich and aid the poor," backed up by concrete instances of famine relief. As a result the key to their survival included protective as well as predatory survival strategies.[14]

The pirates, as creatures of the sea with bases in the islands and coves that ringed the continent, never incorporated such protective mechanisms into their survival strategies. They were not social bandits fighting for justice on behalf of the poor, but predators in search of fast fortunes. Owing in part to their ability to shelter themselves in remote offshore islands, they had little need for continental bases. Although coastal communities were of vital importance as sources of supply and outlets for prizes, it was not imperative that pirates either share their territory or coexist with them on a daily basis. As a result they could afford the luxury of allowing villages to remain as little more than sources of prey, protection money, and provisions.

Thus the pirates made little attempt to garrison communities on the shore and would probably have been unable to have sustained on-shore communities for long even if they had wanted to. The advan tage of their modus operandi was that they could remain mobile, elusive, and difficult to apprehend. But the result was that they remained totally isolated from key elements of society. Aside from the support of a few scattered followers, the pirates never had a solid base within either the gentry or the peasant society onshore. Moreover, peasants constituted no verifiable presence within either the gangs at Chiang-p'ing or the confederation that followed.

Although we cannot generalize on the basis of one example, this study reveals significant differences between banditry and piracy as forms of collective violence. It also suggests that securing bases and winning broad popular support would have created severe if not overwhelming obstacles for any maritime group that dreamed of extending its influence to the shore. One cannot but wonder whether the social distance between maritime troublemakers and villagers of the interior would not have made it difficult (though perhaps not impossible) for "sea bandits" to have become full-fledged continental bandits or rebels had that been their goal.

At first glance the Ch'ing may have seemed wise to have brought the pirates to terms through a policy of pardon and pacification that allowed both sides the luxury of a "victory." But in fact the only victors were the pirates, many of whom stepped into new lives ashore with their proceeds from piracy intact. For the Chi'ng, however, the victory was a Pyrrhic one at best.

On April 20, 1810, the very day of Chang Pao's surrender, the British expressed their reservations: "From such arrangements we cannot be induced to look forward to any permanent relief from piratical depredations."[15] Even the Emperor, referring to the entire surrender procedure as a money-making scheme on the part of Chang Pao, had his doubts.[16] Ironically, the fears of both the British and the Emperor were borne out when, on August 18, the Liang-kuang Governor-general had to delay his return to Canton from the suppression campaign in western Kwangtung because of an insurrection among a group of pirates who had been forced to surrender against their will.[17] In October came reports of other actions by supposedly reformed pirates, and on November 26 the Emperor himself admitted that on several occasions former pirates with no means of livelihood ashore had already returned to the sea.[18]

A much more serious effect of the surrender, however, was that it lulled Ch'ing officials into a false sense of security about the state of their coast. Success in the traditional methods of rebel suppression, instead of awakening the government to the weakness of its maritime

defenses, left it unaware of a problem at all. Instead of taking the
navy's repeated defeats at the hands of the pirates as a warning, Ch'ing
officials were content to make only a few superficial reforms.[19]

The enactment of these measures allowed government officials to
emerge from their bout with the pirates believing that their Mandate
of Heaven was restored and their control of the coast intact, when in
fact the opposite was the case. For rather than serving to restore their
Mandate, the pirate episode of the early nineteenth century marked
the turning point in their loss of it. Thereafter, the Ch'ing were never
able to regain full authority along a coast that was soon to feel pressure from without as well as from within. In less than a decade the
water world was again the scene of turmoil, as foreigners linked up
with secret societies to smuggle opium. From there it was but a short
step to the open confrontation of the Opium War (1839–42).

In this respect the tragedy of the pirate episode was that success in
bringing to terms people not yet so alienated from the Confucian
world as to be unattracted to a place within it enabled government
officials to enter into their first conflict with the West oblivious to the
weakness of their defense and unprepared for the debacle that would
follow. On this occasion China found itself challenged by a strong military power unable to be bought off by the rewards of the Confucian
order. No longer able to rely on pardon and pacification, Chinese soldiers had to fight to the finish, and when at last committed to action,
the country's defenses crumbled quickly. The pirates, it seems, had
taught Ch'ing officials nothing.[20]

Appendixes

A

The Background of the Pirates
in the Study

The data in the following tables are drawn from memorials in the Palace Memorial Archive (Kung-chung tang) of the National Palace Museum, Taiwan, and the Grand Council Reference File (Chün-ch'i-ch'u tsou-che lu-fu) in the First Historical Archives, Peking. These sources are identified by the abbreviations KCT and LF. The LF citations are by file number, those for KCT by reign year, lunar month, and day according to the Chinese calendar. In a KCT citation the form "CC4 iii 2," for example, is to be read as the fourth year of the Chai-ch'ing reign (1796–1820, i.e., 1800), third month, second day. An asterisk next to a month indicates the intercalary month that followed it. Since the KCT memorials, unlike the LF memorials, did not specify the pirates' ages, in table rows based on both sources the number of ages given does not accord with the pirate totals in column 1. Unless otherwise indicated, all place-names are in Kwangtung province.

TABLE A. 1

49 Voluntary Pirates of Known Occupational Background

(Excludes fishermen)

Occupation	No.	No. known to be connected with:		Native place	Age	Source
		VN	CP			
Sailor	11	11	2	Ch'ao-chou(8); Ch'in Chou(2); Hsin-an		KCT 001074, CC1 viii 26; KCT 003611, CC3 i 13
Carrier/porter	8	8	7	Sui-ch'i(5); Jao-p'ing; Ho-p'u; Fukien province	30; 32; 40	KCT 001074, CC1 viii 26; KCT 001392, CC1 x 15; KCT 001656, CC1, xii 11; KCT 001899, CC2 i 28; KCT 001967, CC2 ii 7; LF 3856; LF 3861
Laborer	8	6	4	Sui-ch'i(3); Hsin-hui(2); unknown(2); Tien-pai	29; 32; 35	KCT 001074, CC1 viii 26; LF 3854; LF 3857
Peddler	7	6	4	Vietnam; Chekiang province; Hsin-ning; Hua Chou; Hai-k'ang; Wu-ch'uan; Shih-ch'eng	25; 29; 41; 44	KCT 002010, CC2 ii 4; KCT 002481, CC2 v 16; KCT 004607, CC4 vii 1; LF 3857
Merchant	5	5	0	Hsin-an; Fukien province; Kuei-shan; Ch'eng-hai	14; 34	KCT 001047, CC1 viii 19; KCT 002845, CC2 vii 6; LF 3857
Grasscutter	4	0	0	Hsin-hui(4)		KCT 000292, CC1 iii 10
Store owner; unspecified commerce	4	4	4	Jao-p'ing(2); Kwangtung; Nghe An, Vietnam	33; 34(2)	KCT 001427, CC1 xi 6; LF 3854; LF 3856
Anchorman	1	1	0	Hsin-an		KCT 003749, CC3 ii 29
Ferryman	1	0	0	Po-lo		KCT 002367, CC2 iv 24

NOTE: As shown, 41 of the 49 pirates had Vietnam (VN) connections, and 21 Ch'iang-ping (CP) connections. 9 of the sailors (the ones from Ch'ao-chou and Hsin-an) might have been included in Table A.2 instead; at least they were specifically said to have worked on fishing boats.

TABLE A. 2
44 Fisherman—Voluntary Pirates

No.	No. connected with: VN	CP	Native place	Age	Source
6	6	6	Ho-p'u	23(1); 24(1); 32(1); 36(1)	KCT 00857, CC1 vii 5; KCT 001899, CC2 i 28; LF 3854; LF 3856; LF 3857
5	5	4	Hsin-hui	35(1)	KCT 001092, CC1 viii 30; KCT 001448, CC1 xi 10; KCT 001734, CC1 xii 21; LF 3861
5	2	1	Yang-chiang		KCT 000066, CC1 i 21; KCT 001074, CC1 viii 26; KCT 001176, CC1 ix 21; KCT 001805, CC2 i 8
4	4	3	Wu-ch'uan	26(1); 44(1)	KCT 000137, CC1 ii 9; KCT 001804, CC2 i 8; LF 3857
4	2	0	Ch'eng-hai		KCT 001496, CC1 xi 18; KCT 002531, CC2 v 29; KCT 002779, CC2 vi* 2
3	3	2	Tien-pai	22; 26; 35	LF 3854; LF 3856; LF 3857
2	2	1	Sui-ch'i	30; 35	LF 3857
2	1	1	P'an-yü		KCT 2109, CC2 iii 4; KCT 003347, CC2 xi 2
1	0	0	Chang-p'u, Fukien province		KCT 000067, CC1 i 21
1	1	0	Chao-an, Fukien province		KCT 002848, CC2 vii 6
1	1	0	Ch'ao-yang		KCT 03459, CC2 xii 11
1	1	1	Hai-k'ang	30	LF 3857
1	0	0	Hsin-an		KCT 008158, CC7 v 27
1	0	0	Jao-p'ing		KCT 000981, CC1 vii 29
1	1	1	Mou-ming	28	LF 3861
1	1	1	Tung-kuan	22	LF 3857
5	2	2	Unknown		KCT 000827, CC1 vi 25; KCT 008158, CC7 v 27

NOTE: As shown, 32 of the 44 fisherman-pirates had Vietnam (VN) connections, and 23 had Ch'iang-ping (CP) connections.

TABLE A. 3

62 Voluntary Pirates of Unknown Occupational Background

No.	Native place	Age
15	Ho-p'u	22(2); 28(3); 29(3); 30; 31; 32; 36; 38; 42; 43
11	Wu-ch'uan	23; 30; 32; 33(2); 35; 36; 39(2); 44; 52
5	Sui-ch'i	28; 30; 36; 52(2)
4	Hsin-hui	28(3); 52
4	Shih-ch'eng	33(2); 37; 68
3	Fukien province	27; 31; unknown
3	Tien-pai	32; 35; 39
2	Hai-feng	22; 32
2	Hai-k'ang	33(2)
2	Hsin-an	27; 40
2	Mou-ming	30; 32

1 each from Chia-ying (age 53), Ch'in Chou (36), Ho-p'ing (35), Hua-chou (24), Jen-chou (49), Kuei-shan (20), Shun-te (45), Tung-kuan (58), and Yang-chiang (40)

SOURCES: LF 3854; LF 3856; LF 3861.
NOTE: 59 of these 62 pirates had both Vietnam and Chiang-p'ing connections. 1 of the pirates from Fukien had no known VN or CP connection; and 2 pirates, 1 from Shun-te and 1 from Tien-pai, were not known to be connected with Ch'iang-ping.

TABLE A. 4

26 Captives-Turned-Pirate of Known Occupational Background

(Excludes fishermen)

Occupation	No.	Native place	Age	Source
Sailor[a]	10	Ch'eng-hai(6); T'ung-an, Fukien province(2); Chang-p'u, Fukien province; Wu-ch'uan	24; 30; 31; 39(2); 40; 44; un-known(3)	KCT 002848, CC2 vii 6; KCT 003347, CC2 xi 2; LF 3857
Rice dealer	6	Vietnam		KCT 004602, CC4 v 29
Peddler	4	Ch'in Chou(2); Hai-k'ang; Mou-ming	24; 26; 32; 34	LF 3857
Porter/ carrier	3	Ch'ao-yang; Sui-ch'i; Shun-te		KCT 000981, CC1 vii 29; KCT 001116, CC1 ix 8; KCT 003459, CC2 xii 1
Grasscutter	2	Tien-pai(2)	34; 44	LF 3857
Shoemaker	1	Sui-ch'i	26	LF 3857

NOTE: None of these pirates had any known Chiang-p'ing connections. 24 of the 26 had Vietnam connections; the 2 exceptions were both porter/carriers.
[a] 1 pirate listed as both a sailor and a carrier is included in the porter/carrier category.

TABLE A. 5

26 Fisherman Captives-Turned-Pirate

No.	Native place	No. known to be connected with: VN	CP	Age	Source
5	Ch'eng-hai	4	3	22; 26; 29(2)	KCT 002723, CC2 vi* 7; LF 3854
4	Hsin-an	1	0		KCT 001074, CC1 viii 26; KCT 002723, CC2 vi* 7; KCT 003749, CC3 ii 29; KCT 004516, CC4 vi 21
3	Ho-p'u	3	0	26; 32; 33	LF 3857
3	Tien-pai	3	0	28; 29; 32	LF 3857
2	Hai-k'ang	2	1	28(1)	KCT 003728, CC3 ii 19; LF 3857
2	Hsin-hui	2	1	23(1)	KCT 008517, CC7 vii 14
2	Mou-ming	2	0	30; 39	LF 3857
1	Hai-feng	1	0	34	LF 3854
1	Hai-yang	1	0		KCT 001074, CC1 viii 26
1	Lu-shui	1	0		KCT 008517, CC7 vii 14
1	Sui-ch'i	0	1		KCT 009507, CC7 xi 14
1	Unknown	1	0	29	LF 3856

NOTE: As shown, 21 of the 26 fisherman-captives had known Vietnam (VN) connections, and 6 Chiang-p'ing (CP) connections.

TABLE A. 6

23 Captives-Turned-Pirate of Unknown Occupational Background

No.	Native place	No. known to be connected with: VN	CP	Age
11	Ch'eng-hai	11	10	22(4); 30(2); 32; 33; 36; 45; 68
3	Sui-ch'i	2	1	26; 29; 48
2	Hai-feng	2	2	29; 36
2	Jao-p'ing	2	2	23; 44
2	Wu-ch'uan	2	2	25; 37
1	Hai-yang	1	0	40
1	Kuei-shan	1	1	23
1	Tien-pai	1	0	58

SOURCES: LF 3854; LF 3857.
NOTE: As shown, 22 of the 23 captive-pirates had known Vietnam (VN) connections and 18 Chiang-p'ing (CP) connections.

B

The Pirates' Declaration
of 1809

Three copies of this declaration were posted in Macao and 20 in Canton. On June 10, 1809, the governor of Macao conveyed the translation given below to the British. It is in the Canton Consultations file in the India office, London (Factory Records G/12/100–G/12/174).

We who live on the seas weeping declare that the reason why we are Pirates has been no other but for that in past times all the Mandarins being persons of tyrannical hearts sought for nought but money. There has now arrived at the Metropolis of Canton the most bright and severe sky (a laudatory appellation given by the Ladrones to the new Viceroy) [Pai Ling].

The Mandarin Siam-xan (commonly called Hy-am-san) [Hsiang-shan hsien?] does not know his crimes nor is he aware of the errors he has committed. In the purpose of amendment, he does not perplex himself, nor has he care over his Brother nor even over the people of his Household, who are under his directions and in his own service; since he leaves them to do what they choose according to their will, in such sort that on one occasion when there was a quantity of rice to be transported to Macao, they exacted five candareens of silver for each bag of Rice; in like manner in an instance where there was a portion of Nele (Rice in the husk or paddy) to be conveyed to Canton, they likewise extracted 50 Dollars for each Boat or Vessel on which it is customary to transport the said commodity; at the present time the Mandarin of Hy-am-san has addressed Letters to the substantial traders exhorting them that they should aid with a certain Sum of money such as each of them should choose to give in order that he might buy a portion of rice at the actual and current price in order to enable him at a future time to sell the said Rice to the indigent for a moderate price; we know that this does not proceed from his love of the People nor is it his true Project.

The Mandarin Ouvidor (Judge) of Cou-my-tam [Macao] does not watch over his [illegible] having them at liberty to connect themselves with the Chin chew Chinese in gaining establishments of various descriptions, exacting from the gamblers 50 Tales [sic] each month. We, if we addict ourselves to gambling in that way and at such games, will think of nothing else but play and take no more heed for our subsistence and mode of living—If the Mandarin would not cloak such proceedings he would be spoken of as a good character, but allowing for this to go on he can no longer vaunt his affection for the people.

The Military Mandarins great and small are all afraid of Death. They ask for nothing more than the money of others with the purpose that at a future time when they shall not be able any longer to exercise the charge of Mandarin, being under the necessity of returning to their houses, they shall have by that time amassed money for the expenses of subsistence. If they were not such kind of men as thus specified they ought forthwith to have come out to the open sea in order to fight with us, when they know of our arrival in these parts, instead of seeking for various pretexts as for instance of repairing their Boats, mending their sails, setting this and that to rights, and pretending all this notwithstanding their being aware of our arrival—We as we had notice of the Mandarin Fleet being in Macao seeking various pretexts with deceit return to other places. Furthermore it will be seen that the said Military Mandarins when advised of our retreat will communicate to the Superior Mandarins that we being afraid to fight them have fled elsewhere—

The Superior Mandarins who in past times were Magistrates in the Province of Canton are not men of a similar character to the present Viceroy who in truth is clear as the crystal and [illegible] luminous as a mirror—We are waiting till these warlike Mandarins finish the repair of their Vessels and prepare all that shall be necessary, begging the loan of Guns, etc. After they have made everything ready we hope they may come out to fight us—These very Mandarins after having made all the necessary preparations having out their Vessels close to the Islands such as those of the Taypa, etc. and there they allow them to remain without having the spirit to come out into the open sea to fight us; and in this manner they deceive the Mandarins above them and the Viceroy and others who are in the firm belief that they are gone forth to stop the Ladrones; in like manner do they deceive the people also who have seen them sally forth to stop the Ladrones. When in reality all is Falsehood and deceit. We hope that the Pai Chim Tien (the title given by the Ladrones to the Viceroy of bright and severe heaven) may chastise and deprive all these Mandarins from their offices which they exercise, listening to our first suggestions and complaints; we then will be no longer pirates; rather than go, we will convey our Vessels to a great distance and will not have the audacity to navigate in the seas belonging to the jurisdiction of Pai-Chim-Tien.

We who live upon the Seas with Lamentation have spoken.

C

Pirate Junks

Most of the pirates' seagoing junks were of eight types:

1. *Ch'i-wei hai-fei fei-ch'uan*, or even-masted pirate junks.

2. *Ta-t'iao ts'ao-ch'uan*, great hook or great fish-shaped cargo junks. In Kwangtung the *ts'ao-ch'uan* were a type of commercial or merchant junk, and from the Ming dynasty on, they were one of the larger craft seeking shelter in the Hong Kong harbor.

3. *Pai-ts'ao ch'uan* and *wu-ts'ao ch'uan*, white- and black-hulled junks, respectively (Fig. C.1). First built in Fukien for the transport of wood, they were originally called "Shanghai junks," after the port they most often frequented. These vessels were made of ironwood and were constructed like war junks. Their appearance resembled that of a horse trough (*ts'ao*). According to one account, the character *ts'ao* is a kind of pun derived by substituting the boat radical for the wood radical of the character meaning horse trough. The heads and tails of the *ts'ao-ch'uan* also resembled those of a large whale (*hai-ch'iu*); consequently the ostensible purpose of the two large eyes of either black or white painted on their bow was so that whales seeing them at a distance would take them for other whales and not eat them. The black-hulled junks were used primarily to transport food and salt, the white to catch fish or carry goods.

4. *Shuang-wei ch'uan*, two-masted junks.

5. *Liao-ch'uan*, materials boats, which were probably a type of small transport used for a variety of local produce.

6. *Lao-tseng ch'uan* and *liu-tseng ch'uan*, arrow vessels of a still undetermined type. It appears that these "arrow vessels" may have been a kind of small warship resembling a corvette, ranging in size from 40 by 12 feet to 80 by 21 feet with two masts and a mizzen that was stepped on the port side and had no sail

7. *K'uai-ch'uan* or "fast boats." These were common two-masted vessel of the local type used for both fishing and the coasting trade. They carried a lot of sail and handled well in high seas. The dimensions of the one in Figure C.2 are 27m 50cm from bow to stern, 21m long at the water line, 6m wide outside the bulwarks, 6 m² surface of the rudder, and 16m 30cm high at the tallest mast.

8. *Ta-k'ai-po ch'uan*, "great break-through-the-waves junks." Perhaps these vessels resembled the *hai-po ch'uan*, vessels from Ch'ao-chou that traded t Hainan and Annam; their average cargo capacity was 350 tons, but they wer

known to have been as large as 1,000 tons. Or they may have been similar to the *k'ai-lang ch'uan* ("open-the-waves junks") of Kwangtung, known also as the *ch'ih-shui ch'uan* ("eat-water junks") because of their ability to cut through the waves. Equipped with four oars and a sweep, the *k'ai-lang ch'uan* could move "like flying" and could accommodate between 30 and 50 people (Fig. C.3).

Some of the specific types of river craft employed by the pirates were the following:

1. *Ta-t'o-feng ch'uan,* "great drag-the-wind vessels." Although I have been unable to find any information on *t'o-feng ch'uan,* I think they were a type of *t'o-ch'uan* used primarily to transport passengers. The Chinese government, however, often used them as armed cruisers, for in 1802 Liang-kuang Governor-general Chi-ch'ing was allowed to construct eight of these vessels at a cost of 800 taels each to be used against pirates. Occasionally the *t'o-ch'uan* were used in fishing on the high seas, and after the middle of the nineteenth century they provided the major passenger service between Canton and Hong Kong. The average ones were two-masted vessels 100 feet long by 24 feet wide with an exterior platform five feet in width. The depth of the hold was between nine and ten feet, and their draft between five and ten feet. They carried 28 men.

2. *K'uai-t'ing* or "fast boats" (to be distinguished from the seagoing *k'uai ch'uan*) were a type of gondola ranging from 25 to 50 feet in length and sometimes carried a single mast. They were used by smugglers, police, and customs agents alike. On a platform open in the front, six men could take their place at the oars; on the stern, which was raised high above the water, there was a room for the crew as well as a station for the man in charge (*godilleur*).

3. The pirates' sampans, or "three-board boats," were modeled on those of the Pearl River. They were characterized by slender, pointed bows and were used for fighting in shallow water or mounting onshore attacks. They were armed with old cannon placed on the deck. Their raised sterns formed platforms on which the pilot and helmsman rode, and in the middle of the deck was a mat roof that served as a shelter. With no masts, their only means of propulsion was by sculls.

4. *Ch'ang-lung,* or "long dragons," another type of rowboat, were referred to by the Europeans as "serpent" or "snake" boats because of their elongated forms. They were used by the pirates for navigating in the rivers.

SOURCES: Lo Hsiang-lin, "Hsiang-kang chih hai-wan yü t'e-ch'an chi ch'i-ch'ien tai-li-shu," in Lo Hsiang-lin, ed., *I-pa-ssu-erh nien i-ch'ien chih Hsiang-Kang chi ch'i-tui wai-chiao-t'ung* (Hong Kong, 1959), p. 13; Louis Audemard, *Les Jonques chinoises,* 10 vols. (Rotterdam, 1957–71) 4: 58, 9: 20–22; *Kuang-chou fu-chih,* comp. Tai Chao-ch'en, 163 chüan (1879; Taipei, 1966), ch. 74: 23, 24; Joseph Needham, *Science and Civilization in China,* 6 vols. in 13 parts (Cambridge, Eng., 1954–76), vol. 4, part 3, p. 406.

烏槽

Fig. C.1. Black-hulled junk (*wu-ts'ao ch'uan*). Source: Louis Audemard, *Les Jonques chinoises*, 10 vols. (Rotterdam, 1957–71), 9: 22 (fig. 18).

快船

Fig. C.2. Fast boat (*k'uai-ch'uan*). Source: same as Fig. C.1, 8: 59 (fig. 22).

開浪船圖

Fig. C.3. Open-the-waves junk (*k'ai-lang ch'uan*). Source: same as Fig. C.1, 1: 59 (fig. 13).

D

The Pirate Surrender Document
of 1810

Controversy surrounds the origin of this pirate surrender document. Most scholars have attributed it to Chang Pao, but Yüan Yung-lun, author of *Ching hai-fen chi*, has attributed it to Kuo P'o-tai; and Yeh Lin-feng, author of *Chang Pao-tsai ti ch'uan-shuo ho chen-hsiang*, to the staff of Governor-general Pai Ling, who presumably wrote it on behalf of the pirates. Regardless of its authorship and whether it was the actual petition of Chang Pao or Kuo P'o-tai, the document is a succinct apology for the rise and fall of piracy. It begins by invoking past precedents for the pardoning of serious offenders. After accounting for the rise of piracy, it makes its appeal for sympathy through a pitiful depiction of life at sea. It is a rare and detailed description of the pirates' lives and motivations.

An English-language translation of this document appears in Karl Friedrich Neumann, *History of the Pirates Who Infested the China Sea from 1807 to 1810* (London, 1931), pp. 69–72. Another is available in Chung-shen (Thomas) Chang, "Ts'ai Ch'ien, the Pirate King Who Dominates the Seas: A Study of Coastal Piracy in China, 1795–1810," Ph.D. dissertation, University of Arizona, 1983, pp. 240–44. The translation here was done by the author in consultation with P. S. Ni.

Chinese texts of the document appear in Yüan Yung-lun (Yuen Yung-lun), *Chiang hai-fen chi*, 2 chüan (Canton, 1830), ch. 2: 10b–13; Hu Chieh-yü (Woo Kit-yü), "Hsi-Ying-P'an yü Chang Pao-tsai huo-luan chih p'ing-ting," in Lo Hsiang-lin, ed., *I-pa-ssu-erh nien i-ch'ien chih Hsiang-kang chi ch'i-tui wai-chiao-t'ung* (Hong Kong, 1959), pp. 156–57; and Yeh Ling-feng, *Chang Pao-tsai* (Hong Kong, 1970), pp. 109–10.

The backgrounds of heroes are different. So are the hearts of the officials, for some are benevolent and others have patience. Therefore, the bandits o

Liang-shan were thrice pardoned for pillaging the city and became a pillar of state.* The robbers of Wa-kang on several occasions resisted the soldiers, but when granted amnesty became cornerstones of the country.† Other examples can be found in history: Kung Ming captured Ming Huo several times, and Kuan Kung thrice freed Ts'ao Ts'ao.‡ Ma Yüan never chased a desperate enemy and Yüeh Fei never killed those who submitted.§ Thus, when the heroes of the world surrender, people from far and near are happy. Such events are not one-time occurrences, for their underlying principles are the same.

Now, we "ants" [the pirates' reference to themselves in humble terms] are living in a prosperous age. Originally we were good people, but we became pirates for a variety of reasons. Because some of us were not careful in making friends, we fell into a bad situation and became robbers. Others of us were unable to secure a livelihood or were captured while trading on the lakes and rivers and forced into piracy. Still others because of having committed some crime joined this watery empire to escape punishment. At first we constituted only a small number, but later we increased to a thousand and ten thousand. In addition, as a result of the dearth of the last several years, people had nothing with which to maintain their living, and as time went on could not help but rob in order to live. If we had not resisted the government officials, our lives would have been in danger. Therefore, we violated the laws of the empire and destroyed the merchants. This was unavoidable.

As pirates, we left our native villages. Without families, we floated upon the sea. If we encountered government patrols, their cannon and arrows frightened us. If we encountered rough seas, then we were also frightened. We fled to the east and west, and often tried to avoid the pursuit of warships. Having to live without shelter and eat the wind, we suffered all the bitterness of the sea. At those times, we wanted to leave the robbers and return to our villages, but the inhabitants would not tolerate us. We considered surrendering as a group, but did not know what the officials, with their power, would do to us, so we had to remain on the islands, just looking on and waiting with no decision. Alas! Alas!

Of course our crimes should be punished by death. It is hard to avoid the laws of the government. But our situation is extremely pitiful and if we are to survive, we must depend on men of benevolence. We are happy that you, Governor-general, have come again to Kwangtung to rule, for you regard others as yourself and love them as your sons.

We have respectfully read your proclamation several times. You advise us to surrender and take pity on our reasons for having become pirates. Your principle is to use both severity and leniency, and you understand the virtue of the treasure of life. In your justice you use both extermination and appeasement. Even the bird flying in the dust wants to be quiet, and how can a fish be content in boiling water? On account of this, I have gathered my entire group, and we have sent this petition with all our signatures. We hope that you will

---

*Liang-shan, in Shantung, was the stronghold of a group of bandits who became the heroes of the adventure novel *Shui-hu ch'uan* (*Water Margin*).

† Wa-kang was a bandit-infested marsh in Honan province.

‡ All four references are to historical figures from the late Han dynasty whose stories are told in the novel *San-kuo-chi yen-i* (The Romance of the Three Kingdoms).

§ Ma was a famous later Han general, Yüeh a famous general of the Southern Sung.

pity the remaining life of us "insects and ants"; save us from the flood and fire; pardon our former crimes; and open for us a new way of life from this day forward. We solemnly promise to "sell our swords and buy cows." In appreciation of your greatness, we burn incense and praise you in song. If we dare to act with duplicity, you may kill us at once.

E

Chinese Money, Weights, and Measures

MONEY

All references to dollars in the text are to Spanish dollars.

10 *cash* (*li* or *wen*)	=	1 candareen (*fen*)
10 candareen	=	1 mace (*ch'ien*)
10 mace	=	1 tael (*liang*)
1 tael	=	approx. 1.33 Spanish dollars
1 dollar of foreign or		
Spanish silver (*yüan*)	=	720–50 Chinese *cash*

These equivalents cannot be accepted as firm, for there was considerable regional and local variation. For example, in 1805 20 *yüan* of foreign silver equaled 14 taels, 4 mace. In sycee or pure silver, the same amount equaled 13 taels, 1 mace, 4 candareens, 8 *cash*.

WEIGHTS AND MEASURES

1 catty (*chin*)	=	1.3 pound
10 catties	=	1 picul (*tan*) = 133.33 pounds
1 *ts'un*	=	1 inch
10 *ts'un*	=	1 *ch'ih* = 10 inches
10 *ch'ih*	=	1 *chang* = 8 feet, 4 inches

SOURCE (on money): Na-yen-ch'eng, *Na-wen-i-kung-tsou-i* (1834; Taipei, 1968), 12: 42, CC 10 vii 1.

Notes

Notes

Citations from documentary collections are followed by a date of reign, lunar month, and day according to the Chinese calendar. The Ch'ien-lung reign (1736–95) is abbreviated CL; the Chia-ch'ing reign (1796–1820) is abbreviated CC; and the Tao-kuang reign (1821–50) is abbreviated TK. "CL58 viii 11" is thus to be read Ch'ien-lung 58, eighth month, eleventh day. An asterisk next to the month indicates the intercalary month that followed it. On works that are cited only once, complete information is given in the note. The others are cited in short form. For full authors' names, titles, and publication data on those works, see the References Cited, pp. 220–26. Other abbreviations used in these Notes are as follows:

CanCon   "[Canton] Consultations and Transactions of the Select Committee of Resident Supercargoes Appointed by the Honourable Court of Directors of the United East India Company to Manage Their Affairs in China Together with the Letters Written and Occurrences." Factory Records G/12/100–G/12/174, March 1791 to January 1811. India Office, London.

CHFC   *Yuan Yung-lun. Ching hai-fen chi* [Record of the pacification of the pirates]. 2 *chüan*. Canton, 1830.

CP   *Chu-p'i tsou-che* [Rescripted memorial collection]. First Historical Archives, Peking.

CSK   *Ch'ing-shih kao* [Draft of the Ch'ing dynasty history], comp. Chao Erh-hsün. 536 *chüan*. Peking, 1927–28.

CSL   *Ta Ch'ing li-ch'ao shih-lu* [Veritable records of the successive reigns of the Ch'ing dynasty; Muken, 1937]. 4,485 *chüan*. Taipei, 1964.

CSLC   *Ch'ing-shih lieh-ch'uan* [Biographies of the Ch'ing dynasty]. 80 *chüan*. Shanghai, 1928.

DNCB   *Dai Nam chinh bien liet truyen Nha Tay-son* [First collection of the primary biographies of Imperial Vietnam (the Nguyen dynasty)]. Saigon, 1970. (A reprinted edition of the biographies of the Tayson from the *Dai Nam Chinh bien liet truyen*, with Chinese and Vietnamese texts on opposite pages.)

DNTL   *Dai Nam thuc luc* [Veritable records of Imperial Vietnam (the Nguyen dynasty)]. 20 vols. Tokyo, 1961. (This hard-copy edition of the work contains both the *Dai Nam thuc luc chinh bien* [First collection of the veritable records of the Nguyen dynasty] and the *Dai Nam chinh bien liet truyen* [First collection of the primary biographies of Imperial Vietnam]. Microfilms of the originals in the library of the Ecole Française d'Extrême Orient, A 27, no. 73, and A 35, no. 94.)

HSHC(1)   *Hsiang-shan hsien-chih* [Gazetteer of Hsiang-shan county], comp. Chu Huai. 8 *chüan*. 1827.

HSHC(2)   *Hsiang-shan hsien-chih*, comp. T'ien Ming-yao. 22 *chüan*. 1879.

KCFC   *Kuang-chou fu-chih* [Gazetteer of Kuang-chou prefecture; 1879] comp. Tai Chao-ch'en. 163 *chüan*. Taipei, 1966.

KCT   *Kung-chung tang* [Palace memorial archive]. National Palace Museum, Taipei. An "E" following the memorial number indicates an enclosure of that memorial.

KTHF   *Kuang-tung hai-fang hui-lan* [An examination of Kwangtung's sea defense], comp. Lu K'un and Ch'eng Hung-ch'ih. 42 *chüan*. n.d.

KTTC   *Kuang-tung t'ung-chih* [Encyclopedia of Kwangtung province], comp. Juan Yüan. 334 *chüan*. 1822.

LF   *Chün-ch'i-ch'u tsou-che lu-fu* [Grand Council reference file]. First Historical Archives, Peking.

NHHC   *Nan-hai hsien-chih* [Gazetteer of Nan-hai county; 1872], comp. Cheng Meng-yü. 26 *chüan*. Taipei, 1971.

NYC   *Na-yen-ch'eng, Na-wen i-kung tsou-i* [The collected memorials of Na-yen-ch'eng; 1834]. Taipei, 1968.

STHC(1)   *Shun-te hsien-chih* [Gazetteer of Shun-te county; 1853], comp. Kuo Ju-ch'eng. 32 *chüan*. Taipei, 1974.

STHC(2)   *Shun-te hsien-chih* (1929), comp. Ho Tsao-hsiang. 24 *chüan*. Taipei, 1966.

SYT   *Shang-yü-tang fang-pen* [Imperial edict record book, long form]. National Palace Museum, Taipei.

TKHC   *Tung-kuan hsien-chih* [Gazetteer of Tung-kuan county; 1921], comp. Yeh Chüeh-mai. 102 *chüan*. Taipei, 1969.

INTRODUCTION

1. Dalrymple, *Memoir*, p. 2.
2. Robert B. Forbes, *Personal Reminiscences*, 3d ed. (Boston, 1892), p. 390.
3. CSL 1434: 12b, CL58 viii 11. Fu-k'ang-an, the Liang-kuang Governor-general between 1789 and 1793, was one of the most eminent military commanders of his day. His first major military undertaking was the quelling of a Muslim rebellion in Kansu in 1784. In 1787 he was ordered to Taiwan to put down the uprising of Lin Shuang-wen, and in 1790 he led an expedition to expel the Gurkas from Tibet. Following his tenure as the Liang-kuang Governor-general, Fu-k'ang-an was put in charge of suppressing a Miao uprising in the Szechwan–Kweichow border area. Hummel, pp. 252–55.
4. Koxinga, "Lord of the Imperial Surname," conducted one of the more sustained Ming Loyalist Movements along the coast. His father, Cheng Chih-lung, a native of Ch'üan-chou, Fukien, was a pirate of great renown who had initially come to terms with the Ming government but later made his sub

mission to the Manchus, only to be subsequently betrayed by them. When Koxinga learned of his father's fate, he declared himself an enemy of the Manchus, pledged lifelong allegiance to the Ming, and gathered a force of several thousand men to carry out his resistance. In 1662 he concluded a treaty with the Dutch that ended their rule of Taiwan. From this new base, Koxinga readied himself for a protracted struggle against the Ch'ing, which never materialized because of his unexpected death in June 1662. A rather spiritless resistance was carried on by his son until 1683, when Taiwan fell to the Ch'ing. "Chinese Pirates," pp. 65–66; Ralph C. Croizier, *Koxinga and Chinese Nationalism: History, Myth, and the Hero* (Cambridge, Mass., 1977), pp. 6–27; Hummel, pp. 108–10.

5. The Portuguese translation of the letter in which this boast appears is in Judice Biker, pp. 253–55. The document is dated Dec. 26, 1809.

6. John E. Wills, Jr. "Maritime China from Wang Chih to Shih Lang: Themes in Peripheral History," in Jonathan D. Spence and John E. Wills, Jr., eds., *From Ming to Ch'ing: Conquest, Region, and Continuity in Seventeenth-Century China* (New Haven, Conn., 1979), p. 206.

7. For more information on the administrative and economic regions into which continental China was divided, see G. William Skinner, "Regional Urbanization in Nineteenth-Century China" and "Cities and the Hierarchy of Local Systems," in Skinner, ed., *The City in Late Imperial China* (Stanford, Calif., 1977), pp. 211–52, 275–352.

8. Perry, *Rebels*, pp. 2–4, 149. "Predatory" survival strategies involved some members of the community expanding their resources at the expense of others through such aggressive activities as theft, banditry, smuggling, and organized feuds. "Protective" survival strategies involved defending one's belongings against potential predation through such activities as crop-watching, private vigilantes, village militia, and the construction of fortified communities.

9. Elizabeth J. Perry, "Popular Unrest in China: The State and Local Society," paper presented at the conference on The Role of the State in Development and Change, China, 1880–1980, Washington, D.C., Dec. 14–15, 1981, pp. 9–11.

10. Gosse, pp. 18, 23, 34. For a more detailed account of the competition between the Barbary Corsairs and the Knights of Malta, see Peter Earle, *The Corsairs of Malta and Barbary* (London, 1970).

11. Gosse, pp. 106, 115; Kenneth Andrews, *Elizabethan Privateering: English Privateering During the Spanish War, 1585–1603* (Cambridge, 1964), p. 20. Vindication for the Queen's policies can be said to have come when, in 1588, the British "navy," composed largely of privateers, sailed forth to meet the Armada.

12. For accounts of Henry Morgan, see P. K. Kemp and Christopher Lloyd, *Brethren of the Coast Buccaneers of the South Seas* (New York, 1960), p. 7; Gosse, pp. 154–60; and John Esquemeling, *The Buccaneers of America: A True Account of the Most Remarkable Assaults Committed of Late Years upon the Coasts of the West Indies by the Buccaneers of Jamaica and Tortuga* (New York, 1967), pp. 120–272 (originally published in Dutch and translated into English in 1684–85). For details on the operation of piracy in North America, see Gosse, pp. 176–77; and Botting, pp. 20, 31, 68, 72, 86, 101–27, 137. (Companies of seamen fitted out ships in New England, recruited crews in Newfoundland, obtained provisions in the West Indies, and sailed to the Red Sea, the Persian Gulf, or the

Malabar coast of western India. There they preyed on ships belonging to the Moghul of India and obtained shelter whenever necessary in the pirate republic of Madagascar.)

CHAPTER 1

1. The exact origins of the boat people are unknown, but scholars have speculated that they may be the descendants of the ancient Yüeh, the indigenous inhabitants of the region, or of landsmen who fled to the sea in large numbers during such national crises as the fall of the Northern Sung and Ming dynasties. Anderson, *Essays*, pp. 2, 3; Ward, "Varieties of the Conscious Model," p. 118. "Tanka" was a popular name for the boat people whose dwellings extend from the Min River in Fukien through Kwangtung and on into Hainan and Vietnam. But technically speaking, the term applied solely to the Cantonese speakers; it was not used for the Hoklo or the Hokkien boat people from Fukien. Blake, *Ethnic Groups*, p. 73.

2. T. R. Tregear, *A Geography of China* (London, 1965), p. 256.

3. William Dampier, *A Collection of Voyages*, 4 vols. (London, 1729), 2: 20; "Topography of the Province of Canton," pp. 478, 483; "Description of the City of Canton," *Chinese Repository*, 2: 146 (Aug. 1833).

4. "Topography of the Province of Canton," p. 483; Barth, p. 14.

5. Until 1965, when Kwangsi province was given an outlet to the sea, Kwangtung lay directly adjacent to Vietnam.

6. Cushman, p. 6. See also Mills, pp. 227–29.

7. For information on oceanography in general and the South China Sea in particular, see J. W. Hedgpeth, ed., *Treatise on Marine Ecology and Paleoecology* (New York, 1957); G. L. Pickard, *Descriptive Physical Oceanography* (New York, 1963); P. Groen, *The Waters of the Sea* (New York, 1969); Rhodes W. Fairbridge, ed., *The Encyclopedia of Oceanography* (New York, 1966); and *The Ocean: A Scientific American Book* (San Francisco, 1969).

8. Samuels, p. 23; M. A. P. Meilink-Roelofsz, *Asian Trade and European Influence in the Indonesian Archipelago between 1500 and About 1630*, tr. M. B. Quest (The Hague, 1962), pp. 132, 133, 329, 344, 350, 375–76; Jacob Cornelis van Leur, *Indonesian Trade and Society: Essays in Asian Social and Economic History*, tr. J. S. Holmes and A. van Marle, 2d ed. (The Hague, 1967), pp. 135–37, 197–200.

9. Cushman, pp. 51, 54.

10. For more information on the junk trade, see Leonard; Viraphol, p. 7; and Cushman, pp. 95, 96, 103. The junk trade was distinct from the tribute trade, which was channeled to the port of Canton. Besides the Chinese trade to Southeast Asia, the junk trade included most of the trade from Southeast Asia to China. All of this East Asian commerce of the Nan-yang was eligible for special tax considerations because it was "native trade" (i.e., carried on Chinese-style vessels and conducted by Chinese).

11. Viraphol, p. 7; Cushman, pp. 95, 96, 103; Leonard, p. 60.

12. Wakeman, *Strangers*, p. 43; Viraphol, p. 123; Lamb, pp. 9–40. For an account of the British activity in the water world during the 17th and 18th centuries, see Morse, *Chronicles*, vol. 1.

13. Viraphol, p. 51.

14. Capt. Alexander Hamilton, *A New Account of the East Indies*, 2 vols. (1727; London, 1930), 2: 128.

15. Cushman, p. 94.
16. "Coast of China," p. 343; Schafer, pp. 79–82.
17. Cushman, p. 30; Viraphol, pp. 51, 165, 188, 195; "The Island Hainan," *The Asiastic Journal*, 21.1: 15–16 (1826); Gützlaff, pp. 82–83; Friedrich Hirth, "The Port of Hai-k'ou," *The China Review*, 1.2: 127 (1872).
18. "Coast of China," p. 341.
19. Samuels, p. 23. For additional information on sailing routes to Canton, see Wang Gungwu, "The Nan-hai Trade: A Study in the Early History of Chinese Trade in the South China Sea," *Journal of the Malayan Branch of the Royal Asiatic Society*, 31.2: 72, 73 (June 1958); and Morse, *Chronicles*, 1: 273.
20. Ch'en Lun-chiung, *Hai-kuo wen-chien lu* [Sights and sounds of the maritime countries] (1730; Taipei, 1970), pp. 20–22.
21. Schafer, pp. 73, 79.
22. For a discussion of the theory of how commercialization of the economy and the subsequent polarization of society contribute to pushing people off the land and of how this worked in practice in Kwangtung during the early 20th century, see Edward Friedman, *Backward Toward Revolution: The Chinese Revolutionary Party* (Berkeley, Calif., 1974), pp. 121, 124, 134–35.
23. Wakeman, *Strangers*, p. 57.
24. Edward J. M. Rhoads, *China's Republican Revolution: The Case of Kwangtung, 1895–1913* (Cambridge, Mass., 1975), pp. 12–14; Armando da Silva, pp. 33–35.
25. Armando da Silva, p. 30.
26. Downing, 2: 20–21.
27. For information on life in the floating communities, see Ward, "Floating Villages"; Ward, "Hong Kong Fishing Village"; Blake, "Island"; Hayes, p. 33; and Downing, 2: 20.
28. Downing, 2: 223.
29. Richard, p. 712; Anderson and Anderson, pp. 36, 37, 42, 45; Anderson, *Essays*, p. 7; Armando da Silva, pp. 37–73.
30. For further descriptions of the inner Asian frontier zones, see Owen Lattimore, *Inner Asian Frontiers of China* (New York, 1940), pp. 46, 54, 66–79, 334; and Owen Lattimore, *Studies in Frontier History: Collected Papers, 1928–1958* (London, 1962), pp. 8, 61, 469–70, 503.
31. Ward, "Chinese Fishermen," pp. 278–79; Anderson and Anderson, p. 48; Blake, "Island," p. 8. According to Ward, "Varieties of the Conscious Model," pp. 119, 127, the lack of permanent landed estates, the potential of physical mobility, the absence of literati within the group, and economic dependence on non-kinsmen helped prevent the emergence of lineages among the Tanka. Local deities, not ancestral halls, were the focus of corporate worship among the Tanka.
32. Ward, "Chinese Fishermen," pp. 277–78; Ch'ü T'ung-tsu, *Law and Society in Traditional China* (Paris, 1961), p. 132; Blake, *Ethnic Groups*, p. 13.
33. Ward, "Varieties of the Conscious Model," pp. 118–19.
34. Downing, 2: 224; Blake, "Island," p. 10; Blake, *Ethnic Groups*, p. 13.
35. Overmyer, p. 154. Among peasants, loan associations provided members with a means of insurance against hard times. Old people's societies helped ease the burden of funeral expenses, and annual dues paid to garment societies enabled peasants to purchase winter coats. Perry, *Rebels*, p. 53. In major commercial centers, associations composed of merchants from the

same province or county provided fellow sojourners with entrée into professional circles and surrogate kinships while away from home. Among the tribute grain transporters of the Yangtze River and the Grand Canal, the sutra halls of the Lo sect doubled as boatmen's hostels in the 17th and 18th centuries. David Kelley, "Sect and Society: The Organization and Activities of the Grand Canal Boatmen's Associations in the Mid-Qing," paper presented at the annual meeting of the Association for Asian Studies, Toronto, March 13–15, 1981.

36. Anderson and Anderson, p. 48; Wakeman, "Secret Societies," pp. 29–34; Laffey, "In the Wake of the Taipings," pp. 67, 69.

37. Blake, *Ethnic Groups*, p. 26 and chap. 5.

38. Kani, pp. 71–72.

39. Ward, "Chinese Fishermen," pp. 276–77; Ward, "Hong Kong Fishing Village," p. 301.

40. Blake, "Island," p. 11. For an overview of coastal villages and market towns, see Bruce Swanson, *Eighth Voyage of the Dragon: A History of China's Quest for Seapower* (Annapolis, Md., 1982), p. 19; Ward, "Hong Kong Fishing Village," p. 301; Ward, "Varieties of the Conscious Model," p. 133; Hayes, pp. 37–38; and Anderson, *Essays*, p. 45.

41. For examples of the extreme poverty of the Tanka, see Downing, 1: 106, 144, 210, and 2: 222, 223. To people connected with the fishing industry, "fishmongers" meant the various capitalists they had to deal with, usually on credit and at high rates of interest, including those who bought and sold fish, ran stores selling staples, and built, repaired, outfitted, or fueled fishing junks. Fessler, p. 1.

42. Kani, p. 70.

43. KTHF 2: 17–17b; KTHF 23: 30; KTHF 25: 7; Wang Chih-i, p. 36.

44. KCFC 74: 10.

45. HSHC 4: 18; KTHF 25: 6b; Wo Shih-pu, p. 24. Others saw it as the inevitable result of fishermen being allowed to remain at sea for extended periods, and thus urged that inshore fishing junks be required to return to port once every 20 days, and deep-sea junks once a month. KTHF 33: 14b. In 1810, in fact, the Liang-kuang Governor-general attributed piracy in Kwangtung specifically to those poorest of poor Tanka who went out in fleets of nine or ten to net fish. Trouble arose, he thought, because the personal junks that stood by to transport each net partner's catch to shore used their spare time to set upon any approaching craft. When they could not complete a strike on their own, the fishermen would come to their aid. KTHF 33: 8–8b.

CHAPTER 2

1. Chiang-p'ing, situated almost exactly on the Sino-Vietnamese border, remained under Vietnamese jurisdiction until 1885, when it was transferred to China and attached to Kwangtung province in the settlement of the Sino-French War. In 1965 it became Kwangsi province's outlet to the sea. P. J. M. Geeland and D. C. Twitchett, *The Times Atlas of China* (New York, 1974), pp. 81–83; *Kham dinh Viet su thong giam cuong muc* [Mirror of the complete history of China and Vietnam; Taipei, 1969], 324: 26–26b.

2. Shao Yang-wei, "Yüeh-nan chiang-yü k'ao" [An investigation of the Vietnamese border region], in *Hsiao Fang-hu chai yü-ti ts'ung-ch'ao* [Collected docu-

ments on geography from Hsiao Fang-hu, 1877–97; Taipei, 1975]; Suzuki, "Re (Lê) chō," p. 480.

3. Many of the Chinese in Vietnam in the late 18th century were descendants of the several thousand supporters of the Ming dynasty who fled the country when China fell to the Manchus in 1644. Ch'en Ching-ho, "Ch'ingch'u Cheng Ch'eng-kung ts'an-pu chih i-chih nan-ch'i" [The migration of the partisans of Cheng Ch'eng-kung to South Vietnam during the early Ch'ing], *The New Asia Journal*, 5.1: 433–59 (Aug. 1960). Woodside, pp. 270–71, also confirms the presence of the Minh Hu'ong, or Ming Loyalists in Vietnam and distinguishes them from the Chinese who lived in congregations (*pang*) with their own headmen. Of the two groups, the Minh Hu'ong were far more assimilated into Vietnamese society. They could enter the Vietnamese examination system and become bureaucrats. It was possible, however, for sons and grandsons of congregation Chinese born in Vietnam who did not wear the queue or shave their heads to become Minh Hu'ong.

4. KCT 001656, CC1 xii 11; KTHF 26: 5b, CC9. Even today the precise location of Pai-lung-wei is difficult to determine. The *Dai Nam nhat-thong-chi* says it is an island 50 kilometers east of Van Ninh Chau. On the map showing the routes from Annam (Vietnam) to China during the Mongol dynasty in Deveria's *Histoire*, it appears as a peninsula slightly northeast of Van Ninh Chau. But even Deveria acknowledges that the map is probably apocryphal. On the map of Republican China published in Tainan, Taiwan in 1963 (*Chung-ua min-kuo tai-t'i-t'u*), Pai-lung-wei appears as a narrow fjord between China and Vietnam. Its location at the border is corroborated by the *Kuang-tung u-shuo* [Plates and description of Kwangtung; 1866], comp. Mao Hung-pin Taipei, 1967), 62: 9, which states that it was a strategic point on the western maritime frontier with Vietnam.

5. Suzuki, "Re (Lê) chō," p. 480.

6. James M. Coyle, personal communication, Oct. 14, 1984. According to n ancient map of the Hong Duc reign (1491), the peninsula of Van Ninh hau was an administrative division of An Quang province. In 1822, during he reign of Minh Mang, the name was changed to Quang Yen, and in 1906 he province Hai Ninh was carved out of its territory. Truong Buu Lam, ed., *ong Duc Ban Do* (Saigon, 1962), pp. 45, 196, 207.

7. For a discussion of Chinese perceptions of the border, see Laffey, "In the ake of the Taipings," p. 71; and Lloyd Eastman, *Throne and Mandarins: ina's Search for a Policy During the Sino-French Controversy, 1880–85* (Camidge, Mass., 1967), pp. 35–36.

8. Laffey, "In the Wake of the Taipings," pp. 70–71.

9. Discussing the difficulties of oceanic research as they related to his study Ma Huan, Mills says (p. 227): "The attempt to study the mediaeval Chinese eans is attended by certain difficulties. First, the dictionaries are wrong in ting that *yang* means 'the ocean'; for Chinese maps are studded with the mes of small sea areas which are designated *yang*. . . . It seems that the meeval Chinese made no distinctions between *yang* 'ocean' and *hai* 'sea.'"

10. Such indeterminateness prevails also in descriptions of sea-related acties, where, for example, the terms for pirates—*hai-tao, yang-tao; hai-fei, g-fei*; and *hai-tsei, yang-tsei*—are often used synonymously in the same ument. In part this seeming imprecision in the use of the terms *hai* and

TABLE TO NOTE 15
KCT Memorials on Vietnamese Cities as Pirate Market Centers

000066, CC1 i 21	001734, CC2 xii 21	002845, CC2 vii 6
000137, CC1 ii 9	001804, CC2 i 8	002848, CC2 vii 6
000465, CC1 iv 14	001899, CC2 i 28	003347, CC2 xi 2
000827, CC1 vi 25	001967, CC2 ii 7	003459, CC2 xii 1
000857, CC1 vii 5	002010, CC2 ii 14	003611, CC3 i 13
001047, CC1 viii 19	002012, CC2 ii 14	003728, CC3 ii 19
001074, CC1 viii 26	002074, CC2 ii 27	003749, CC3 ii 29
001092, CC1 viii 30	002481, CC2 v 16	003963, CC3 v 11
001302, CC1 x 15	002531, CC2 v 29	004516, CC4 v 21
001427, CC1 xi 6	002636, CC2 vi 7	004602, CC4 v 29
001488, CC1 xi 10	002723, CC2 vi* 7	005965, CC6 viii 28
001656, CC1 xii 11	002779, CC2 vi* 21	008158, CC7 v 27

yang may be a product of geography. From north to south, China's coast is ringed at distances of several tens or a few hundred miles by the islands of Japan, the Ryukyus, Taiwan, the Philippines, and Borneo, which have the effect of enclosing its coastal waters. Hence, these bodies of water are technically speaking seas, not part of the ocean.

11. Leonard, p. 65.
12. Samuels, p. 22. See also pp. 32–40, 42–47.
13. KCT 001656, CC1 ii 11; Suzuki, "Re (Lê) chō," p. 480.
14. KTHF 26: 1–2b, CC4 ix 5.
15. The table above lists the KCT memorials describing the use of Vietnamese cities as pirate market centers.
16. Downing 2: 222–23. For examples of outlaws who fled from China and became pirates at Chiang-p'ing, see KCT 000137, CC1 ii 9; KCT 000465, CC1 iv 14; and KCT 002531, CC2 v 29.
17. For examples of malcontents attracted to piracy see KCT 000066, CC1 i 21; KCT 001074, CC1 viii 26; KCT 001392, CC1 xi 1; KCT 001656, CC1 xi 11; and KCT 002481, CC2 v 16.
18. KCT 001427, CC1 xi 6. For other examples, see KCT 002845, CC2 vii 6; and KCT 004607, CC4 vii 1.
19. KCT 000066, CC1 i 21.
20. Ch'en Ya-hui's and Ch'en Te-sheng's confessions, LF 3889.
21. Wu Ya-sheng's confession, LF 3856.
22. KCT 000981, CC1 vii 29; KCT 001496, CC1 xi 18.
23. Ch'en Ya-hui's confession, LF 3889.
24. Among bandit groups, double shares of loot were customarily presented to leaders as well as to suppliers of special resources or equipment such as horses or guns. Among the Nien, all plundered loot except that given the banner chiefs was divided among the participants in a given raid, with two parts going to the cavalrymen and one part to the foot soldiers. Perry, *Reb.* pp. 136–37.
25. Huang Wen-sheng's and Lin Chang's confessions, LF 3890.
26. KCT 002109, CC2 iii 4. See also KCT 002845, CC2 vii 6.
27. Wakeman, *Strangers*, p. 14; Naquin, *Millenarian Rebellion*, p. 281; Wa. p. 364.

28. Susan Mann Jones and Philip A. Kuhn, "Dynastic Decline and the Roots of Rebellion," in Vol. 10 of Denis Twitchett and John K. Fairbank, eds., *The Cambridge History of China* (Cambridge, 1978) pp. 108–9.

29. Wakeman, *Strangers*, p. 179.

30. Viraphol, pp. 162, 167. In 1805 passage from Kwangtung to Penang cost 20 Spanish silver dollars.

31. Ibid., p. 123, based on information in *Chang-chou fu-chih* [Gazetteer of Chang-chou prefecture; 1877], comp. Wu Lien-hsün (Taipei, 1964), 33: 64–65, and *Chang-p'u hsien-chih* [Gazetteer of Chang-p'u county], comp. Ch'en Ju-chien (1876), 22: 28–28b.

32. KTTC 180: 22.

33. Morse, 1: 161; 2: 11, 12, 29, 35, 40, 50. For information on the intervening years, see, for example, 1: 171, 176.

34. Suzuki, "Kenryū Annan," p. 102.

35. Woodside, pp. 272–73.

36. Suzuki, "Kenryū Annan," p. 102.

37. Suzuki, "Re (Lê) chō," pp. 101, 103; Barrow, *Voyage*, p. 350; Deveria, p. 48.

38. Suzuki, "Kenryū Annan," pp. 103–4.

39. Ibid.; Takeda, p. 532. One other interesting example of an officially sponsored smuggler-turned-pirate is Lo Ya-san, a Chinese whose family had resided in Vietnam for three generations. In July 1796 a Tay-son official ordered him to sell some rice in Chiang-p'ing and use the money to procure a cargo of medicine, porcelain, and cotton. Although Lo had originally intended to report back at once with his cargo, his vessel was attacked en route by pirates, and all his goods were stolen. Not daring to return empty-handed, Lo and a companion made their way to Chiang-p'ing, where they sought out a friend, the pirate leader Liang Erh-shih. They asked Liang for a junk and some weapons so that, by turning to piracy, they could make up the value of their lost cargo. Liang gave them the junk and 13 of his own recruits as well. A few days later Lo Ya-san began his career as a pirate. KCT 002010, CC2 ii 14.

CHAPTER 3

1. Maybon, pp. 183–85.   2. Woodside, pp. 3, 52, 57.

3. Le-thanh-Khoi, pp. 288–302.   4. Maybon, pp. 290–93, 297–98.

5. Woodside, pp. 2–3; Maybon, pp. 297–99. For detailed accounts of the Chinese expedition to Vietnam in 1788–89, see Truong, pp. 165–79; and Suzuki, "Kenryū Annan," p. 102.

6. Like the Tay-son, the Nguyen recruited Chinese pirates as privateers, but their sponsorship seems to have been neither so extensive nor so significant as the Tay-son's. One example of Nguyen sponsorship of Chinese pirates occurred when Nguyen Phuc Anh, returning to Vietnam from his second exile in Siam, was aided by Ha Hi Van (Ho Hsi-wen), "the infamous Szechwan-born pirate and member of the Triad Society." Woodside, p. 17. Ha Hi Van first contacted Phuc Anh when his fleet was anchored off Poulo Condore Island and Phuc Anh accepted his protection. On the night of Aug. 13, 1787, entrusting himself to the care of his pirate mentor, Phuc Anh embarked for Long Xuyen. There he began assembling the troops to stage his comeback and in the process enlisted several other pirate chiefs and their followers to his cause. Maybon, p. 223. Ha Hi Van's official biography can be found in

DNCB 28: 7ff. Further evidence that the Nguyen were sponsoring pirates, and even imitated the Tay-son in issuing seals and certificates, is afforded by Chinese sources. A number of pirates captured in Kwangtung and Fukien provinces in 1796 and 1797 had in their possession seals that bore the inscription "issued by the Gia Hung Vuong [Chia-hsing wang] and the Chieu Quang Vuong [Chao-kuang wang]." KCT 002012, CC2 ii 14. According to the testimony of these captured pirates, the two "Kings" (Vuong) were the "Nguyen bandit leaders" at Dong Nai and Tran Ninh, who had presented these documents to them. KCT 001848, CC2 i 16; KCT 002051, CC2 ii 20.

7. The account of Chi T'ing and Li Ts'ai in service of the Tay-son is drawn from Maybon, pp. 185, 186, 189; and DNCB 30: 4, 4b, 5b, 6b, 8, 9–10b.

8. The following account is based on Ch'en T'ien-pao's and Liang Kuei-hsing's depositions, LF 3855, LF 3857; and KCT 008517, CC7 vii 14.

9. Woodside, p. 3; Le-thanh-Khoi, p. 311.

10. Le-thanh-Khoi, pp. 309, 311; Deveria, p. 48.

11. Deveria, p. 48; Wei Yüan, 8: 24b–25; TKHC 26: 5b; TKHC 33: 21b–22; DNTL 6: 5b.

12. Maybon, pp. 308, 319.

13. Ibid., pp. 310–12; DNTL 6: 5b, 7; Wei Yüan, 8: 24b–25; TKHC 33 21b–22. Besides having an excellent harbor, Qui Nhon had symbolic impor tance, for it was the site of the former Cham capital of Vijaya. It was also re ferred to as Xa Ban or Cha Ban in Vietnamese. Qui Nhon was also the sym bolic capital of the Tay-son, for it was the headquarters of the group's mos able leader, Nguyen Van Nhac. Van Nhac, the eldest of the three rebel broth ers, established his rule over the provinces from Quang Nam to Binh Dinl He referred to himself as the "Emperor of the Center" and remained at Qu Nhon until his death in 1792. Maybon, p. 313; Lamb, p. 145.

14. T'ang Te's and Ch'en T'ien-pao's depositions, LF 3855, LF 3857.

15. DNTL 9: 20b–21; KCT 003611, CC3 i 13.

16. Ch'en T'ien-pao's deposition, LF 3855.

17. Lo Ya-san's deposition, LF 3854.

18. KCT 005050, CC5 ii 15.

19. DNTL 10: 3b.

20. DNTL 10: 38b; Maybon, pp. 324–25. Among the defectors from tl Tay-son camp in the aftermath of this defeat were a number of Chinese rates who, taking advantage of a proclamation of amnesty, surrendered to t Ch'ing officials and were pardoned and resettled. For information on F Wen-ts'ai, see KCT 008517, CC7 vii 14; and DNTL 13: 22b.

21. Maybon, pp. 325–28; DNTL 10: 39b; DNTL 11: 16–16b.

22. KCT 004980, CC5 ii 6.

23. Maybon, pp. 329–31; Barrow, *Voyage*, p. 274.

24. DNTL 12: 10b, 20, 27.   25. NYC 13: 66b, CC10 xi 22.

26. Wei Yüan, 8: 25b.   27. Hummel, p. 255.

28. Ibid., p. 233. For more information on the White Lotus, see Daniel Overmyer, *Folk Buddhist Religion: Dissenting Sects in Late Traditional Ch* (Cambridge, Mass., 1976).

29. NYC 6: 1–79b, CC8 n.d.

30. KCT 004790, CC5 i 20. Chi-ch'ing was a Manchu of the Goro c who was sent to Kwangtung in 1796 to replace the demoted Liang-kua Governor-general, Chu Kuei. He remained there fighting pirates until death some six years later. (On Dec. 14, 1802, he committed suicide by fo

ing a snuff bottle down his throat in the presence of the provincial governor.)
Hummel, p. 584; Morse, 2: 396.

31. KCT 005244, CC5 ii 11. For a criticism of this policy, see Wei Yüan,
8: 25b.

32. For descriptions of the tributary system in operation, see John K. Fairbank, ed., *The Chinese World Order* (Cambridge, Mass., 1968); and Immanuel
C. Y. Hsü, *The Rise of Modern China* (New York, 1970), pp. 174–78.

33. KCT 000385, CC1 iv 2.

34. Lo Ya-san's deposition, LF 3854; Maybon, p. 321.

35. Among the inscriptions most commonly appearing on the pirate permits were the words "Canh-Thinh Reign Fourth Year" (Canh Thinh Tu Nien).
Upon inquiry the Chinese were informed that Canh Thinh was the reign title
of the Tay-son Emperor Quang Toan, who had been invested in 1793, and
that the fourth year of his reign corresponded to 1796, or the first year of the
Chinese Emperor Chia-ch'ing's reign. KCT 002012, CC2 ii 14.

36. *Annam-tang*, p. 23, CC1 viii 3 edict. In his deposition Lo Ai-i testi-
fied that his authorization had come from Wang Hsin-chang, a pirate from
Kwangtung who had become powerful enough to issue seals on his own in
Annam. KCT 001212, CC1 ix 29; KCT 002636E, CC2 vi 17.

37. *Annam-tang*, pp. 24–28, CC1 viii 3 edict.

38. KCT 002334, CC2 iv 16; KCT 002368, CC2 iv 24; CSL 17: 1b–2, CC2
v 1. For a detailed account, including both the testimony and the disposition
of the 63 pirates, see KCT 002481, CC2 v 16.

39. Truong Buu Lam, pp. 165–79.

40. KCT 002636E, CC2 vi 17.

41. KCT 002767, CC2 v* 16.

42. Because Chinese rulers were unable to conduct sustained naval operations within coastal seas, they usually made "sea defense" (*hai-fang*) rather
than "sea war" (*hai-chan*) the cornerstone of their maritime defense policy.
One argument raised against a long-term policy of "offensive" rather than
"defensive" coastal defense was that "sea war" was too expensive, necessitat-
ing specialized vessels that required continuous upkeep and knowledgeable
pilots and helmsmen. In addition, it was fraught with problems of logistics
and mobility. One vessel could not go everywhere. Most coastal or river vessels
were not seaworthy; seagoing vessels were not suitable for shallows. Once at
sea, it was often difficult to locate the enemy or position the fleet for war. Even
if an adversary was located, he could not be engaged in unfavorable weather.
The complexity of the geography and the vast expanses of water often made
it difficult to send in reinforcements. Given the ease with which adversaries
could use a favorable wind to vanish, Chinese officials believed that maritime
battles were seldom conclusive. KTHF 25: 7; Ch'eng Han-chang, p. 37b.
What emerged instead was a strategy centered on static defenses and barriers
to contact, so that for inshore waters, garrisons, not gunboats, became the bas-
ion of Chinese defense.

43. *Annam-tang*, pp. 13 (CC1 ii 1), 23–24 (CC1 viii 3 edict), 37 (CC1 ix 18
edict); KTHF 25: 23b, CL60 xii 20.

44. In this respect cases involving bandits and rebels (and pirates) were ex-
ceptional. No other offenders could be tried and executed on the spot without
resort to Peking. Derk Bodde, *Law in Imperial China* (Cambridge, Mass., 1967),
p. 134, 142; *Annam-tang*, p. 37, CC1 ix 18 edict.

45. KTHF 26: 3–4, CC4 ix 5.

46. For a discussion of the pacification policy as it was employed in response to the Wako pirate challenge of the 16th century, see Charles Hucker, "Hu Tsung-hsien's Campaign Against Hsü Hai, 1556," in Frank A. Kierman, Jr., and John K. Fairbank, eds., *Chinese Ways in Warfare* (Cambridge, Mass., 1974), pp. 282—83. For an application of the policy vis-à-vis the pirate Wang Chih, see Kuan-wai So, *Japanese Piracy in Ming China During the 16th Century* (East Lansing, Mich., 1975), pp. 297—304.

47. The rationale for "pardon and pacification" is systematically discussed in Ch'eng Han-chang, pp. 47b—48.

48. KTHF 25: 21—22b, CL59 ii 5. Ch'ang-lin, a Manchu of the imperial clan, was a collateral descendant of the father of Ch'ing dynasty founder Nurhachi. In early 1793 he was appointed governor-general of Fukien and Chekiang, and in September he was promoted to the post of governor-general of Kwangsi and Kwangtung. In August 1795 he was transferred back to Fukien and Chekiang. He died in 1811. J. L. Cranmer-Byng, ed., *An Embassy to China; Being the Journal Kept by Lord Macartney During His Embassy to the Emperor Ch'ien-Lung, 1793—1794* (Hamden, Conn., 1963), pp. 51, 373.

49. KCT 004963, CC5 ii 5; KCT 004980, CC5 ii 6.

50. KCT 004980, CC5 ii 6; Von Krusenstern, 2: 306—7.

51. KCT 005230, CC5 ii 27 edict; CSL 60: 28—28b, CC5 ii 27 edict.

52. CSL 68: 22b, CC5 v 25.

53. Maybon, p. 336.

54. Ibid.; DNTL 13: 21b; KCT 008517, CC7 vii 14.

55. DNTL 14: 34b; KCT 005965E, CC6 viii 28.

56. CHFC 1: 1b—2b; KCT 007451, CC7 ii 21. The term *szu-ma*, or vexillary as translated by W. H. Medhurst, derives from the *Chou-li*. According to S. Y. Teng, p. 88, the *liang-szu-ma* served as a kind of pastor, teacher, or judge in the army, and such officials were used by the Taiping as well as the Tay-son. On the long list of Tay-son ranks in DNCB 31: 40b, the *szu-ma* is ranked fourth.

57. KCT 006453, CC6 x 22; KCT 006211E, CC6 ix 23; SYT 129, CC6 x 8.

58. DNTL 16: 1—1b; Laurent de Barisy to the British East India Company, CanCon, July 31, 1802. DNTL says that 100 Chinese pirate boats participated in this battle.

59. For an account of this mission, see Trinh Hoai Duc, *Can trai thi tap* [Collected poems of Can Trai; Hong Kong, 1962], pp. 129—31. Trinh Hoa Duc, a descendant of a Chinese immigrant family from Foochow, served as the Nguyen's minister of finance and was entrusted with the diplomatic mission to the Ch'ing court in 1802—3. See also DNTL 18: 5, which says tha Cheng Ch'i was beheaded; and KCT 008978, CC7 x 11.

60. KCT 006211E, CC6 ix 23; KCT 006793, CC6 xi 28.

61. KCT 000827, CC1 vi 25.

62. KCT 005050, CC5 ii 15. The practice of using fictive kinship was no unique to pirates. In the 18th century Wang Lun, a rebel leader in Shantung used his network of White Lotus sects to create fictive kinship ties. Just as pi rates incorporated new gang members by adoption, so Wang made new pupil his "godsons" and "goddaughters," eventually acquiring some 20 fictive chil dren. Naquin, *Shantung Rebellion*, pp. 40, 44, 58. Members of bandit gang who were not actually related often took oaths of brotherhood and subse quently addressed one another as relatives. One bandit chief, Wu Ju-wen o

the Anhui–Kiangsu border region, boasted of more than 100 adopted sons. Perry, *Rebels*, p. 69.

63. KCT 005050, CC5 ii 15; KCT 008052, CC7 v 12. Granting female captives to subordinates was practiced by other outlaw groups. The 18th-century rebel leader Wang Lun, for example, on being presented with desirable female prizes, habitually granted them to his followers as rewards. Naquin, *Shantung Rebellion*, p. 106.

64. James C. Scott, "Patron-Client Politics and Political Change in Southeast Asia," in Steffen W. Schmidt et al., eds., *Friends, Followers, and Factions: A Reader in Political Clientelism* (Berkeley, Calif., 1977), p. 126.

65. KCT 000066, CC1 i 21; KCT 001496, CC1 xi 18; KCT 000857, CC1 vii 5.

66. KCT 001091, CC1 viii 30.

67. For the 22 memorials containing incidents of homosexuality, see the table below. Although the documents do not identify the specific motivation in every case, it is worth noting that penal servitude instead of decapitation was the punishment meted out to those who were merely victims. According to Withers, p. 224, homosexuality was widespread among the Taiping rebels as well.

68. KCT 001427, CC1 xi 6; KCT 003728, CC3 ii 19; KCT 003749, CC3 ii 29; KCT 008517, CC7 vii 14; KTHF 26: 4, CC7.

69. Wen Hsiung-fei, *Nan-yang huo-ch'iao t'ung-shih* [Complete history of overseas Chinese; Shanghai, 1929], p. 146. Wen's account is based on Wei Yüan's *Sheng-wu-chi.*

70. KCT 002637, CC2 vi 17; Wu-ya Erh's deposition, LF 3854.

71. KCT 001804, CC2 i 8; KCT 002637, CC2 vi 17.

72. KCT 008715, CC7 vii 14.

73. KCT 008978, CC7 x 11.

74. KCT 001448, CC1 xi 10.

75. *Kao-chou fu-chih* [Gazetteer of Kao-chou prefecture], comp. Huang An-t'ao (1827), 11: 33b–34; *Wu-ch'uan hsien-chih* [Gazetteer of Wu-ch'uan county], comp. Li Kao-k'uei (1825), 9: 28. The account presented in the text was compiled from entries in local gazetteers. The memorial to the Emperor

TABLE TO NOTE 67

50 Documented Cases of Homosexuality Among Pirates

KCT memorial	No. of people convicted	KCT memorial	No. of people convicted
000066, CC1 i 21	1	002531, CC2 v 29	1
000137, CC1 ii 9	1	002637, CC2 vi 17	6
000827, CC1 vi 25	2	002723, CC2 vi* 7	2
000857, CC1 vii 5	4	002845, CC2 vii 6	3
001047, CC1 viii 19	3	003347, CC2 xi 2	1
001091, CC1 viii 30	1	003459, CC2 xii 1	1
001092, CC1 viii 30	2	003728, CC3 ii 19	2
001392, CC1 xi 1	2	003749, CC3 ii 29	1
001448, CC1 xi 10	6	004578, CC4 v 10	1
001496, CC1 xi 18	2	004725, CC5 i 11	4
002481, CC2 v 16	3	005050, CC5 ii 15	1

concerning this affair was written by Liang-kuang Governor-general Chi-ch'ing and differs considerably. According to him, the sublieutenant, looking out from the fort, saw in the distance several pirate junks harassing merchant vessels. Thereupon, he and his men set off to arrest them. As their rowboats drew near, the soldiers opened fire and killed several pirates. The pirates attempted to board the sublieutenant's rowboat, but became afraid and were forced to withdraw. They continued to resist arrest, however, and in the battle the sublieutenant and a soldier were killed. KCT 005965, CC6 viii 28. At issue is whether the battle took place on land or sea. In all likelihood it took place on land, and the true facts were concealed from the Emperor by the provincial officials, who risked censure when such incidents took place within their jurisdictions.

76. KCT 006211, CC6 ix 23. *Hai-feng hsien-chih* [Gazetteer of Hai-feng county], comp. Ts'ai Feng-en (1873), 2: 33b.

77. For examples, see KCT 004516, CC4 vi 21; and KCT 003611, CC3 i 13.

78. Wei Yüan, 8: 25b.

79. The conferring of rank and titles was widely employed by bandit and rebel leaders as a part of their recruiting endeavors on shore. In 1774 the Shantung rebel Wang Lun created a system of ranks and titles that granted positions of power and prestige normally beyond his followers' grasp. Naquin, *Shantung Rebellion*, p. 58. The Taiping (1850–64) used similar practices to confer status within their own ranks, where the title "King" or "Wang" designated the movement's five major commanders. Jen Yu-wen, pp. 80, 102. On the Taiping practice, see also Winters, pp. 167–68. In much the same way that the Tay-son bestowed rank on the pirates, the Taiping conferred titles on Nien leaders in 1860–61. Perry, *Rebels*, p. 120; S. Y. Teng, pp. 86–89.

80. Lo Ya-san's confession, LF 3854.

81. CP 1121/03, CC12 i 13; Liang Kuei-hsing's deposition, LF 3857.

82. CP 1120/01, CC14 x 29; CP 1121/17, CC15 vii 12; CP 1140/22, CC10

83. Alexander B. Woodside, "The Tay-son Revolution in Southeast Asian History" (Mimeo of an undated paper in the Watson Collection, Olin Library, Cornell University), pp. 5–6.

84. Truong Buu Lam, p. 177; DNCB 30: 41.

85. The Chinese in fact ascribed the phenomenon to two sources: the Tay-son's sponsorship of such activities and Chinese profit-seekers' encouragement of the Vietnamese-backed pirates when, after 1791, they operated between Chiang-p'ing and Kwangtung. For examples see KCT 001212, C11 i 29; KCT 001334, C11 x 19; KTHF 25: 23, 24, CL60 xii 20; KTHF 26: 1, 5, CC14 ix 5; Ch'eng Han-chang, p. 37; and Wang Chih-i, p. 34.

CHAPTER 4

1. CP 1058/2. The English term confederation was first used to describe this force by the British captive Richard Glasspoole, officer of the HCS *Marquis of Ely*. The Chinese used the term *tang* to refer to the organization.

2. Chinese accounts that refer to six major pirate fleets include CHFC 2b–3; and Chu Ch'eng-wan, p. 20b. Westerners, by contrast, have referred five fleets. According to the chief mate of the *Tay*, the most powerful fleet banner was a red triangle with a white scalloped border; the second-most powerful one flew a black triangle with a white scalloped border, the third square red banner with a plain yellow border, the fourth a red triangle with

plain yellow border, and the fifth a square with blue and white horizontal stripes. Turner, pp. 66–67. Richard Glasspoole, captured by the pirates in 1809, also reported the existence of five major pirate fleets. Glasspoole, "Substance," p. 40.

On the banner units of the Manchus, the Nien, and the Taiping, respectively, see Frederic Wakeman, Jr., *The Fall of Imperial China* (New York, 1975), pp. 72–80; S.-t. Chiang, pp. 24, 28; and S. Y. Teng, pp. 81–89. On bandits' use of banners units, see Perry, "Social Banditry," p. 367; and Perry, *Rebels*, p. 64.

3. KTHF 42: 31b–32, CC15 i; NYC 13: 32, CC10 x 2; NYC 13: 45–47, CC10 x 22; NYC 13: 65b, CC10 xi 22; KCT 013190, CC5 iii 8; Glasspoole, "Brief Narrative," p. 127; Turner, pp. 48, 59, 66; CSL 223: 26b–27b, CC14 xii 28.

4. For information on squadrons and squadron leaders, see NYC 12: 81b–82, CC10 viii 28; NYC 13: 35b–37, CC10 x 12; NYC 13: 57, CC10 xi 6; Glasspoole, "Brief Narrative," pp. 103, 105, 106, 115–17; and Turner, p. 68.

5. NYC 13: 57, CC10 xi 6.

6. KCT 001656, CC1 ii 11; KCT 001734, CC1 xii 21; KCT 003459, CC2 xii 1; KCT 011447, CC13 vii 5; KCT 013512, CC14 iii 5. By 1808 and 1809 the majority of apprehended pirates seem to have been allied to various *lao-pan*, who were in turn under the various fleet leaders. This contrasted with the earlier situation, where a *lao-pan's* influence seldom extended beyond a single vessel. KCT 012021, CC13 ix 20.

7. Turner, p. 68.

8. KCT 003611, CC3 i 13; KCT 003728, CC3 ii 19; KCT 004602, CC4 v 29; Turner, p. 68; NYC 13: 32, 36, CC10 x 2.

9. Gützlaff, pp. 54–55; Cushman, pp. 140–47.

10. KCT 003611, CC3 i 13; KCT 005364, CC5 iii 17; KCT 004602, CC4 v 29.

11. KCT 004602, CC4 v 29.

12. CSL 137: 176, CC9 xi 24.

13. Turner, p. 68; KCT 002531, CC2 v 29; KCT 003728, CC3 ii 19; CHFC 1: 6b.

14. KCT 002531, CC2 v 29; KCT 003728, CC3 ii 19.

15. Hsü Chien-ping, pp. 133, 139.

16. Ibid., pp. 133, 139–40; Hu Chieh-yü, pp. 152–60; Hsiao, fol. 25.

17. Hsiao, fols. 23, 27; Hu Chieh-yü, p. 161; *Yang-chiang hsien-chih* [Gazetteer of Yang-chiang county], comp. Li Yün (1822; Taipei, 1974), 8: 18b; KCT 008517, CC7 vii 14.

18. KCT 008432E, CC7 vii 2; DNTL 18: 5. One of Cheng Ch'i's sons, Cheng Pao-yang, headed a squadron of several junks in China during the first decade of the 19th century, and the other, Cheng Wei-feng, was invested by the Tay-son at age 17 as the "Golden Jade Marquis" (Chin-yü-hou). In 1805 Wei-feng was wanted by the Ch'ing officials for posting a document containing "rebellious words" and bearing his name. To avoid arrest he fled to Vietnam, where he was involved in a series of uprisings against the Gia-long Emperor. KTHF 42: 26–26b, CC15 i; NYC 11: 26–26b, CC9 xi 23.

19. Hsü Chien-ping, p. 133; Hu Chieh-yü, pp. 151, 152, 160, 161; NYC 2: 91, CC10 ix 20; NYC 13: 65b, CC10 xi 22; NHHC 25: 20b; Hsiao, fol. 25; Hu Ch'eng-wan, p. 20b.

20. CHFC 1: 3, 10b; CP 1121/17, CC1 vii 12. For a general discussion about all the fleets, see NYC 13: 65–67, CC10 xi 22.

21. CP 1121/14, n.d.

22. CP 1121/13, CC15 vi; CP 1121/17, CC15 vii 12.

23. CHFC 1: 3; Chu Ch'eng-wan, p. 21; KTHF 42: 35.

24. CHFC 1: 1b, 3; Chu Ch'eng-wan, p. 20b; Yeh Lin-feng, p. 11; KTHF 42: 28; NYC 13: 46, CC10 x 22.

25. NYC 13: 65b, CC10 xi 22; NHHC 14: 21; CHFC 1: 3b.

26. In Western language sources Kuo P'o-tai's name has appeared variously as O Po-tai, O Po-tae, Ya Po-tai, A Po-tsye, A Pao-tai, Kwo Po-tae, Qua-a-Pou, and Opo-tai. For more information see KTHF 42: 31b–32, CC15 i; Chu Ch'eng-wan, pp. 20–20b; Hsiao, fol. 20; Hu Chieh-yü, p. 164; CHFC 1: 3; NYC 13: 60, CC10 xi 6; CP 1139/5, CC11 iv 30; and CP 1121/08, CC12 xi 11.

27. CP 1140/29, CC10 xii 2; CP 1140/30, CC10 i n.d.

28. Chu Ch'eng-wan, p. 20b; Hu Chieh-yü, p. 151; CHFC 1: 3b; NYC 12: 47, CC10 vii 1; NYC 12: 83–83b, CC10 viii 28; NYC 13: 4b, CC10 ix 4.

29. NYC 12: 6b, CC10 v 16; NYC 12: 92b, CC10 ix 2; NYC 13: 59b, CC10 xi 6; Hsiao, fol. 25.

30. KTHF 42: 28, CC15 i n.d.; NYC 12: 6b, CC10 v 16; NYC 12: 92b, CC10 ix 2; NYC 13: 1b, CC10 ix 4; NYC 13: 59b, CC10 xi 6; KCT 005050, CC5 ii 15; KCT 008052, CC7 v 12; CHFC 1: 3; Chu Ch'eng-wan, p. 20b.

31. CHFC 1: 4b; KTHF 42: 32–33, CC15 i n.d.; Maughan, p. 12.

32. Lo Hsiang-lin, "Tun-men yü," pp. 21–28; KCFC 64: 25–25b. The exploits of the pirates in this stronghold were commemorated in a song still sung in the 20th century by the Tanka of T'ai-ao (Tai-o). It tells how Cheng I's widow, Lady Cheng I Sao, and her confederate Chang Pao-tsai held off an attack of the government vessels for a week in the Tung-yung Harbor. S. F. Balfour, "Hong Kong Before the British," *T'ien Hsia Monthly* 11.5: 464 (April–May 1941).

33. Balfour, as cited above, pp. 454, 460.

34. Von Krusenstern, 2: 276.

35. Fay, p. 15. The terms outer and inner were used by the East India Company to describe these two principal passages from Macao to Canton.

36. HSHC 8: 56b; Hunter, *Bits of Old China*, p. 84.

37. CHFC 1: 14–14b; Chu Ch'eng-wan, p. 20b; Turner, p. 67; NYC 13 1b, CC10 ix 4.

38. CHFC 1: 15; KCT 010976, CC13 v* 19; NHHC 25: 20b.

39. For background information on Cheng I Sao, see Chu Ch'eng-wan, p. 20b; NHHC 25: 20b, 26b; CHFC 1: 15; KTHF 42: 26b, CC15 i n.d. KTHF 32b, CC15 ii n.d.; Hu Chieh-yü, p. 161; and Hsiao, fol. 22.

40. KTHF 42: 26b, 32; CHFC 1: 5–5b; Hsiao, fol. 28; Chu Ch'eng-wan p. 20b; Lin Tse-hsü, memorial of TK20 v 15 (July 14, 1840), reproduced i Yeh Lin-feng, p. 69.

41. "Code of laws" is the term used by the captive Maughan (p. 28). Alon the same lines, according to Yüan Yung-lun, though Chang Pao is known t have established three regulations or provisions (*san-t'iao*) for governing h fleet; whether or not they were put in writing is uncertain. CHFC 1: 5b.

42. CHFC 1: 6b.

43. Maughan, p. 29; CHFC 1: 5b.

44. Maughan, p. 29.

45. CHFC 1: 5b–6b; Turner, p. 71; Maughan, p. 29.

46. Turner, p. 71.

47. Glasspoole, "Substance," pp. 44–45. See also Sainte-Croix, 2: 57. For other accounts of the pirates' bravery, see Maughan, p. 15; and CanCon, Aug. 18, 1809.

48. Glasspoole, "Substance," p. 44.

49. Ibid., p. 40; Glasspoole, "Brief Narrative," p. 113; Andrade, p. 81; Montalto de Jesus, *Historic Macao*, p. 238. Similar practices prevailed among the Nien. See S. Y. Teng, pp. 83–97.

50. Maughan, p. 29; Hill, p. 310. Although religion was an important means of achieving organizational unity among the pirates, it was not the raison d'être as it was in sectarian movements like the White Lotus Society, where charismatic leaders were able to mobilize their followers for "great undertakings" with promises of a better world to come. For accounts of the Wang Lun Uprising of 1774, the Eight Trigrams Insurrection of 1813, and the Taiping Rebellion of 1850–64, all of which grew out of religiously inspired movements, see Naquin, *Shantung Rebellion*; Naquin, *Millenarian Rebellion*; and Jen Yu-wen, *Taiping Revolutionary Movement*.

The pirates' religious practices were those common to the boatmen society from which they sprang. As we have seen, that society did not maintain ancestral halls or assemble as a body to read sutras, burn incense, or eat vegetarian meals. Its religious rites centered on the departure and completion of a voyage and were limited to the crews of a junk or two.

According to the early-19th-century account of Gützlaff (*Journal of Three Voyages*, pp. 57–60), on nearly every junk there was an image of the Sea Goddess (Ma-tzu or T'ien-hou), before whom a lamp was always kept burning. On board ship, her care was entrusted to a priest (or someone acting as a priest) who burned incense to her every morning. It was also his duty to invoke the help of the proper spirits on those occasions when the junk reached a promontory or encountered contrary winds. Such were the concerns of the boatmen that they never set forth without properly consulting the deities. When a vessel was about to get under way, the Sea Goddess was taken in procession to a temple, where various offerings were displayed before her. A service ensued in which the priests offered prayers, the mate made several prostrations, and the captain appeared in full dress before her. Afterward the goddess was treated to a theatrical performance before finally being returned to the vessel.

51. CHFC 1: 6b–7. This legend was picked up by Hill. In "Pirates," p. 310, he says that when the Portuguese destroyed Chang Pao's floating pagoda in 1809, on it were "his priests and a wonderful image which his followers had been unable to lift from its pedestal in an ancient temple, but which came willingly as soon as Chang Pao touched it."

52. Glasspoole, "Brief Narrative," p. 113.

53. CHFC 2: 6b–7.

54. Hu Chieh-yü, pp. 162–63.

55. Turner, p. 55.

56. Montalto de Jesus, *Historic Macao*, p. 236; Turner, p. 48; Glasspoole, "Brief Narrative," pp. 112, 116.

57. Glasspoole, "Substance," p. 43.

58. Glasspoole, "Brief Narrative," p. 127.

59. Andrade, p. 33. Chang Pao's desire to overthrow the dynasty is also mentioned in the 20th-century account of Luis G. Gomes (*Páginas*, pp. 139, 140, 154).

60. Frederic Wakeman, Jr., argues in his article "The Secret Societies of Kwangtung, 1800–1856," that during the early 19th century Triad groups invoked the fan-Ch'ing, fu-Ming (overthrow the Ch'ing and restore the Ming) ideology to gain "social respectability that put them a cut above gangsterism." He also argues that in providing a kind of illegitimate "legitimacy," the ideology transformed local bandits (*t'u-fei*) into genuine rebels (*ni-fei*), which made "this social myth . . . as potent as the struggling scholar's examination dream" (p. 35).

Hsiao, fol. 25, asserts that the pirates were specifically influenced by this ideology, and that their Sea Goddess temple at Li-yü-men functioned as the headquarters of their "fan-Ch'ing fu-Ming" activities. According to Woodside ("The Tayson Revolution," mimeo of an undated paper in the Wason Collection, Olin Library, Cornell University, p. 3), 20th-century Vietnamese scholars have echoed this theme and "have even gone so far as to assert that the Tayson incorporated overseas Chinese soldiers into their army and established links with members of the Chinese White Lotus and Triad movements as far away as Szechwan . . . in order to essay the complete overthrow of the Ch'ing dynasty in China and to reestablish the Ming court, which could then be propped up by Vietnamese military power." Woodside does not document this point, so it is not clear which scholars he means, but similar ideas appear in Luong-duc-Thiep, *Viet-nam tien-hoa su* [History of Vietnamese feudalism]; Hoang-thuc-Tram (under pseud. Hoa Bang), *Quang Trung anh hung dan toc, 1788–92* [Quang Trung, a national hero, 1788–92; Saigon, 1958]; and the *Lich-su-phong kien Vietnam* [History of Vietnamese feudalism]. In my own reading of the DNTL, DNCB, and *Dai Nam nhat thong-chi*, I have failed to uncover any references to the Tay-son's desire to conquer China or overthrow the Ch'ing dynasty.

61. Personal communication, Ch'in Pao-ch'i, professor at People's University, Peking, summer 1984. Information on early secret societies in Fukien and their spread to Kwangtung appears in the following documents in the First Historical Archives; none mentions *fan-Ch'ing, fu-Ming* as part of either the ideology or the activity of these early groups: CP 632/1–15, CL56–TK6; CP 641/1–7, CL56–CC10; CP 642/1–24, CL57–CC10; CP 649/1–5, CL57–CC5.

62. At best, the size of the pirate force can only be estimated. See the accompanying table for the range of figures culled from both Western and Chinese sources. Note that the two 1804 estimates predate the confederation. Although it is impossible to know which, if any, of these figures is accurate, two of the British reports—those of the East India supercargo and the captive Turner—appear to me to be the most reliable. Unlike the Chinese, the British would have felt little pressure either to minimize or exaggerate the magnitude of the pirate problem for political purposes. They were on the scene primarily as observers, whose main interest was in keeping the channels of trade open. Throughout the course of this study, their observations and statistics have provided a useful counter to official Chinese documents, which tend to minimize the problem, and to local gazetteers, which tend to inflate its importance. Portuguese reports on all fronts proved to be so untrustworthy that I have accepted them only if they were corroborated by other accounts. In the case, Gomes's estimate on the number of junks appears to be reasonable, but the estimate of a pirate force of 80,000 men in 1805 seems large to me. Th

TABLE TO NOTE 62
Estimates of the Size of the Pirates' Forces

Vessels	Manpower	Date where given	Source
4,000	200–300 on large junks, 30–50 otherwise	—	Von Krusenstern, 2: 309
1,800 (800 large)	—	1809	Glasspoole, "Brief Narrative," p. 127
1,000 (future Red, Blue, Black fleets)	—	1804	*Hsin-an hsien-chih*, comp. Wang Ch'ung-hsi (1819), 13: 59
600–800	80,000	1805	Dalrymple, *Memoir*, p. 43; Artur Gomes, p. 301
600–700	—	1804	East India Co. supercargo, in Dalrymple, *Further Statement*, p. 4.
500	25,000	1804–5	Turner, p. 64
300	—	1805	Gov.-gen. Na-yen-ch'eng, NYC 11: 30b, CC10 ii 21
—	150,000		Russian captain, in Dalrymple, *Memoir*, p. 42

Russian figures, too, strike me as being highly exaggerated. (At the time of the Armada the Spanish fleet had 130 ships, with 8,000 men, and the English fleet 197 ships, with 16,000 men.)

63. Maughan, p. 26.

64. Demetrius C. Boulger, *History of China*, 3 vols. (London, 1881–84), 3: 28. French, Russian, and British observers have uniformly identified "mandarin oppression" as a major cause of piracy. Sainte-Croix, 2: 53; Von Krusenstern, p. 281; Glasspoole, "Brief Narrative," p. 126; Turner, p. 66. For additional information on why people became pirates, see the surrender document in Appendix D.

65. Turner, p. 66; Glasspoole, "Brief Narrative," p. 103.

66. Turner, p. 66; Glasspoole, "Brief Narrative," p. 126.

67. Turner, p. 66.

68. Glasspoole, "Brief Narrative," pp. 114–15; Turner, p. 52.

69. Maughan, p. 26; Turner, pp. 70–71; Sainte-Croix, 2: 82.

70. Turner, pp. 70–71. Although in some bandit and rebel groups members were branded behind the ear or were forced to adopt certain hairstyles as a means of identification, there is no evidence that the pirates resorted to such practices. Elizabeth Perry, "When Peasants Speak," *Modern China*, 6: 79–80 (Jan. 1980).

71. NYC 12: 54, CC10 vii 1.

72. Turner, pp. 48, 50, 53, 54; Glasspoole, "Brief Narrative," pp. 116, 172.

73. Reported by Sainte-Croix, 2: 58, based on an interview with Turner.

74. Turner, p. 71. The second part of the quotation is again not Turner's own report but words ascribed to him by Sainte-Croix, 2: 57.

75. Glasspoole, "Substance," p. 41.

76. CHFC 1: 10b. China has had a long tradition of women warriors in fact as well as fiction. Among women warriors of fiction, Hua Mu-lan and Mu Kuei-ying figure large in China's pantheon of legendary heroines. The historical record ranges from Ch'iao-kuo-fu-jen of the Sui dynasty, who led an army of 100,000 into battle in the south, to the two women who, with clubs in hand, confronted the bandit chief White Wolf (Pai Lang) in 1914, an encounter that cost him two teeth. See Wei Cheng, *Shi Shu* (Peking, 1973), *lieh-ch'üan* 45, pp. 1800–1805; and Perry, "Social Banditry Revisited," p. 374, on these two incidents. For details on women's activities in the Ming and Ch'ing eras, specifically, see Overmyer, p. 166; T'ao Hsi-sheng, pp. 7–8 (I am grateful to Joanna Handlin for having called my attention to the incident covered in these two sources); Naquin, *Shantung Rebellion*, pp. 84–85, 133–34; Jen Yu-wen, pp. 67, 120; and Elizabeth Perry, "Worshippers and Warriors: White Lotus Influence on the Nien Rebellion," *Modern China*, 2: 12, 13 (Jan. 1976).

77. Maughan, p. 26; Glasspoole, "Brief Narrative," p. 128.

78. Turner, pp. 61–62; Glasspoole, "Brief Narrative," p. 107.

79. Course, p. 140; Glasspoole, "Brief Narrative," p. 128. The Chinese in Canton were known for "preferring" to eat a particular type of large, whitish rat.

80. Glasspoole, "Substance," p. 45.

81. Glasspoole, "Brief Narrative," p. 128; Course, p. 140.

CHAPTER 5

1. For full accounts of the pirates' tactics, see Dalrymple, *Further Statement*; Glasspoole, "Brief Narrative"; Maughan, pp. 7–32; and Turner, pp. 46–74.

2. "Chinese Pirates," pp. 70–71; Audemard, 3: 20–21.

3. Maughan, p. 28; Glasspoole, "Brief Narrative," p. 102.

4. Glasspoole, "Brief Narrative," pp. 117–18; Glasspoole, "Letter," p. 35.

5. Audemard, 8: 69.

6. CanCon, July 27, 29, 1802; Glasspoole, "Letter," p. 38.

7. Turner, pp. 52, 70.

8. Glasspoole, "Brief Narrative," p. 105; Maughan, p. 28. Turner, p. 50, however, contends that the fleet leader's junk did not play much of a role in combat and seemed to fight only when first attacked.

9. Glasspoole, "Substance," p. 40; Glasspoole, "Brief Narrative," p. 123. The pirates' use of magic, spells, charms, and special rites to ensure their success in battle was a well-established practice. In the Wang Lun Uprising of the 18th century, Wang boasted to his followers that on meeting an enemy, they had merely to recite the words he gave them, and they would find themselves impervious to muskets, knives, and arrows. Naquin, *Shantung Rebellion*, pp. 99–100, 134. Likewise, the Nien rebels often girded themselves for combat by reaffirming their brotherhood through a rite in which they added a little blood from their fingertips to their wine and swore that they would fight to the finish. S. Y. Teng, pp. 84–85. The Boxers' well-known claim of invulnerability to bullets can be added to the list.

10. KCT 004602, CC4 v 29; NYC 12: 39b–40, CC10 vii 1.

11. Maughan, p. 27.   12. Turner, p. 70.

13. CHFC 1: 9, 10.   14. CanCon, Oct. 17, 1805.

15. NYC 12: 25–27b, CC10 vi 15.   16. NYC 12: 12b, CC10 v 16.

17. CanCon, Nov. 2, 1805.   18. CSL 186: 31–31b, CC12 x 26.

19. KCT 000981, CC1 vii 29; NYC 12: 41, CC10 vii 1.

20. Sainte-Croix, 2: 54; NYC 14: 23, CC10 iv 20.
21. Glasspoole, "Brief Narrative," pp. 113, 114.
22. Turner, p. 72.
23. Glasspoole, "Brief Narrative," p. 123.
24. Turner, pp. 49–61; CanCon, Feb. 26, 1810.
25. Glasspoole, "Brief Narrative," pp. 102–6, 116–17, 123–24; CanCon, Feb. 26, 1810.
26. KCT 001271, CC1 x 8.
27. KCT 000827, CC1 vi 25; KCT 001092, CC1 viii 30; KCT 001176, CC1 ix 21; KCT 001334, CC1 x 19; KCT 002723, CC2 vi* 7.
28. KCT 013189, CC5 iii 19; KCT 006211, CC6 ix 23.
29. Dobell, *Travels*, 2: 153; SYT 275, CC10 v 21; NYC 12: 60, CC10 vii 25.
30. NYC 12: 31b–32, CC10 vi 15; CanCon, April 4, 1805.
31. STHC(1) 27: 1b (the year in this account is incorrectly given as 1804); SYT 15, CC10 xi 5.
32. SYT 15, CC10 xi 5; SYT 99, CC10 xi 9.
33. Dobell, *Travels*, 2: 153.
34. James Bromley Eames, *The English in China; Being an Account of the Intercourse and Relations Between England and China from the Year 1600 to the Year 1843; and a Summary of Later Developments* (London, 1909), pp. 234, 236. For more information on the early opium trade, see Chang Hsin-pao, *Commissioner Lin and the Opium War* (Cambridge, Mass., 1964).
35. CanCon, June 1, 1795, Nov. 19, 1803; Secret Consultations, Nov. 19, 1803.
36. CSL 186: 30, CC12 x 26; SYT 318, CC11 xi n.d.; Wei Yüan, 8: 25b. According to Maughan, p. 30, the pirates extorted "blackmail" (*ta-tan-ch'ien*) from merchant ships and "harbor fees" (*kang-kuei*) from fishing boats.
37. Maughan, pp. 30, 69; Von Krusenstern, 2: 310; NYC 12: 32, CC10 vi 15; Wei Yüan, 8: 25b; Meadows, p. 178.
38. Dalrymple, *Memoir*, p. 17.
39. Ibid., p. 26; Turner, p. 69; Glasspoole, "Brief Narrative," p. 108.
40. Turner, p. 69. Von Krusenstern, 2: 310, reports the amount at 500 *piastres*.
41. Maughan, p. 27; CHFC 1: 15.
42. Glasspoole, "Brief Narrative," pp. 107, 109, 110, 112; CHFC 1: 15; Hunter, *Bits of Old China*, p. 61.
43. Maughan, p. 30; CSL 186: 30, CC12 x 26; Turner, p. 72.
44. For these and other examples of pirate suppliers (*chien-fei*), see NYC 12: 51–52b, CC10 vii 1; and NYC 12: 67b, CC10 vii 25.
45. NYC 12: 68, CC10 vii 25.
46. NYC 11: 36b, CC10 iii 9.
47. CHFC 1: 6.
48. Boris Novikov, "The Anti-Manchu Propaganda of the Triads, ca. 1800–1860," in Jean Chesneaux, ed., *Popular Movements and Secret Societies in China, 1840–1950* (Stanford, Calif., 1972), p. 49.
49. Wakeman, "Secret Societies," p. 31.
50. CSL 97: 19, CC7 iv 18.
51. Tenuous evidence of pirate membership in secret societies has been uncovered by W. P. Morgan, a former sub-inspector of the Hong Kong police force. Morgan discovered that the hierarchy of rank employed by the Triads in Hong Kong differed from that more commonly found in South China. Ac-

cording to him, this discrepancy dates back to Chang Pao's time, when the pirate leader had held one title but performed the duties associated with another. Thereafter, he contends, the ranks of the "Red Stick and White Paper Fan" offices were confused in Hong Kong. W. P. Morgan, *Triad Societies in Hong Kong* (Hong Kong, 1960), p. 46.

52. Wei Yüan, 8: 25b; Von Krusenstern, 2: 310–11; KTHF 26: 4.

53. For examples of pirate–secret society collusion, see CP 1118/05, CC9 vi 4; CP 1144/77, CC9 xii 5; LF 3909; LF3877; and NYC 12: 30, CC10 vi 15.

54. Sainte-Croix, 2: 55.

55. Dalrymple, *Memoir*, p. 17; CSL 216: 13b, CC14 vii 27.

56. NYC 12: 19b–20, CC10 vi 26.

57. Sun Yü-t'ing, *Yen-hsi-t'ang chi*, 1: 44–44b; SYT 265, CC10 vi* n.d.; CSL 164: 9b, CC11 vii 8. For an English-language account of Lin Wu, see Meadows, pp. 177–82.

58. CSL 164: 10–10b, CC11 vii 8; SYT 265, CC10 vi* 19.

59. Glasspoole, "Brief Narrative," p. 127; Glasspoole, "Letter," p. 33.

60. The usage on seagoing as against oceangoing vessels is not consistent in the sources, but in general seagoing junks (*hai-ch'uan*) can be thought of as those used in the inner ocean and oceangoing junks (*yang-ch'uan*) as those used in the outer ocean. For more information on the distinction between them, see Fredrick Mayers, "Chinese Junk Building," *Notes and Queries on China and Japan*, 1.12: 170–72 (1867); and Cushman, p. 66. On the difficulties of categorizing Chinese seagoing craft, see Cushman, pp. 64, 68, 69, 79, 80; and Audemard, 4: 58. Other craft sometimes employed in the junk trade from Kwangtung were the *t'o-feng*, which sailed from Chiang-men, and the *hai-po*, which sailed from Ch'ao-chou; their average cargo capacity was 350 tons. Cushman, p. 80. For more information, see Appendix C.

61. Parkinson, pp. 335–38, 344, 348.

62. For more information on seagoing pirate craft, see Turner, p. 63; Montalto de Jesus, *Historic Macao*, p. 231; Course, p. 139; and Maughan, pp. 24–25.

63. Montalto de Jesus, *Historic Macao*, p. 231. See also Maughan, pp. 24–25. According to Turner, p. 63, the largest carried 12 cannon of mostly 6- to 12-pounders with a few 18-pounders.

64. Howard Chapelle, *The History of American Sailing Ships* (New York, 1935), pp. 11, 15; CanCon, Aug. 23, 1809.

65. Turner, p. 65.	66. Audemard, 8: 40.
67. Ibid., p. 69.	68. Turner, p. 49.
69. Glasspoole, "Letter," p. 33.	70. Ibid., pp. 33–34.
71. "Chinese Pirates," p. 70.	72. Turner, p. 65.

73. On the pirates' use of these types of cannon, see NYC 12: 81b, CC10 viii 28; and Sainte-Croix, 2: 56.

74. CSL 189: 7–8b, CC12 xii 2; NYC 14: 19b, CC10 v 20; Sainte-Croix, 2: 56; SYT 171, CC11 vi 9. Cannon might be purchased from groups of private individuals who, for the purposes of some "easy money," pooled their resources, formed a partnership, and engaged in the wholly illegal business of casting cannon. One such group was formed in April 1800 by Yang Tsankung, a resident of Hai-yang district, who got four friends to join him in putting up 20 silver *yüan* apiece for the project. After going around to various village markets to purchase iron, they built a small shanty with a forge outside Tung-ti village and hired six blacksmiths to do the casting. Over the next four years the group cast 43 cannon, ranging in size from 250 catties to 500 catties.

which they sold for 2,284 *yüan*. The blacksmiths' bill came to 427 *yüan* leaving a tidy sum of 371 *yüan* for each of the partners. *NYC* 12: 16–16b, CC10 vi 26. A similar group formed under Ch'en A-tou, who in July 1801, on learning of Yang Tsan-kung's venture, decided to go into business for himself. He and four friends put up 16 *yüan* each, and hired a man to purchase scrap iron in the various villages and Yang's six blacksmiths to do the casting. They built their forge in a secluded mountain at Hu-tzu-chou. Between 1801 and 1804 they cast 20 cannon, ranging in size from 200 catties to 500 catties, which fetched 946.5 *yüan*. Of this amount, 208.5 went to the blacksmiths, leaving 738 to be divided among the five business partners. NYC 12: 17b, 18, CC10 vi 26.

75. Turner, p. 63; G. R. G. Worcester, p. 44; Fay, p. 345; Brown, p. 79.
76. Glasspoole, "Brief Narrative," p. 112.
77. Turner, pp. 63–64; Maughan, p. 25; Sainte-Croix, 2: 56.
78. Turner, p. 63; Maughan, p. 25.
79. NYC 12: 53, CC10 vii 1.
80. Glasspoole, "Substance," p. 45.
81. Brown, p. 23.
82. Turner, p. 65; KCT 014890, CC14 vii 23; Glasspoole, "Substance," p. 42.
83. Glasspoole, "Substance," p. 45; Maughan, p. 25.
84. NYC 12: 81b–82, CC10 viii 28; NYC 13: 35b–36, CC10 x 2.
85. NYC 13: 57, CC10 xi 6.
86. Oberschall, pp. 129, 143–44.

CHAPTER 6

1. One of the country's leading proponents of sea defense (*hai-fang*) was Sun Yü-t'ing, the governor of Kwangtung. In a memorial to the throne written in the summer of 1804 he argued that the sea-war policy of tracking down the pirates one by one made little sense for a force that could easily come together and disperse over an expanse of 3,000 *li*. There were always problems in deploying the soldier boats (*ping-ch'uan*), Sun argued, for if they proceeded individually, they possessed only the strength of a single ship, and if they sailed together, they could pursue only one pirate group at a time, allowing the rest to escape. Furthermore, when a fleet of soldier boats did manage to engage in combat, they were at the mercy of weather conditions that often drove them so close together that they collided or so far apart that they were ineffective. Thus, Sun concluded, the most important aspect of coastal defense was to "guard the ports and increase the garrisons." It was also important to cut off the pirates' onshore sources of supply and prevent the people on land from communicating with them. This would force hungry pirates onshore in search of food. For these expeditions, they would have to rely on sampans, which could not accommodate many men, so theoretically the soldiers in the forts ought to have had an advantage over them. As the pirates approached, the soldiers could give the signal for villagers to assemble their braves (*hsiang-yung*). Having advanced, the pirates would experience difficulty in withdrawing. Without food, they would soon be unable to attack and would therefore perish of their own accord. Sun Yü-t'ing, *Yen-hsi-t'ang chi*, 1: 49–51b.
2. Hummel, pp. 584–85.
3. KCFC 74: 7b. Detailed geographical descriptions of the east, middle, and west districts can be found in the preface and *chüan* 2, 3, and 4 of KTHF.

Additional information is available in *chüan* 8: 1–2 and 14: 4–4b. The Kwang-tung coast was divided into three districts during the Chia-ching reign of the Ming dynasty. Later, the western district was further divided into upper and lower *lu*, and in 1810, after the pirates were brought to terms, the eastern district was likewise divided.

4. Rawlingson, p. 7; Wade, pp. 254, 319, 320.

5. Rawlingson, pp. 7–8; H. S. Brunnert and V. V. Hagelstrom, *Present-Day Political Organization of China* (Shanghai, 1912), p. 337.

6. Rawlingson, pp. 7, 8, 12.

7. Barrow, *Travels*, p. 274.

8. This fleet to defend the creeks and harbors included six-oared boats (*liu-lu ch'uan*), rowboats (*chiang-ch'uan*), and fast boats (*k'uai-ch'uan*). KTTC 179: 15.

9. KTHF 23: 39, CC15 viii 6. For estimates of the size of the confederation, see the table on p. 197, above.

10. Worcester, pp. 52–53; CSL 46: 6, CC4 vi 2; SYT 424, CC11 iii 25; KCT 007808, CC7 iv 8.

11. NYC 11: 31b–32, CC10 ii 21. For more information on the unkempt state of the water forces, see CSL 129: 12, CC9 v 12.

12. Von Krusenstern, 2: 308–9.

13. Ch'eng Han-chang, p. 38.

14. Barrow, *Travels*, pp. 200–201; Rawlingson, p. 6; "Military Skill," p. 167.

15. CSK 142: 3, 4, 10; Wade, p. 377; KTHF 23: 44–44b, CC15 viii 6; Yen Ju-i, 2: 2.

16. CSK, 142: 3, 4, 10; KTHF, 23: 31b–32; Wade, p. 378.

17. KTHF, 23: 31b–32, CC5 ii n.d. The edict is also reproduced in Yen Ju-i, *Yang-fang chi-yao*, 2: 5b. In that same *chüan* Yen enumerates the various punishments for naval officers who lost vessels at sea and failed to arrest pirates within a specified period. See also SYT 291, CC9 vi 24.

18. Secret Consultations, Nov. 24, 1804.

19. CSL 129: 12, CC9 v 12.

20. CSL 130: 27, CC9 vi 22; Sun Yü-t'ing, *Yen-hsi-t'ang chi*, 1: 50b.

21. CSL 137: 16b, CC9 xi 24; Dalrymple to Viscount Melville, Feb. 27, 1805, Melville Muniments GD 51/3/534, Scottish Record Office, Edinburgh.

22. HSHC(2), 14: 37b; SYT 1, CC8 x 1. Huang Piao, originally of Nan-ao in Ch'ao-chou prefecture, Kwangtung, grew up in Hsiang-shan, and having been raised almost on the water, was fully conversant with sea routes. He began his military career in 1780 as a second captain in the Hsiang-shan Regiment and demonstrated such extraordinary ability that, 10 years later, Liang-kuang Governor-general Fu-k'ang-an put him in charge of anti-pirate campaigns a Wei-chou and Dog's Head Mountain (Kou-t'ou shan), for which he earned a promotion to first captain. Thereafter he continued to arrest pirates with a vengeance while serving in a number of military posts in the province, and in 1798 he reached the apex of his career with his appointment as brigade general of the Left Wing Brigade (Tso-i-chen). A year later he was awarded a peacock feather for his pirate-suppression endeavors. He died in 180? HSHC(2), 14: 37–38.

23. Sun Ch'üan-mou, a native of Lung-ch'i, Fukien, began his career in the Ch'ing navy in 1770, serving as a sergeant in the middle fleet of the Fukienes naval commander-in-chief. He moved up through the ranks and served continuously in Fukien until 1787, when for his role in suppressing Lin Shuang

wen's uprising on Taiwan, he was promoted to the position of colonel and transferred to the Lo-ting Regiment in Kwangtung. Subsequently, he took up posts in Taiwan (1788) and, as a brigade-general, in Chekiang (1795), where he remained until his appointment as the provincial commander-in-chief of Kwangtung in January 1797. At that point, his major responsibility was fighting pirates, and his career rose and fell in proportion to his success at sea. CSLC 27: 25b–30.

24. CSL 130: 31b–32, CC9 vi 26; NYC 11: 31b, CC10 ii 21; NYC 12: 1–1b, CC10 iv 20.

25. NYC 12: 3, CC10 v 12; CSL 146: 10b, CC10 vi* 8; CSLC 27: 26b. As provincial commander-in-chief, Ch'ien Meng-hu outlasted his two predecessors by remaining in that office until June 11, 1809, when he was replaced by Sun Ch'üan-mou.

26. Dalrymple, *Memoir*, p. 17; CanCon, Oct. 10, 1804, June 22, 1805; Sun Yü-t'ing, *Tzu-ting nien-p'u*, 1: 19b–21; NYC 11: 29, CC10 i 24.

27. KTTC 179: 16b.

28. NYC 11: 42b, n.d.; NYC 13: 79–81, n.d. For examples of people who responded to Na's proclamation, see NYC 13: 50b–52, CC10 xi 6; *Hsin-hui hsien-chih*, 14: 4b; and HSHC(2), 6: 78.

29. Huo T'ao (1487–1540) was a native of Nan-hai county, Kwangtung. A *chin-shih* (1514) who held mainly metropolitan offices, he was a member of the clique who supported Emperor Chu Hou-ts'ung in the Ta-li-i controversy, in which the Emperor decided to ascend the throne, not as an adopted son, but by right of succession. Huo continuously pointed out the corrupt practices of the bureaucracy. L. Carrington Goodrich, ed., *Dictionary of Ming Biography, 1368–1644* (New York, 1976), pp. 679–83.

30. KTHF 33: 1.   31. KTHF 33: 9.

32. KTHF 33: 11b–13b.   33. KTHF 33: 5–5b.

34. For cases of gentry organizing their villages against pirate raids, see *Lien-chou fu-chih* [Gazetteer of Lien-chou county], comp. Chang Yü-chün, 26 *chüan* (1833), 21: 55b; *Hsin-hui hsien-chih*, 14: 4; and STHC 27: 16, 17b.

35. Kuhn, pp. 41–50.

36. NYC 11: 38b–39, CC10 ii 24; SYT 109, CC10 vi 9.

37. NYC 11: 38b–39, CC10 ii 24; NYC 11: 40–43, n.d.

38. NYC 11: 39, CC10 ii 24; NYC 11: 40–43, n.d.

39. NYC 11: 44–48b, n.d.

40. NYC 11: 47b, n.d.

41. CanCon, April 3, 1804. The Portuguese sent out an armed longboat to convoy boats from the vicinity of Nine Islands, and relief came on April 4, when a small supply of rice was brought to Macao from the adjoining villages. Ibid., April 4, 9, 1804. Commenting on the weak state of Macao's defenses, Von Krusenstern, 2: 286, quotes the remarks of one inhabitant: "We have more priests here than soldiers."

42. CanCon, March 30, April 3, April 11, 1804.

43. Ibid., April 11, May 19, 1804. The expedition returned to Macao on May 19.

44. Ibid., Sept. 3, Oct. 10, 1804. The Chinese fleet was said to have been built and equipped with money jointly contributed by Chinese officials, salt merchants, and Hong merchants.

45. CanCon, June 22, 1805.

46. *Ch'ing Chia-ch'ing-ch'ao wai-chiao shih-liao*, 1: 22b–23, CC10 iii 3.

47. Parkinson, p. 60; CanCon, March 24, 1804; Secret Consultations, Oct. 8, 1804.

48. Morse, 2: 423–27; Great Britain, FO 233/189/77, p. 145b, CC10 vi* 21, edict of governor-general; Secret Consultations, Oct. 8, 1804.

49. Secret Consultations, Oct. 25, 27, 1804.

50. Ibid., Nov. 19, 1804.

51. *Ching Chia-ch'ing-ch'ao wai-chiao shih-liao*, 1: 21b–22, CC10 ii 7, from the translation in Lo-shu Fu, *A Documentary Chronicle of Sino-Western Relations (1644–1820)* (Tucson, Ariz., 1966), p. 360.

52. CanCon, July 13, Aug. 15, 16, 1805; SYT 15, CC10 xi n.d.

53. When the pirates invaded Shui-tung in May 1805, the magistrate of Tien-pai led the braves to repel them; and in Shih-ch'eng a member of the gentry, Yang Kuang-p'u, led villagers in keeping watch and defending the harbors. *Tien-pai hsien-chih* [Gazetteer of Tien-pai county; 1825], comp. Chang Hung, 20 *chüan* (Taipei 1967), 13: 17. In Hsiang-shan the local gentry aided Magistrate P'eng Chao-lin in devising plans for the city's defense. But in none of these cases was there any mention of *t'uan-lien*. And it is also clear in the case of Shun-te, where, after a pirate invasion in late 1805, members of the local elite were instrumental in procuring a cannon for the defense of the village, that there was no recourse to *t'uan-lien*. HSHC(1), 14: 44–44b; STHC 27: 14.

54. NYC 12: 90b–92, CC10 ix 2; CP 1119/6, CC10 viii 21; CP 1140/24, CC10 ix 26.

55. SYT 15, CC10 xi n.d.

56. NYC 12: 93b–95, CC10 ix 20; CP 1119/6, CC10 viii 21.

57. NYC 12: 92b, CC10 ix 2; CP 1118/9, CC11 vi 27.

58. NYC 12: 94b, CC10 ix 2.   59. NYC 13: 1b, CC10 ix 4.

60. SYT 15, CC10 xi 5.   61. NYC 13: 74–79b, n.d.

62. NYC 12: 81b, CC10 viii 28.   63. NYC 13: 78b–79, n.d.

64. NYC 12: 56b, CC10 vii 20; NYC 86b–87, CC10 ix 19; SYT 467, CC10 xii 25; CSL 156: 13b–14, CC11 i 9; CSL 158: 12b, CC11 iii 10.

65. NYC 12: 84b–86, CC10 viii 28; NYC 13: 3b–6b, CC10 ix 4; NYC 13: 31–37, CC10 x 2.

66. NYC 13: 72–72b, n.d.

67. NYC 12: 3b, CC10 v 16; NYC 12: 15, CC10 vi 26; NYC 12: 42b, CC10 vii 1; NYC 12: 59, CC10 vii 25.

68. NYC 12: 25–29b, CC10 vi 15; SYT 11, CC10 ix 2.

69. SYT 15, 10 xi 15; SYT 469, CC10 xii 25.

70. Sun Yü-t'ing, *Yen-hsi-t'ang chi*, 1: 53–55b; Sun Yü-t'ing, *Tzu-ting nien p'u*, pp. 22b–23b.

71. CSL 151: 25, CC10 x 22.

72. For more details on Na-yen-ch'eng's abrogation of the pacification policy and his subsequent dismissal from office, see NYC 13: 54–59b, CC10 x 16; SYT 372, CC10 xi 28; SYT 469, CC10 xii 25; SYT 101, 102, CC11 i 6; SYT 307, 321, 325, CC11 i 27; SYT 327, CC11 i 28; SYT 68, CC11 ii 4; SYT 120–21, CC11 iii 8. Li Chung-yü's confession and testimony are translated in C.-s. Chang, Appendixes D–F, pp. 257–64.

CHAPTER 7

1. Reports of the battle can be found in KCT 009666, CC13 i 6, and KC 009676, CC13 i 8.

2. CanCon, Feb. 4, 1808; Secret Consultations, June 1, 1808; KCT 009839, CC13 i 28; KCT 009917, CC13 ii 8. For the Chia-ch'ing Emperor's response to Li Ch'ang-keng's death, see CSL 191: 15b–17b, CC13 i 21; and Hummel, pp. 446–48. Following their victory over Li Ch'ang-keng, Ts'ai Ch'ien's group sailed to eastern Kwangtung, where they eventually joined forces with Chu Fen, the pirate of the Kwangtung–Fukienese border, and Wu-shih Erh, the leader of the Blue Flag Fleet. As a result, the naval forces from Fukien and Chekiang had to stay in Kwangtung for several weeks thereafter. On Feb. 17, 1808, Chang Chien-sheng, the commander from Fukien, set out for Tien-pai from Macao at the head of a squadron composed of forces from Fukien, Chekiang, and Kwangtung. KCT 009839, CC13 i 28. On March 26 and 27 they met with some pirates near Wei-chou Island and captured 509 of them. The pirates suffered a further loss when the coffin of Wu-shih Erh's father was burned to ashes. KCT 011082, CC13 v* 25. In the aftermath of this battle, Ts'ai Ch'ien and Wu-shih Erh fled on April 13 to Vietnam, where they joined the partisans of the former Tay-son Emperor Quang Toan in an abortive attempt to reconquer the country. SYT 109, CC13 v 9; KCT 010867, CC13 v 25. The cooperation between Ts'ai Ch'ien and Wu-shih Erh was only temporary, however. Although Ts'ai Ch'ien and Chu Fen continued their piratical activities, their gangs operated mainly in Fukien and Chekiang and seldom, if ever, cooperated with the pirates in Kwangtung. Thus, a complete discussion of them is beyond the scope of this study. For an account of their activities, see Chang Chung-shen; Chi Shih-chia, "Ch'ing chün-chi-ch'u 'Ts'ai Ch'ien fan-ch'ing tou-cheng hsiang' tang-an shu-lüeh" [Outline summary of Grand Council materials on Ts'ai Ch'ien's anti-Ch'ing resistance], *Li-shih tang-an* [Historical Archives], 1: 115–19 (Feb. 1982); and Chi Shih-chia, "Lüeh-lun Ts'ai Ch'ien ti fan-ch'ing tou-cheng" [Outline summary of Ch'ing Grand Council materials on Ts'ai Ch'ien's anti-Ch'ing resistance], *Chung-kuo ku-tai shih* [Ancient Chinese history], 1982, no. 6: 103–10.

3. CSL 191: 11b, CC13 i 19; KCT 010974, CC13 v* 9; KCT 014217, CC14 v 17.

4. CanCon, July 13–30, 1808. On July 13 Magistrate P'eng Chao-lin of Hsiang-shan county had approached the supercargoes of the East India Company about the possibility of their cruisers *Antelope* and *Discovery* joining a squadron he was outfitting. But nothing came of the request. The governor-general did not favor the proposal and ultimately sealed its fate by refusing to supply the British with an official written application for their assistance.

5. SYT 33, CC13 vi 3.

6. CHFC 1: 7–9. Brief summaries of this encounter are also found in KCT 011083E, CC13 v* 25; KCT 011879E2, CC13 viii 29; and KCT 012562, CC13 xi 26. There are also accounts in various printed sources (e.g. KTHF 42: 10), but all err on the date of the battle. In most cases the mistake can be traced to CHFC 1: 7, which places the event in the seventh lunar month, or sometime in late August or early September. This date is obviously wrong, since we have the precise date of the battle (July 15) from the official memorial Wu Hsiung-kuang submitted on July 18. That date also appears in other unpublished memorials referring to the battle (e.g., in addition to the memorials cited above, SYT 277, CC13 vi 18). The dating error is significant because a number of local gazetteers, in their own renditions of the pirates' story, based their accounts heavily on the CHFC and inadvertently perpetuated the error. See, for example, *P'an-yü hsien-chih*, 22: 15b; TKHC 33: 23; and KCFC 81: 16. The

last states that the battle occurred on Sept. 11 (CC13 vii 21) and then reproduces the CHFC account. KTHF goes so far as to place the event in the wrong year: on Aug. 31, 1807, rather than in 1808.

7. KCT 011111, CC13 v* 25; KCT 012562, CC13 xi 26; CHFC 1: 8b–9.

8. SYT 277, CC13 vi 18. On Sun's career, see note 23 to Chap. 6, above.

9. KCT 011083E, CC13 v* 25; KCT 011111, CC13 v* 27; KCT 011243E, CC13 vi 15.

10. Hsiao, fol. 30; CHFC 1: 9b.

11. Maughan, p. 19; KCT 013354, CC14 ii 16.

12. CSLC 32: 24b, 25. For Pai Ling's complete biography, see *chüan* 32: 24–35.

13. KCT 014217, CC14 v 17.

14. KCT 014384E, CC14 v 28; KCT 014560, CC14 vi 19.

15. KCT 014085, CC14 v 1. The governor-general proposed to hire the soon-to-be-idle salt junks to fight the pirates. It appears that these measures were put into place in late May and early June 1809. However, the dates given in KCFC 81: 18b–19 and CHFC 1: 12b–13b imply that the embargo came into being as a consequence of Hsü T'ing-kuei's defeat in July (see below).

16. CHFC 1: 14b; Chu Ch'eng-wan, p. 21; STHC(1), 31: 18–18b.

17. KCT 014384E, CC14 v 28.

18. Ibid.; KCT 014651E, CC14 vi 19; STHC(1), 27: 18b; *Hsin-ning hsien-chih* (1893), 7: 18b, 14: 16b; KCFC 81: 17–17b.

19. KCT 013513, CC14 iii 5; KCT 014384, CC14 v 28.

20. Morse, 3: 116; Chu Ch'eng-wan, pp. 21b–22; KTHF 42: 28, CC15 i n.d.

21. For accounts of this battle, see CHFC 1: 12b–13b; KCT 014559, CC14 vi 19; KTHF 42: 17, n.d. (which is a reprint of parts of KCT 014559); Chu Ch'eng-wan, p. 21b; TKHC 33: 25b; KCFC 81: 17b–18; and HSHC(1), 8: 58b. For the Emperor's response to the battle, see CSL 215: 24–27, CC14 vii 10. The account in CHFC differs from the others in two respects: it puts the number of vessels at 200, not 300, and it says that Hsü T'ing-kuei, seeing that there was no hope, slit his own throat, where the others indicate he died in battle.

22. KCT 014560, CC14 vi 19; KCT 014804, CC14 vii 15; CSL 215: 25–25b, CC14 vii 10.

23. Chu Ch'eng-wan, p. 21b; KCT 014560, CC14 vi 19.

24. HSHC(1), 20: 5b; CanCon, Aug. 16, 1809.

25. NHHC 15: 8, 10.

26. STHC(1), 27: 18, 20b.

27. STHC(1), 27: 16–17b; STHC(1), 31: 18b–19; KCFC 81: 19.

28. TKHC 33: 25b–26; Yeh Lin-feng, p. 23. For examples of other setbacks, see Chu Ch'eng-wan, p. 22.

29. CHFC 1: 18–18b; TKHC 33: 26; KCFC 81: 20b–21.

30. CHFC 1: 17b–18.

31. Dalrymple, *Further Statement*, pp. 74–75.

32. HSHC(1), 6: 79b; HSHC(1), 8: 58b–59; KCFC 81: 19–20; CanCon, Aug. 16, 18, 1809; CHFC 1: 15.

33. The term *chin* used in the text to denote the amount of money is probably an error, for *chin* were of such little value that 3,000 equaled 1 tael. Probably the reference was to taels or Spanish dollars.

34. CHFC 1: 15b, 17. *P'an-yü hsien-chih,* 22: 16, states the death toll was 54 village braves (a figure that is picked up in KCFC 81: 20.)

35. KCFC 81: 20b (citing STHC[1], 81: 20b); CHFC 1: 17–17b. There is some question about who conducted the campaigns against Ma-chou, San-shan, and P'ing-chou. The CHFC account implies the raids were led by Kuo P'o-tai, whereas KCFC states that Chang Pao led them. I have followed the former because it is consistent with the fact that Kuo was operating in the Inner Passage at the time.

36. STHC(1), 27: 4–4b, 71b; STHC(1), 31: 18b–19; KTHF 42: 21b, CC14 x 14; Chu Ch'eng-wan, p. 22. For a biography of Ho Ting-ao, see STHC(1), 27: 78b; and HSHC(1), 6: 78.

37. Andrade, pp. 33–34; CanCon, Aug. 16, Sept. 27, 1809.

38. TKHC 33: 26. According to CHFC 1: 17b, more than 1,000 people were killed in this encounter, but TKHC calls the figure "unfactual hearsay."

39. KCT 015184E, CC14 viii 23. A more fanciful version of the Ta-fen encounter is found in TKHC 33: 26–26b.

40. CanCon, Sept. 17, 1809.

41. *P'an-yü hsien-chih,* 22: 17. This account is picked up in KCFC 81: 21b.

42. CHFC 1: 19; Glasspoole, "Brief Narrative," pp. 109–10.

43. Glasspoole, "Brief Narrative," pp. 110–11.

44. Ibid., p. 111.

45. CHFC 1: 19b–20; Chu Ch'eng-wan, p. 22.

46. CHFC 1: 21b–22; KTHF 42: 20.

47. CHFC 1: 21b–22; CanCon, Oct. 5, 1809.

48. STHC(1), 27: 20b; CHFC 1: 22–24. After several months the villagers ransomed the women for 15,000 taels. CHFC 1: 23b states that 1,140 captives of both sides were seized, but the number may well be inflated.

49. Glasspoole, "Brief Narrative," p. 115; CHFC 2: 1; STHC(1), 27: 78b; STHC(1), 31: 19–19b; KTHF 42: 21.

50. Glasspoole, "Brief Narrative," pp. 117, 119; CHFC 2: 2–3. Glasspoole states that this engagement occurred at "Little Whampoa."

51. CanCon, Aug. 28, Sept. 17, 1809; Secret Consultations, Sept. 19, 1809; Dalrymple, *Further Statement,* p. 75. For other appraisals of the situation, see Supercargoes to Lord Minto, CanCon, Nov. 27, 1809; and Montalto de Jesus, "Macao's Deeds of Arms," p. 153.

52. CanCon, Oct. 4, 1809; Secret Consultations, Nov. 19, 1804.

53. CanCon, Nov. 21, 1809.

54. Supercargoes to Lord Minto, CanCon, Oct. 3, 1809. See also CanCon, Oct. 1, 26, 28, Nov. 4, 1809.

55. Innis to Dundas, March 10, 1810, with extracts of a letter from Canton dated Sept. 30, 1809, Melville Muniments, G287/292/1, Scottish Record Office, Edinburgh.

56. CanCon, Sept. 1, 2, 5, 1809; CHFC 1: 17b; KCT 015184, CC14 viii 23; L. G. Gomes, pp. 140, 141; Andrade, p. 34; Montalto de Jesus, *Historic Macao,* p. 236.

57. Andrade, p. 35; L. G. Gomes, pp. 143–44; CanCon, Sept. 5, 7, 8, 9, 11, 12, 1809.

58. L. G. Gomes, p. 148.

59. Andrade, pp. 34–44; L. G. Gomes, pp. 143–44.

60. Dalrymple, *Further Statement,* p. 76; CanCon, Sept. 17, 1809.

61. For the Chinese version of this communication, see Great Britain, FO 682/483/1, CC14 viii 4, and for the English translation, see CanCon Sept. 17, 1809. This communication was transmitted by the Hong merchants to the supercargoes on Sept. 15 and to Capt. Thomas Jones a couple of days before.

62. CanCon, Sept. 19, 1809; Dalrymple, *Further Statement*, p. 76; *Asiatic Annual Register*, 11: 190.

63. Dalrymple, *Further Statement*, pp. 76, 84; CanCon, Sept. 22, 1809, letter of John Williams.

64. CanCon, Oct. 25, 28, 1809.

65. Secret Consultations, Dec. 10, 1809. For the Chinese text of the agreement, see Great Britain, FO 682/483/1, CC14 x n.d. For its terms, see Andrade, pp. 44–45; L. G. Gomes, p. 160; Montalto de Jesus, *Historic Macao*, p. 240; and Judice Biker, 11: 251. See also Dalrymple, *Further Statement*, pp. 77–78; CanCon, Nov. 2, 1809; and CP 1120/02, CC14 x n.d. The Chinese signatories were the magistrate of Nan-hai, the magistrate of Hsiang-shan, and the assistant prefect of Ch'ien-shan, commonly known as the "Mandarin of Casa Branca." Ouvidor Miguel de Arriaga Brum da Silveira and Procurador José Joaquim da Barros signed for the Portuguese. Teixeira, p. 262; Artur Gomes, p. 309; Andrade, pp. 44–45; L. G. Gomes, p. 160. The Portuguese squadron consisted of the *Inconquistavel*, flagship of the commander-in-chief, Captain Alcoforado, 400 tons, 26 guns, and 160 men; the *Pala Conceicão* under Capt. Luis Carlos de Miranda, 18 guns, 130 men; the *Indiano* under Capt. Anacleto José de Silva, 24 guns, 120 men; the *Princess Carlota* under Capt. Antonio José Gonsalves Carocha, 16 guns, 100 men; the *São Miguel* under Capt. José Felix dos Remedios, 16 guns, 100 men; and the *Belisario* under Capt. José Alves, 18 guns, 120 men. For an excellent summary of the Portuguese literature on the subject, see Teixeira, pp. 65–70. See also Andrade, p. 47; L. G. Gomes, pp. 164–65; and Montalto de Jesus, *Historic Macao*, p. 240. For more details on the "ancient privilege" claim, see Ljungstedt, pp. 109–16.

66. Glasspoole, "Brief Narrative," p. 119.

67. Ibid., p. 120.

68. Ibid.

69. CHFC 2: 4b; Glasspoole, "Brief Narrative," p. 121.

70. Glasspoole, "Brief Narrative," p. 122.

71. Ibid., p. 123. Chinese accounts of the siege can be found in KTHF 42: 216–22; and CP 1120/01, CC14 x 29.

72. CanCon, Dec. 9, 1809.

73. CP 1120/01, CC14 x 29.

74. Glasspoole, "Brief Narrative," p. 122.

75. Ibid., p. 123.

76. The Portuguese translation of Chang Pao's letter containing this offer appears in Judice Biker, 11: 253–55 (dated Dec. 26, 1809). I have not found any references to it in the Chinese sources, let alone a Chinese text.

CHAPTER 8

1. Hu Chieh-yü, p. 155; CHFC 2: 8; Yeh Lin-feng, pp. 9, 26.

2. Kuo P'o-tai's confession, LF 3865, CC15 ii 15.

3. Maughan, p. 22; HSHC(1), 8: 61; CSK (ch. 363), p. 4506; CHFC 2: 9–10b.

4. CP 1126/06, CC14 xii 7.

5. Ibid.; CHFC 2: 9–9b; Yeh Lin-feng, p. 26; SYT 95, CC15 i 15; KTHF 42: 39, n.d.; CSL 223: 27, CC14 xii 28. Four of the 16 junks Kuo P'o-tai took from Chang Pao were official rice carriers that had been captured and put to use by the pirates. Of the 321 prisoners he captured, 82 were volunteer pirates, 150 were captives impressed into service; 67 had been imprisoned in the hold and held for ransom; and 9 were women who had been captured and raped. The background of the other 13 is not known. CP 1120/11 CC15 i 22. The account in CSL errs in reporting the capture of 14 instead of 16 vessels. On the Portuguese role in the battle, see L. G. Gomes, p. 165; Montalto de Jesus, "Macao's Deeds of Arms," p. 154; and Andrade, p. 49.

6. CP 1120/06, CC14 xii 7; Kuo P'o-tai's confession, LF 3865, CC15 ii 15.

7. Ibid.; KTHF 42: 39, n.d.; SYT 95, CC15 i 15; CSL 233: 26b–29, CC14 xii 28. Arriaga's participation in the surrender process is not mentioned in the Chinese sources, but is confirmed by the English as well as the Portuguese accounts. For additional details, see CanCon, Dec. 28, 1809, and Jan. 4, 1810; L. G. Gomes, p. 167; and Teixeira, p. 71.

8. SYT 95, CC15 i 15; CSL 223: 28b–29, CC14 xii 28. After disgrace and demotion in 1809 (following the breaking of the blockade at Lantao), Sun Ch'üan-mou again worked his way back up from the rank of second captain (1810) to become provincial commander-in-chief of Kwangtung one more time in 1816, shortly before his death. CSLC 27: 25b–30.

9. *Yang-chiang hsien-chih* (1822, 8: 22b; 1925, 20: 92) states that the Black Fleet leader Chang Jih-kao surrendered with 79 followers and 2 vessels, and Feng Yung-fa and Kuo Chiu-shan with more than 1,000 men and several dozen ships.

10. CP 1120/12, CC15 i 22; CHFC 2: 14; CanCon, Jan. 17, 29, 30, 31, Feb. 5, 1810; Dalrymple, *Further Statement*, p. 80; Ljungstedt, p. 113; Teixeira, p. 71; STHC(1), 31: 20.

11. CP 1120/12, CC15 i 22.

12. KTHF 42: 28b, CC15 i n.d.

13. CHFC 2: 17b. Chou Fei-hsiung was a native of Hunan who moved during his childhood to Kwangtung, where he made his living by selling methods of medical treatment. Known to be close to the pirates, he had been one of several emissaries sent by the governor-general to proclaim amnesty to them. He not only played a major role in the surrender of Chang Pao, but later helped bring in Wu-shih Erh as well. He remained in Kwangtung as the acting deputy magistrate of Hsiang-shan county and was in charge of Macao for about 10 years until his death at the age of 53. *Kuo ch'ao ch'i-hsien lei-cheng ch'u-pien* [Biographies of the eminent men of the Ch'ing], comp. Li Huan, 720 *üan* (1884–90), 247: 38–39. See also HSHC(1), 8: 61b–62.

14. L. G. Gomes, p. 174; Andrade, p. 57. While Arriaga was in the midst of the negotiations for the surrender of Chang Pao, a contretemps arose when a new *ouvidor* arrived in Macao. According to the law, Arriaga then yielded his post, but Chang Pao and the Chinese officials informed the governor of Macao that they would parley only with Arriaga. Accordingly, it was arranged that he would continue in his role of mediator despite his unofficial status. For details this controversy, see L. G. Gomes, pp. 175–76; and Teixeira, pp. 77–82.

15. Ljungstedt, p. 114. The Mandarin of Casa Branca was the assistant prefect of Ch'ien-shan and the Chinese official in charge of Macao. Dalrymple, *Further Statement*, pp. 81–82.

16. CanCon, Feb. 20–21, March 1, 1810; Maughan, p. 22; Dalrymple, *Fur-*

ther Statement, pp. 81–82. The surrender date of Feb. 21, 1810, given in many Portuguese sources, is incorrect. Teixeira, p. 71.

17. CHFC 2: 18b–20a; CSK (ch. 363), p. 4506. According to CanCon, Feb. 23, 1810, the Hong Merchant Puiqua (known also as P'ei-kuan and Wu Ping-chün) returned to Canton from the Bogue that day convinced that the pirates would soon surrender.

18. CP 1120/13, CC15 iii 6; CHFC 2: 19b; CSL 227: 1b, CC15 iii 1. CHFC claims it was Portuguese ships, not English vessels, that frightened the pirates.

19. KTHF 42: 40–41, n.d. This source also states that Chang Pao was ordered to present his boats and weapons to the authorities and to scatter his followers onshore before proceeding to attack the pirates, and that he did not agree to these terms. The biography of the Han bannerman Chu-erh-keng-o states that Chang Pao asked to keep a force of 3,000 men to lead in pursuit of Wu-shih Erh. CSK (ch. 363), p. 4507. CHFC 2: 17b states that during Chang Yü-chih's visit, Chang Pao asked to retain several dozen boats to kill other pirates and to atone for his crimes.

20. CSL 225: 21–22, CC15 ii 15.

21. CanCon, Feb. 25, March 8, 12, 16, 1810; Maughan, p. 22.

22. CanCon, March 16, 24, 27, 1810.

23. HSHC(1), 8: 60b; CanCon, March 27, 1810.

24. *Hsin-hui hsien-chih* (1840/1956), 14: 5b; *Hsin-ning hsien-chih* (1893), 14 16b.

25. CP 1120/13, CC15 iii 6.

26. Ibid.; CanCon, April 8, 1810; CHFC 2: 20b.

27. CP 1120/13, CC15 iii 6; CHFC 2: 20b (according to which Cheng I Sao requested that Chang Pao be allowed to retain 80 vessels for himself and 4(for use in the salt trade); CanCon, April 15, 1810; Morse, 3: 123.

28. CP 1120/14, CC15 iii 24.

29. CanCon, April 10, 1810; L. G. Gomes, p. 181. The Mong Ho pagoda the site of the conference, can be visited today.

30. CP 1120/15, CC15 iv 9, For other accounts of the surrendered item and people, see L. G. Gomes, p. 189; CSL 227: 21b–22, CC15 iii 23; Ljung stedt, pp. 114–15 (which says 360 vessels, 22,000 people, 1,200 cannon, an 700 firelocks); SYT 251, CC15 iv 27 (430 junks, 5 principal chieftains, mo than 30 large cannon, and 12,000 weapons); and KTHF 42: 41 (480 junk 36,000 weapons, and 26,000 men). Ambiguity still surrounds the question whether or not Chang Pao submitted the document of surrender given in A pendix D.

31. CanCon, April 20, Oct. 24, Nov. 12, 26, 1810; HSHC(1), 8: 61b; A drade, pp. 69–71; L. G. Gomes, p. 192.

32. L. G. Gomes, pp. 187, 191; Ljungstedt, p. 115; Andrade, p. 67; Ca Con, April 20, 1810.

33. L. G. Gomes, pp. 191, 193–94; Andrade, pp. 71–73. Chinese sour omit all mention of Chang Pao's visit to Macao and indicate that the western e pedition got under way on May 20. CHFC 2: 22–23; KTHF 42: 41b, n.d.

34. *Lien-chou fu-chih*, 21: 58b–59b.

35. KTHF 42: 41, n.d.; SYT 105, CC15 i 12; CHFC 2: 12, 22; CanC(May 24, 1810. CHFC 2: 22 states that those chosen to lead the expediti were Grain Intendant Wen Ch'eng-chih and the military commander of Lei-Lien-Ch'iung circuit, Chu-erh-keng-o.

36. CHFC 2: 22b says the encounter at Fang-chi occurred on May 29, 1810; KTHF 42: 41b, n.d., says it occurred on May 28.

37. CP 1121/17, CC15 vii 12; Andrade, pp. 73–74; L. G. Gomes, pp. 194–95; SYT 5, CC15 vi 1; CHFC 2: 23b; KTHF 42: 42b, n.d.; CSL 231: 22b, CC15 vi 29. CHFC states that Wu-shih Erh had more than 100 junks at Nao-chou, that these were attacked by Sun Ch'üan-mou and his men, and that more than 20 of the junks were sunk and between 200 and 300 of the pirates captured.

38. CP 1121/17, CC15 vii 12; CHFC 2: 22–25b; KTHF 42: 42b–43, n.d. The sources differ on the exact date of the Blue Fleet's demise. KTHF 42: 41b, n.d., states that Chang Pao's campaign against Wu-shih Erh began on May 29. CHFC 2: 22–22b indicates that Pai Ling arrived in Kao-chou on June 5, and that the battle against Wu occurred after that date. In addition to the 128 women, the 490 captives or prisoners handed over at the Lei-chou rendezvous included 6 accountants and other pirate officers, 6 of Wu-shih Erh's wives (and their children), 2 of Wu-shih Ta's wives (and their children), 107 volunteers who had engaged in piracy several times, 7 people who had received booty twice, 158 people who had received booty once, and 69 people who had been imprisoned and forced to render service.

39. CP 1121/17, CC15 vii 12. According to the CanCon files, this surrender occurred around July 17, 1810.

40. CSL 231: 23b–24, CC15 vi 29; SYT 332–33, CC15 vi 29; CanCon, Aug. 9, 1810.

41. CP 1137/23, CC15 vii 21.

42. Andrade, p. 66.

43. CP 1120/06, CC14 xii 7; CP 1120/10, CC15 i 22; CP 1120/12, CC15 i 2; CP 1120/13, CC15 iii 6; CP 1120/14, CC15 iii 24; CP 1121/14, n.d.

44. Wakeman, *Strangers*, p. 24.

45. Montalto de Jesus, "Macao's Deeds of Arms," p. 154 (this account erroneously dates the encounter as having taken place on April 12, 1810, instead of Jan. 21, 1810); Andrade, p. 56; L. G. Gomes, p. 174.

46. CHFC 2: 14; STHC(1), 31: 20. In mid-January proclamations were posted at Canton asking all nations to import rice. *Asiatic Annual Register*, 12: 56. An English translation of the edict allowing the import of rice free of port charges appears in CanCon, Jan. 31, 1810. The price by then had reached mace for 100 catties, and the shortage was attributed in great measure to the failure of parts of the coast to recover from their repeated devastation by the pirates. For the Chinese text of the edict, see Great Britain, FO 682/483 CC14 14. See also Maughan, p. 22; HSHC(1), 8: 61; CP 1120/06, CC14 xii 7; and CP 1120/10, CC15 i 22.

47. CP 1120/18, n.d.; CP 1120/12, CC15 i 22; Judice Biker, pp. 253–55.

48. Nathan, "Factionalism Model," p. 44.

49. Oberschall, p. 143.

50. Nathan, "Factionalism Model," pp. 43–44.

51. CSL 231: 23b, CC15 vi 29; NHHC 25: 20b–21; CanCon, Nov. 12, 26, 30.

52. CanCon, April 1, 1815.

53. The memorial of Lin Tse-hsü, written during the second lunar month 1820, is reproduced in full in Yeh Lin-feng, pp. 72–73. The information on Chang's career in the Pescadores is from this source.

54. Two other accounts of Chang Pao's end—both false—can be found in Andrade, pp. 75–76, and Dobell, *Sept années*, pp. 154–55.

55. NHHC 25: 20b; memorial of Lin Tse-hsü, in Yeh Lin-feng, pp. 69–71.

56. Lin Tse-hsü, in Yeh Lin-feng, pp. 69–71.

57. "Chinese Pirates," p. 82.

58. Hu Chieh-yü, p. 164.

CONCLUSION

1. It is possible that one of the sailing tribes known as the Joasmees, who operated along the 150-mile "Pirate Coast of Oman" between the 16th and 19th centuries, may have had such "dynasties," but by current data their leadership cannot be traced beyond two generations. Gosse, pp. 253–64; Col. S. B. Miles, *The Countries and Tribes of the Persian Gulf* (London, 1919), 2: 300–325. The acclaimed "dynasty of pirates" of the Mahratta family along the Malabar coast at the end of the 17th century seems to have lasted only two generations. Gosse, pp. 244, 246, 250–51; Col. John Biddulph, *The Pirates in Malabar and an Englishwoman in China 200 Years Ago* (London, 1907), pp. 70–84, 119–60.

2. For a more extended discussion of female pirates, see Linda Grant De Pauw, *Seafaring Women* (Boston, 1982); Henry Musnik, *Les Femmes pirates aventure et legendes de la mer* (Paris, 1934); Gosse, pp. 202–205; Botting, p. 51; and Daniel Defoe, *A General History of the Robberies and Murders of the Most Notorious Pyrates and also their Policies, Discipline, and Government from their first Rise and Settlement in the Island of Providence in 1717 to the present Year 1724* (London, 1724), reprinted and edited by Manuel Schonhorn (Columbia, S.C., 1972), pp. 148–65.

3. For more information on the role of women in sectarian societies and as leaders of rebellion, see Naquin, *Millenarian Rebellion*, pp. 22, 44, 84–8, 133–34; and Overmyer, pp. 165–67. For discussions of other women pirates in Chinese history, see Course, pp. 151, 161; Admiral Rt. Hon. Sir John Ha, *The Suppression of Piracy in the China Seas* (London, 1889); and Aleko E. Liliu, *I Sailed with Chinese Pirates* (New York, 1931).

4. For an example of power passing into the hands of a female bandit chi upon the death of her husband, see Jen Yu-wen, p. 67.

5. Ibid., p. 2; Elizabeth J. Perry, ed., *Chinese Perspectives on the Nien Rebelli* (New York, 1980), p. 2. See also Kwang-chih Liu, "World View and Peasa Rebellion: Reflections on Post-Mao Historiography," *Journal of Asian Stud* 11: 295–326 (Feb. 1981).

6. Chi Shih-chia, p. 110.

7. For examples, see Perry, *Rebels*, pp. 70–72; Naquin, *Millenarian Rel lion*, p. 121; Phil Billingsley, "Bandits, Bosses, and Bare Sticks," p. 240; S Chiang, p. 21; and Perry, "Social Banditry." For a discussion of social bandi and the near impossibility of it either adapting to or being absorbed by mo ern social movements, see E. J. Hobsbawm, *Primitive Rebels: Studies in Arcl Forms of Social Movement in the 19th and 20th Centuries* (New York: 1959).] spite the "pre-political" nature of many of the movements he describ Hobsbawm "was often able to trace implicit ideas of revolution in local fe ings of discontent." Roy Foster, "Master of Exceptions," a review of *Work Worlds of Labor*, by Eric Hobsbawm, in the *New York Review of Books* 32.19 (Dec. 5, 1985). For a hierarchy of social dissidence that culminates in rebel

or revolution, see Albert Feuerwerker, *Rebellion in Nineteenth-Century China* (Ann Arbor, Mich., 1975), pp. 3, 73–78.

8. S.-t. Chiang, pp. 18–20.

9. Ibid., pp. 60–61.

10. Perry, *Rebels*, pp. 141–45; S.-t. Chiang, p. 31; S. Y. Teng, p. 89.

11. Perry, *Rebels*, pp. 99, 121.

12. Ibid., p. 129; S.-t. Chiang, pp. 20–31.

13. Kuhn, p. 180 (see also pp. 165–81); Perry, *Rebels*, p. 71. A similar thing happened to White Wolf (Pai Lang), one of the most famous 20th-century bandits of northern China. Despite a brief flirtation with revolutionaries after the movement began pulling them away from their homes, most of White Wolf's followers insisted on abandoning the cause. Perry, "Social Banditry Revisited," p. 378. For more on the difficulties of transforming banditry into rebellion and on the tendency of bandits to be readily bought out by the state, see Billingsley, "Bandits, Bosses, and Bare Sticks," pp. 239, 250–54, 268.

14. Perry, *Rebels*, pp. 122–27; S.-t. Chiang, pp. 32–44, 58.

15. CanCon, April 20, 1810.

16. CSL 227: 21b–23, CC15 iii 23.

17. CanCon, Aug. 18, 1810.

18. Ibid., Oct. 24, 1810; CSL 235: 32b–33.

19. For details on these reforms, see KTHF 23: 37–42b, CC15 viii 6; KCFC 30: 1; CSK, p. 1666; and KTTC 179: 20b.

20. Evidence for such a view is provided by Fred Drake, who argues that 'the Confucian literati who governed China were unprepared, intellectually as well as militarily, to meet the growing challenge of the West. When the Opium War broke out, the officials who were ordered by the court to control the troublesome barbarians along the coast had little inkling of the true nature of the threat. Though a considerable literature on the maritime barbarians from the West had grown up as a result of China's contacts with European nations, China's literati for the most part had remained indifferent. They had neglected the signs of the scientific and technological transformations that had produced powerful Western states." *China Charts the World: Hsü Chi-Yu and His Geography of 1848* (Cambridge, Mass., 1975), pp. 1–2.

Bibliographic Material

Bibliographic Essay

Locating sources is a paramount problem in studying social dissidence. Troublemakers in general and pirates in particular have left behind few written records. As a result, what scanty records we have of their lifestyles and attitudes come primarily from the hands of their enemies, those who were charged with or interested in their suppression. These accounts are obviously biased and must be supplemented so far as possible with more objective sources. The sources used in this study fall into four principal categories.

1. *Official sources: views from above.* Much information on the origins of piracy, its connection to the Tay-son Rebellion in Vietnam, and its escalation in Kwangtung is contained in the palace memorials (*tsou-che*) sent by high provincial officials to the Emperor. These documents are split into two collections: the Palace Memorial Archive (Kung-chung tang) in the national Palace Museum, Taipei, and the Rescripted Memorial Collection (*Chu-p'i tsou-che*) in the First Historical Archives, Peking.

Although the testimony of apprehended pirates is often available in summarized form in the palace memorials, their original depositions can sometimes be found as unrescripted enclosures to copies of the original documents in the Grand Council Reference Files (Chün-chi ch'u tsou-che lu-fu) or the *lu-fu* collection, in the First Historical Archives. The published memorials of Na-yen-ch'eng and Sun Yü-t'ing, the governor-general and governor of Kwang-tung, respectively, in the years 1804 and 1805, are useful supplements to these archival materials.

The Emperor's response to the palace memorials can be found in the *Ta Ch'ing li-ch'ao shih-lu* [Veritable records of the successive reigns of the Ch'ing dynasty] and in the *Shang-yü-tang fang-pen* [Imperial edict record book]. Copies of the *Shang-yü-tang* are available both in the National Palace Museum and in the First Historical Archives. The strength of these documents lies in the quantity of background information they contain and in the insights one gains from following the dialogues between the Emperor and his officials as they wrestled with the piracy problem. However, with rare exceptions, these communications are episodic and detail what at first appear to be only isolated reports of pirates unskilled enough to get caught.

2. *Official sources: views from below.* The richest sources for viewing the pirates from outside Peking are provincial, prefectural, and county gazetteers.

Often the dates, locations, and numbers of people involved in pirate raids can be found in sections on previous events or rebellions. Accounts of local suppression attempts are available in the military and biographical sections, but again the accounts tend to be episodic. They are written almost entirely from the local perspective, with little attempt to integrate them into a more comprehensive narrative. Events are simply chronicled, and the information must be used with care because statistics are often inflated. One very welcome exception is the biography of Chu Ch'eng-wan in the gazetteer of Nan-hai county, which contains an entire essay on the pirates.

3. *Nonofficial Chinese-language sources.* Two of the most interesting and useful sources I found fall into this category. The first is Yüan Yung-lun's *Ching hai-fen chi* [Record of the pacification of the pirates], which gives a detailed chronological account of the Red and Black Flag fleets beginning in 1808 and contains a wealth of sociological data that is not to be found in other Chinese sources. After its publication in 1830, *Ching hai-fen chi* rapidly became the standard reference on which many local gazetteers based their accounts. The book aroused so much interest that it quickly appeared in two English-language translations. One was the translation of Karl Neumann (Charles Fried), published the following year, under the title *History of the Pirates Who Infested the China Sea from 1807 to 1810.* The other was John Slade's "A Record of the Pacification of the Seas," which appeared serially in the *Canton Register* in 1838. Neumann's translation has circulated widely and has become the standard English-language reference on the pirates. As a result, its errors have been reproduced in nearly every secondary account.

The second nonofficial Chinese-language source that proved helpful is most unusual manuscript, in that its author, the Hong Kong scholar Hsiao Wan-om (Hsiao Yün-han), chose to give it an English title, "Research in the History of the Pirates on the China Sea, 1140–1950." Of particular value was the genealogical table of the Cheng family, which Hsiao copied in 1952 from the clan register of Cheng Chin-shui, a collateral descendant of the pirate family who was then living in Canton. A considerable portion of Hsiao's manuscript is based on sources to which I have no access, so it is impossible to verify the accuracy of every statement, but where our research overlaps our findings are consistent.

4. *First-hand Western-language sources.* A surprising number of Westerners have left informative accounts of their encounters with the pirates. Among the most valuable of these are the diaries and transactions of the East India Company's supercargoes stationed in China. Their "Canton Consultations" and "Secret Consultations" are now preserved in the India Office Library, London, as a part of the China Factory Records. They provide a perspective on the magnitude of the problem so lacking in the Chinese sources and, at the same time, illustrate the extent to which pirates interfered with Western shipping.

Portuguese sources are of mixed utility. The official account of the Portuguese debates and proceedings against the pirates can be found in the Archives of the Senate of Macao (Leal Senado Archives), now housed in the Archivo Historico in Macao. Many of the documents have been published in the journal *Arquivos de Macau*, but the editors' failure to identify them by original Leal Senado number means one must still spend considerable time the archives double-checking related material.

Two of the most exciting documents I unearthed in the course of my research are the accounts of the captured English seamen Turner and Glasspoole. The "Account of the Captivity of J. Turner, Chief Mate of the Ship *Tay*,
Amongst the Ladrones" was first published in 1812. Glasspoole's "A Brief
Narrative of My Captivity and Treatment Amongst the Ladrones" appeared
two years later, in *Sketches of Chinese Customs and Manners in 1811–1812*,
edited by George Wilkinson. Rich in their detail of life aboard ship, both narratives provide an intimate glimpse of daily life among the pirates. The Glasspoole work is particularly useful because it accords perfectly with the *Ching
hai-fen chi* chronology of pirate activities for the summer and autumn of 1809.

Finally, the accounts of such early China travelers as Sir John Barrow, Alexander Dalrymple, Peter Dobell, Adam Johann Von Krusenstern, and Marquis
Carloman Renouard de Sainte-Croix added many colorful anecdotes to the
pirates' story.

References Cited

The following list contains only works that are cited more than once in the Notes.

Anderson, Eugene N. *Essays on South China's Boat People.* Taipei, 1972.

Anderson, Eugene N., and Marja Anderson. *Mountains and Water: Essays on the Cultural Ecology of South Coastal China.* Taipei, 1973.

Andrade, José Ignacio de. *Memoria dos feitos macaenses contra os piratas da China: e da entrada violenta dos inglezes na cidade de Macáo.* 2d ed. Lisbon, 1835. First published as *Memoria sobre a destruição dos piratas da China. . . .* Lisbon, 1824.

An-nam tang [Record book of Annam]. National Palace Museum, Taipei, Taiwan.

Armando da Silva. *Tai Yu Shan: Traditional Ecological Adaptation in a South Chinese Island.* Taipei, 1972.

Arquivos de Macau. Series 1, vol. 1 (June 1929); series 2, vol. 1 (Nov.–Dec. 1941); series 3, vol. 1 (Feb. 1964).

Asiatic Annual Register: Or, a View of the History of Hindustan, and of the Politics, Commerce, and Literature of Asia. 12 vols. London, 1799–1811.

Audemard, Louis. *Les Jonques chinoises.* 10 vols. Rotterdam, 1957–71.

Barrow, Sir John. *Travels in China, Containing Descriptions, Observations, and Comparisons Made and Collected in the Course of a Short Residence at the Imperial Palace of Yuen-min-yuen, and on a Subsequent Journey Through the Country from Pekin to Canton.* 1st American ed. Philadelphia, 1805.

———. *A Voyage to Cochinchina in the Years 1792 and 1793. . . . To Which Is Annexed an Account of a Journey Made in the Years 1801 and 1802, to the Residence of the Chief of the Booshuana Nation.* London, 1806.

Billingsley, Phil. "Bandits, Bosses, and Bare Sticks," *Modern China* 7: 235–88 (July 1981).

Blake, C. Fred. *Ethnic Groups and Social Changes in a Chinese Market Town.* Honolulu, 1981.

———. "Island in the China Sea," in *Faces of Change: China Coast # 1.* Hanover, N.H., 1976. [Scripts of the film series.]

Botting, Douglas. *The Pirates.* Alexandria, Va., 1978.

Brown, Edward. *Cochin-China, and My Experience of It; a Seaman's Narrative of His Adventures and Sufferings During a Captivity Among Chinese Pirates, on the*

Coast of Cochin-China, and Afterwards During a Journey on Foot Across That
Country, in the Years 1857–58 (London, 1861). Taipei, 1971.

Chang, Chung-shen (Thomas). "Ts'ai Ch'ien, the Pirate King Who Dominates
the Seas: A Study of Coastal Piracy in China, 1795–1810." Ph.D. dissertation, University of Arizona, 1983.

Ch'eng Han-chang. "Shang Pai chih-chün teng pan hai-fei shu" [On the handling of pirates by Governor-general Pai Ling and others], in Ho Ch'ang-ling, ed., cited below, ch. 85: 37–48b.

Chi Shih-chia. "Lüeh-lun Ts'ai Ch'ien ti fan-Ch'ing tou-cheng" [Summary of
Ts'ai Ch'ien's struggles against the Ch'ing], Chung-kuo ku-tai shih [Ancient
Chinese history], 1982, no. 6: 103–10.

Chiang, Siang-tseh. The Nien Rebellion. Seattle, 1954.

Chinese Pirates: Ching Chelung; His Son Cheng Ching-kung; Combination
of Gangs in 1806; Narratives of J. Turner and Mr. Glasspoole; Chinese and
Portuguese Join Their Forces Against the Pirates; Divisions Among Them,
and Their Submission to the Government," Chinese Repository, 3: 62–83
(June 1834).

Ch'ing Chia-ch'ing-ch'ao wai-chiao shih-liao [Foreign relations of the Chia-ch'ing
reign]. 10 vols. Peking, 1932.

Chu Ch'eng-wan. "Chi-ssu p'ing-k'ou" [Suppressing the pirates in 1809], in
Nan-hai hsien-chih [Gazetteer of Nan-hai county; 1872], comp. Cheng
Meng-yü. 26 chüan. Taipei, 1971.

Coast of China; Present Degree of Knowledge Concerning It; Desirableness
of Having It Surveyed; Its General Outline and Divisions; with a Brief Description of the Principal Places on Its Southern Line," Chinese Repository, 5:
337–51 (Dec. 1836), 6: 8–16 (May 1837).

Course, A. G., Capt. Pirates of the Eastern Seas. London, 1966.

Cushman, Jennifer. "Fields from the Sea: Chinese Junk Trade with Siam During the Late Eighteenth and Early Nineteenth Centuries." Ph.D. dissertation, Cornell University, 1975.

Dai-Nam nhat-thong-chi [Gazetteer of Imperial Vietnam], comp. Cao-xuan-Duc. 17 chüan. 1909.

Dalrymple, Alexander. Further Statement of the Ladrones on the Coast of China
Intended as a Contribution of the Accounts Published by Mr. Dalrymple. London,
1812.

———. Memoir Concerning the Pirates on the Coast of China Drawn Up at the Desire
of Hon. William Fullarton Elphinstone, Chr. Court of Directors of E.I.C.; and
Supplement to the Memoir Concerning the Pirates on the Coast of China. London,
1806.

Deveria, Gabriel. Histoire des relations de la Chine avec l'Annam-Viêtnam du XVIe
au XIXe siècle. Paris, 1880.

Dobell, Peter. Sept années en Chine; nouvelles observations sur cet empire, l'archipel
Indo-Chinois, les Philippines et les Iles Sandwich, tr. E. Galitzin. Paris, 1842.

———. Travels in Kamtchatka and Siberia; with a Narrative of a Residence in China.
2 vols. London, 1830.

Downing, Charles Toogood. The Fan-Qui in China in 1836–37. 3 vols. London,
1838.

Fay, Peter Ward. The Opium War, 1840–42. Chapel Hill, N.C., 1975.

Glasspoole, Richard. "A Brief Narrative of My Captivity and Treatment
Amongst the Ladrones," in Karl Friedrich Neumann, tr., History of the Pirates, cited below, pp. 97–128. [Glasspoole's "Brief Narrative" was first pub-

lished in George Wilkinson, ed., *Sketches of Chinese Customs and Manners in 1811–1812. . . .* Bath, 1814].

———. "Glasspoole's Letter to the President of the East India Company's Factory," Dec. 8, 1809, in Dalrymple, *Further Statement of the Ladrones,* cited above, pp. 33–39.

———. "Substance of Mr. Glasspoole's Relation, upon His Return to England Respecting the Ladrones," in Dalrymple, *Further Statement of the Ladrones* cited above, pp. 40–45.

Gomes, Artur Levy. *Esboço da história de Macau 1511 a 1849.* Macao, 1957.

Gomes, Luis G. *Páginas da história de Macau.* Macao, 1966.

Gosse, Philip. *The History of Piracy.* New York, 1934.

Great Britain, Admiralty Archives. Admiralty and Secretariat Papers. Formerly known as Secretary's Department: In-letters. 1660–1934. 8,779 vol

———, Foreign Office. FO 17. General correspondence before 1906. 1815 1905. 1,768 vols.

———, ———. FO 233. Embassy and Consular Archives, China Miscellane: 1759–1935. 189 vols. [Catalog of embassy archives 1727–1857, trade an intelligence reports, miscellaneous papers of the Chinese Secretary's O fice.] Vol. 189: Entry Book of miscellaneous papers relating to activities c merchants in China (East India Company). Chinese text.

———, ———. FO 682. Embassy and Consular Archives, China: Papers i the Chinese Language. Vol. 68/1: Public papers of 1819 [*sic*] concernir trade at Canton [all dated documents are Chia-ch'ing 15, which is 181c Vol. 483/1: Canton Trade: Letters from Chinese officials and Hong Kor [*sic*] Merchants. 1809–13. Vol. 526: Unnamed letters. 1811.

Gützlaff, Charles Friedrich. *A Journal of Three Voyages Along the Coast of China 1831, 1832, and 1833, with Notices of Siam, Corea, and the Loo-Choo Islan* (London, 1834). Taipei, 1968.

Hayes, James. *The Hong Kong Region, 1850–1911: Institutions and Leadership Town and Countryside.* Hamden, Conn., 1977.

Hill, Samuel Charles. "Pirates of the China Seas," *Journal of the American A atic Association,* 24.4: 306–10 (April 1924).

Ho Ch'ang-ling, ed. *Huang-ch'ao ching-shih wen-pien* [Statecraft writings of t Ch'ing period]. 120 *chüan.* 1827.

Hsiao, Wan-om (Hsiao Yun-han). "Research in the History of the Pirates the China Sea, 1140–1950." Unpublished manuscript in Chinese, Sep 1976.

Hsin-hui hsien-chih [Gazetteer of Hsin-hui county; 1840], comp. Lin Hsii chang. 14 *chüan.* Taipei, 1956.

Hsin-ning hsien-chih [Gazetteer of Hsing-ning county], comp. Lin Kuo-ker 20 *chüan.* 1893.

Hsü Chien-ping (Hui Kim-bing). "Shih-tzu-ling yü Ch'ing-ch'u Hsiang-ka Chiu-lung, Hsin-chieh chih ch'ien-hai yü fu-chieh" [The Lion Rock and ' abandonment of the coastal strip and its subsequent reoccupation dur early Manchu rule], in Lo Hsiang-lin, ed., 1959, cited below, pp. 129–

Hu Chieh-yü (Woo Kit-yü). "Hsi-Ying-P'an yü Chang Pao-tsai huo-luan c p'ing-ting" [Hsi-Ying-P'an and the end of the ravages of the pirate Cha Pao-tsai], in Lo Hsiang-lin, ed., 1959, cited below, pp. 151–70.

Hummel, Arthur, ed. *Eminent Chinese of the Ch'ing Period, 1644–1912.* Wa ington, D.C., 1943–44.

Hunter, William C. *Bits of Old China*. London, 1885.
———. *The "Fan Kwae" at Canton Before Treaty Days, 1825–44* (London, 1882).
   Taipei, 1970.
Jen Yu-wen. *The Taiping Revolutionary Movement*. New Haven, Conn., 1973.
Judice Biker, Julio Firmino. *Collecção de tratados e concertos de pazes que o estado da India Portugueza fez com os reis e senhores com quem teve relações nas partes da Asia e Africa e Oriental desde o principio da conquista até ao fim do seculo XVIII*. Vol. 11, Lisbon, 1886.
Kani Hiroaki. *A General Survey of the Boat People in Hong Kong*. Hong Kong, 1967.
Kuhn, Philip. *Rebellion and Its Enemies in Late Imperial China*. Cambridge, Mass., 1980. Paperback.
Laffey, Ella. "In the Wake of the Taipings: Some Patterns of Local Revolt in Kwangsi Province, 1850–75," *Modern Asian Studies*, 10.1: 65–81 (Feb. 1976).
Lamb, Alastair. *The Mandarin Road to Old Hue: Narratives of Anglo-Vietnamese Diplomacy from the 17th Century to the Eve of the French Conquest*. Hamden, Conn., 1970.
Le-thanh-Khoi. *Le Viet-Nam, histoire et civilisation*. Paris, 1955.
Leonard, Jane Kate. *Wei Yuan and China's Rediscovery of the Maritime World*. Cambridge, Mass., 1984.
Lien-chou fu-chih [Gazetteer of Lien-chou prefecture], comp. Chang Yü-ch'un. 26 *chüan*. 1833.
Ljungstedt, Anders. *An Historical Sketch of the Portuguese Settlements in China; and of the Roman Catholic Church and Mission in China*. Boston, 1836.
Lo Hsiang-lin. "T'un-men yu ch'i-ti tzu T'ang chih Ming chih hai-shang chiao-t'ung" [The maritime communications of T'un-men and its environs from the T'ang to the Ming dynasties], in Lo Hsiang-lin, ed., 1959, cited below, pp. 21–46.
———, ed. *I-pa-ssu-erh nien i-ch'ien chih Hsiang-kang chi ch'i-tui wai-chiao-t'ung* [Hong Kong and its external communications before 1842]. Hong Kong, 1959.
Maughan, Philip. "An Account of the Ladrones Who Infested the Coast of China," in Dalrymple, ed., *Further Statement of the Ladrones*, cited above, pp. 7–32.
Maybon, Charles B. *Histoire moderne du pays d'Annam, 1592–1820*. Paris, 1919.
Meadows, Thomas Taylor. *Desultory Notes on the Government and People of China and on the Chinese Language; Illustrated with a Sketch of the Province of Kwangtung, Shewing Its Division into Departments and Districts*. London, 1847.
"Military Skill and Power of the Chinese; Actual State of the Soldiery, Forts, and Arms; Description of the Forts on the River of Canton; Army and Navy of China; Modes of Warfare; Offensive and Defensive Arms, etc.," *Chinese Repository*, 5: 165–78 (Aug. 1836).
Mills, J. V. G., ed., *Ma Huan: Ying-yai sheng-lan 'The Overall Survey of the Ocean's Shores' [1433]*. Cambridge, 1970.
Montalto de Jesus, C. A. *Historic Macao: International Traits in China Old and New*. 2d ed. Macao, 1926.
———. "Macao's Deeds of Arms," *The China Review*, 21: 146–59 (1894–95).
Morse, Hosea Ballou. *The Chronicles of the East India Company Trading to China, 635–1834*. 5 vols. Cambridge, Mass., 1926–29.

Murray, Dian. "Sea Bandits: A Study of Piracy in Early Nineteenth Century China." Ph.D. dissertation, Cornell University, 1979.

Naquin, Susan. *Millenarian Rebellion in China: The Eight Trigrams Uprising of 1813*. New Haven, Conn., 1976.

———. *Shantung Rebellion: The Wang Lun Uprising of 1774*. New Haven, Conn., 1981.

Nathan, Andrew J. "A Factionalism Model for CCP Politics," *China Quarterly*, 53: 34–66 (Jan.–March 1973).

Neumann, Karl Friedrich (Charles Fried), tr. *History of the Pirates Who Infested the China Sea from 1807 to 1810*. Translation of Yüan Yung-lun (Yuen Yung-lun), *Ching hai-fen chi*. London, 1831.

Oberschall, Anthony. *Social Conflict and Social Movements*. Englewood Cliffs N.J., 1973.

Overmyer, Daniel L. "Popular Religious Sects in Chinese Society," *Modern China*, 7: 153–90 (April 1981).

P'an-yü hsien-chih [Gazetteer of P'an-yü county; 1871], comp. Li Fu-t'ai. 5 chüan. Taipei, 1967.

Parkinson, C. Northgate. *Trade in the Eastern Seas, 1793–1813*. Cambridge 1937.

Perry, Elizabeth J. *Rebels and Revolutionaries in North China, 1845–1945*. Stanford, Calif., 1980.

———. "Social Banditry Revisited: The Case of Bai Lang, a Chinese Brigand," *Modern China*, 9: 355–82 (July 1983).

Rawlingson, John L. *China's Struggle for Naval Development, 1839–1895*. Cambridge, Mass., 1967.

"Recent Exploits of the Ladrones," *Naval Chronicle*, 23: 278–79 (1810).

Richard, M. l'Abbé Jerôme, "History of Tonquin," in Vol. 9 of John Pinkerton, ed., *A General Collection of the Best and Most Interesting Voyages and Travels All Parts of the World*, pp. 708–71. London, 1811. [Originally published Paris, 1778.]

Sainte-Croix, Carloman Louis François Felix Renouard de, *Voyage commercial et politique aux Indes Orientales, aux îles Philippines, à la Chine, avec des notions sûr la Cochinchine et le Tonquin, pendant les années 1803–1804. . . .* 2 vo Paris, 1810.

Samuels, Marwyn. *Contest for the South China Sea*. New York, 1982.

Schafer, Edward H. *Shore of Pearls*. Berkeley, Calif., 1969.

Secret Consultations, Letters, and Transactions of the Select Committee of the Honourable East India Company, 1803–1810, Vols. 2–5. China Records, India Office, London.

Slade, John, tr. "A Record of the Pacification of the Seas." This article, a translation of Yüan Yung-lun (Yuen Yung-lun), *Ching hai-fen chi*, appeared rially in *The Canton Register*, beginning Feb. 20, 1838.

Sun Yü-t'ing. *Tzu-ting nien-p'u* [Autobiographical chronology]. 1834.

———. *Yen-hsi-t'ang chi* [Collected works of the Yen-hsi-t'ang]. 8 chüan. 18

Suzuki, Chusei. "Kenryū Annan ensei ko" [An investigation of Ch'ien-lung military expedition to Annam], *Tōyō Gakuho* [Reports of the Oriental Society], 50.3: 1–23 (Sept. 1967); 50.4: 79–106 (Dec. 1967).

———. "Re (Lê) chō yoki no shin to no kankei" [Vietnam's relations with Ch'ing in the late period of the Le dynasty, 1682–1804], in Yamamoto suro, ed., cited below, pp. 405–92.

Takeda, Ryoji. "Gen chō (Nguyen) shoki no shin to no kankei" [Vietnam's relations with the Ch'ing in the early period of the Nguyen dynasty, 1802–70], in Yamamoto Tatsuro, ed., cited below, pp. 493–550.

T'ao Hsi-sheng. "Ming-tai mi-lao pai-lien-chiao chi ch'i-t'a 'yao-tsei'" [Complete account of White Lotus and other women robbers of the Ming dynasty], in Pao Tsun-p'eng, ed., *Ming-tai tsung-chiao* [Religion of the Ming dynasty], pp. 5–16. Taipei, 1968.

Teixeira, Manuel. *Miguel de Arriaga*. Macao, 1966.

Teng, S. Y. *The Nien Army and Their Guerrilla Warfare, 1857–68*. Paris, 1961.

"Topography of the Province of Canton; Notices of the Islands from the Borders of Fukien to the Frontiers of Cochinchina," *Chinese Repository*, 12: 477–85 (1843).

Truong Buu Lam. "Intervention Versus Tribute in Sino-Vietnamese Relations, 1788–1790," in John K. Fairbank, ed., *The Chinese World Order*, pp. 165–79. Cambridge, Mass., 1968.

Turner, J. "Account of the Captivity of J. Turner, Chief Mate of the Ship *Tay*, Amongst the Ladrones; Accompanied by Some Observations Respecting Those Pirates," in Dalrymple, ed., *Further Statement of the Ladrones*, cited above, pp. 46–73. [This account was first published in 1808 in the *Naval Chronicle*, 20: 456–72.]

Viraphol, Sarasin. *Tribute and Profit: Sino-Siamese Trade, 1652–1853*. Cambridge, Mass., 1977.

Von Krusenstern, Adam Johann. *Voyage Round the World in the Years 1803, 1804, 1805, and 1806 by Order of His Imperial Majesty Alexander the First, on Board the Ships Nadeshda and Neva*, tr. A. B. Hoppner. 2 vols. London, 1813.

Wade, Thomas Francis. "The Army of the Chinese Empire; Its Two Great Divisions, the Bannermen or National Guard and the Green Standard or Provincial Troops; Their Organization, Locations, Pay, Condition, etc.," *Chinese Repository*, 20: 250–80, 300–340, 363–422 (May–July 1851).

Wakeman, Frederic, Jr. "The Secret Societies of Kwangtung, 1800–1856," in Jean Chesneaux, ed., *Popular Movements and Secret Societies in China*, pp. 29–48. Stanford, Calif., 1972.

———. *Strangers at the Gate: Social Disorder in South China, 1839–61*. Berkeley, Calif., 1966.

Wang Chih-i. "I hai-k'ou ch'ing-hsing shu" [Discussion of the seaport situation], in Ho Ch'ang-ling, ed., cited above, ch. 85: 33–36b.

Ward, Barbara E. "Chinese Fishermen of Hong Kong: Their Post-Peasant Economy," in Maurice Freedman, ed., *Social Organization: Essays Presented to Raymond Firth*, pp. 271–88. London, 1967.

———. "Floating Villages: Chinese Fishermen in Hong Kong," *Man: A Monthly Record of Anthropological Science*, 59: 44–45 (March 1959).

———. "A Hong Kong Fishing Village," *Geographical Magazine*, 31: 300–303 (Oct. 1958).

———. "Varieties of the Conscious Model: The Fishermen of South China," in Michael P. Banton, ed., *The Relevance of Models for Social Anthropology*, pp. 113–37. London, 1968.

Wei Yüan. Sheng-wu-chi [Record of Ch'ing military exploits; 1846]. 14 *chüan*. 1849.

Withers, John L., II. "The Heavenly Capital: Nanjing Under the Taiping, 1853–64." Ph.D. dissertation, Yale University, 1983.

Woodside, Alexander B. *Vietnam and the Chinese Model: A Comparative Study of Nguyen and Ch'ing Civil Government in the First Half of the Nineteenth Century.* Cambridge, Mass., 1971.

Worcester, G. R. G. *Sail and Sweep in China: The History and Development of the Chinese Junk as Illustrated by the Collection of Junk Models in the Science Museum.* London, 1966.

Yamamoto Tatsuro, ed. *Betonamu chūgoku kankei shi* [History of the international relations between Vietnam and China]. Tokyo, 1975.

Yang-chiang hsien-chih [Gazetteer of Yang-chiang county; 1822], comp. Li Yün. 8 *chüan.* Taipei, 1974.

Yang-chiang hsien-chih [Gazetteer of Yang-chiang county; 1925], comp. Chang I-ch'eng. 39 *chüan.* Taipei, 1974.

Yeh Lin-feng. *Chang Pao-tsai ti ch'uan-shuo ho chen-hsiang* [The legends and facts about Chang Pao-tsai]. Hong Kong, 1970.

Yen Ju-i. *Yang-fang chi-yao* [Essentials of ocean defense]. 24 *chüan.* 1838.

Yüan Yung-lun (Yuen Yung-lun). *Ching hai-fen chi* [Record of the pacification of the pirates]. 2 *chüan.* Canton, 1830. [Also published under the title *Chang Pao-tsai t'ou-chiang hsin-shu* (Another account of Chang Pao-tsai's surrender). The book was translated into English twice. See Neumann, *History of the Pirates*, and Slade, "A Record," cited above.]

Character List

The romanization used in this Character List is Wade-Giles. Where appropriate, Vietnamese or Chinese equivalents are given in brackets; parentheses are used for alternative names and for identifying glosses.

A-kuei　阿桂
A P'o-tai, *see* Kuo P'o-tai
an-chia-yin　安家銀
An-nan kuo-wang　安南國王
An Quang　安廣
　[An-kuang]
ao-chang　澳長
ao-chia　澳甲
Bach Viet　百粵
　[Pai Yüeh]
Binh Ba Vuong　平波王
　[P'ing-po wang]
Binh Dinh　平定
　[P'ing-ting]
Binh Thuan　平順
　[P'ing-shun]
Canh Thinh　景盛
　[Ching-sheng]
Canh Thinh Tu Nien　景盛四年
　[Ching-sheng szu-nien]
Chan Ya-szu　詹亞四
Chang Chien-sheng　長見壁
Chang-hua　章化
Chang Jih-kao　張日高
Chang Kuan-hsing　張觀興

Chang Kuang-ch'i　張廣其
Chang Lien-k'o　張連科
Ch'ang-lin (governor)　長麟
Chang-lin (place-name)　漳林
ch'ang-lung　長龍
chang-mu　賬目
Chang Pao　張保
Chang Pao-tsai　張保仔
Chang Pao-tzu　張抱子
ch'ang-ping tao　長柄刀
Chang-p'u　漳浦
Ch'ang-sha　長沙
Chang Sheng-tzu　張生子
Chang Wei-chiang　張維江
Chang Ya-an　張亞安
Chang Ya-liu　張亞六
Chang Yü-chih　張子之
Chang Yüan　張元
Chao-an　詔安
chao-an (pacification)　招安
Chao-ch'ing　肇慶
Ch'ao-chou　潮州
chao-fu　招撫
Ch'ao-yang　潮陽
Ch'en (village)　陳

Ch'en A-ch'ang　陳阿長
Ch'en A-ch'i　陳阿齊
Ch'en A-hsia　陳阿夏
Ch'en A-tou　陳阿斗
Ch'en A-tsung　陳阿聰
Ch'en A-wei　陳阿為
Ch'en A-yang　陳阿養
Ch'en A-yu　陳阿有
Chen-an　鎮安
Ch'en Ch'ang-fa　陳長發
Ch'en I-ching　陳裔經
Ch'en Jih-shih　陳日始
Ch'en Kang　陳剛
Ch'en Kuan-hsiang　陳觀詳
chen-piao　陳標
Ch'en San-ch'iu　陳三九
Ch'en Sheng　陳勝
Ch'en Te-sheng　陳得盛
Ch'en T'ien-pao　陳添保
Ch'en Wei-nung　陳為農
Ch'en Wu　陳五
Ch'en Ya-hui　陳亞輝
Ch'en Ya-kuang　陳亞廣
Ch'en Ya-nan　陳亞南
Ch'en Ya-t'ien　陳亞添
Ch'en Yao　陳要
Ch'en Yü-pao　陳玉保
Cheng An-pang　鄭安邦
Cheng Ch'eng-kung　鄭成功
Cheng Ch'i　鄭七
　(Cheng Yao-huang　鄭耀煌)
Cheng Chien　鄭建
Cheng Chih-lung　鄭芝龍
Cheng Chin-shui　鄭金水
Cheng Ching-hao　鄭景豪
Cheng Ching-ta　鄭景大
Ch'eng-hai　澄海
Cheng Ho-ch'ang　鄭和長
Cheng Hsiung-shih　鄭雄石
Cheng I　鄭一
　(Cheng Wen-hsien　鄭文顯)

Cheng I Sao　鄭一嫂
　(Shih Yang　石陽, Shih
　Hsiang-ku　石香姑)
Cheng Kuei-p'i　鄭桂皮
Cheng Kuo-hua　鄭國華
Cheng Lai-mei　鄭來妹
Cheng Lao-tung　鄭老童
　(Liu T'ang-pai　劉唐柏,
　Cheng Liu-t'ang　鄭流唐)
Cheng Lien-ch'ang　鄭連昌
Cheng Lien-fu　鄭連楅
Cheng Liu-t'ang, *see* Cheng Lao-tung
Cheng Min-ta　鄭敏達
Cheng Pang-ch'ang　鄭邦昌
Cheng Pao-yang　鄭保養
Cheng San　鄭三
Cheng Su-chung　鄭蘇忠
Cheng Ta-ch'eng　鄭大成
Cheng Tsung-fu　鄭從富
cheng-t'uan-tsung　正團總
Cheng Wan-ch'ang　鄭萬昌
Cheng Wang-jen　鄭往認
Cheng Wei-ch'ang　鄭衛昌
Cheng Wei-feng　鄭維豐
Cheng Wei-min　鄭衛民
Cheng Wei-ming　鄭衛明
Cheng Wei-p'eng　鄭衛明
Cheng Wen-hsien, *see* Cheng I
Cheng Ya-lu　鄭亞鹿
Cheng Ya-pao　鄭亞保
Cheng Yao-chang　鄭耀章
Cheng Yao-hsing　鄭耀星
Cheng Yao-huang, *see* Cheng Ch'i
Cheng Yao-i　鄭耀一
Cheng Yao-jih　鄭耀日
Cheng Yao-ming　鄭耀明
Cheng Yao-yü　鄭耀煜
Cheng Yao-yüeh　鄭耀月
Cheng Ying-shih　鄭英石
Cheng Ying-yüan　鄭應元
Cheng Yü-lin　鄭玉麟

Chi-ch'ing 吉慶
Ch'i-hsing 七星
chi huy (chih-hui) 指揮
Chi-shui-men 急水門
Chi T'ing 集亭
[Tap Dinh]
Ch'i-wei hai-fei fei-ch'uan 匪桅
海匪匪船
chia (used for *pao-chia*) 甲
chia (home, house) 家
chia-chang 甲長
Chia-ch'ing 嘉慶
Chia-ying 嘉應
chiang-ch'uan 槳船
Chiang-men 江門
Chiang-p'ing 江坪
[Giang Binh]
chiao-fu 剿撫
Ch'iao-kuo-fu-jen 譙國夫人
Chieh-shih 碣石
chien-fei 奸匪
Ch'ien-lung 乾隆
Ch'ien Meng-hu 錢夢虎
chien-pi ch'ing-yeh 堅壁
清野
Ch'ien-tsung 千總
[Thien tong]
Chieu Quang Vuong 昭光王
[Chao-kuang wang]
Ch'ih-ao 赤澳
Chih hui 指揮
[Chi huy]
Ch'ih-li-chiao 赤鱲角
[Chep Lap Kok]
Ch'ih-shui (ch'uan) 吃水
Ch'ih-shui (fort name) 赤水
chin 斤
Ch'in Chou 欽州
Chin-kang 金崗
Chin Ku-yang 金古養
(Li Hsiang-ch'ing 李相清,

Li Shang-ch'ing 李尚青,
Hsia Mo-yang 蝦蟆養)
chin-shih 進士
Chin-yü-hou 金玉候
Ch'ing-hai ta-chiang-chün 清海大將軍
[Thanh hoi dai tuong quan]
Ch'iung-chou 瓊州
Chou 州
Chou Fei-hsiung 周飛熊
Chou Ho-sheng 周和聖
Chou T'ien 周添
Chu A-erh 朱阿二
Chu-chou 竹州
Chu-erh-keng-o 朱爾賡額
Chu Fen 朱濆
Chu Hou-ts'ung 朱犀熜
chü-jen 舉人
Chu Kuei 朱珪
Chu-kung 主公
chu-p'i tsou-che 硃批奏摺
Chu Ya-pao 朱亞寶
Ch'üan-chou 泉州
chuang-ting 壯丁
chuang-yung 壯勇
chün-chi ch'u tsou-che lu-fu
軍機處奏摺錄副
Chung Hsiu 鍾秀
Chung T'ien-chien 鍾添見
Dai Chiem 大占
[Ta-chan]
Dai nguyen soai 大元帥
[Ta yüan-shuai]
Dai Ty Ma 大司馬
[Ta-szu-ma]
Dinh Khanh 定慶
[Ting-ch'ing]
do doc [tu-tu] 都督
Doan Mien 短棉
[Tuan-mien]
Dong Hoi 洞海
[Tung-hai]

Dong Hoi Vuong 東海王
[Tung-hai wang]

Dong Nai 農耐
[Nung-nai]

Duong (Prince) 陽

e-wai wai-wei 顯外外委

Erh-t'ou 二頭
[Nhi dau]

fan-Ch'ing fu-Ming 反清復明

fan-k'u ch'i-pu-hsiang 潘庫緝捕項

Fan Kuang-shan 范光善

Fan Wen-ts'ai 樊文才

Fang-ch'eng 防城

Fang-chi 放雞

Fang Wei-fu 方為嵩

Feng Ch'ao-ch'ün 馮超群

Feng Pang-chieh 馮邦傑

Feng Ya-szu 馮亞四

Feng-yü 鳳嶼

Feng Yung-fa 馮用發
(sometimes Feng Fa)

Fo-shan 佛山

fu 府

fu-chiang 副將

fu-i 夫役

Fu-k'ang-an 福康安

Fu Pang-ching 傅邦景

fu-piao 撫標

fu-t'ou-mu 副頭目

fu-t'uan-tsung 副團總

Fu-yung-sha 芙蓉沙

Gia Hung Vuong 嘉興王
[Chia-hsing-wang]

Gia-long 嘉隆

Giang Binh 江平

Ha Hi Van 何喜文
[Ho Hsi-wen]

hai 海

hai-chan 海戰

Hai-ch'eng 海澄

hai-ch'iu 海鰌

hai-ch'uan 海船

hai-fang 海防

hai-fei 海匪

Hai-feng 海豐

Hai-k'ang 海康

Hai-k'ou 海口

Hainan 海南

Hai Ninh 海寧
[Hai-ning]

hai-po (ch'uan) 海波

hai-tao 海盜

Hai-t'ou 海頭

hai-tsei 海賊

Hai-yang 海陽

Hang Chung 沆忠

hao-shui 號梲

Hei-lung-chiang 黑龍江

Heng-tang 橫檔

Hiep Duc Hau 合德侯
[Ho-te-hou]

Ho Lao-chien 何老見

Ho-p'u 合浦

Ho Sung 何送

Ho Ting-ao 何定鰲

Ho Ying 何英

hsi-kua 西瓜

Hsia Mo-yang, *see* Chin Ku-yang

Hsia T'ien-jung 夏天軍

hsiang 鄉

Hsiang-shan 香山

Hsiang-shan Erh 香山二
(Hsiao Chi-lan 蕭稽蘭)

hsiang-yung 鄉勇

Hsiao Chi-lan, *see* Hsiang-shan Erh

Hsiao Pu-ao 蕭步鰲

Hsieh Ku-shun 謝谷順

hsieh-piao 協標

hsien 縣

hsien-feng 先鋒

hsien-feng t'ou-mu 先鋒頭目

Hsin-an 新安

Hsin-hui 新會

Hsin-ning 新寧

Hsin-tsao 新造

Hsing-p'ing 興平

Hsü T'ing-kuei 許廷桂

Hsü-wen 徐聞

Hsü Wen-mo 許文謨

Hsü Ya-san 許亞三

hsü-yu t'ou-fa 蓄有頭髮

Hsüan 玄

hsün 汛

Hu-men 虎門

Hu-t'iao 虎跳

Hu-tzu-chou 湖子州

Hua Chou 化州

Hua Mu-lan 花木蘭

Huang 黃

Huang Cheng-sung 黃正嵩

Huang Fei-p'eng 黃飛鵬

Huang Ho 黃鶴

Huang Kuo-hsien 黃幗賢

Huang-lien 黃連

Huang Piao (pirate) 黃棒

Huang Piao (Brigade-general) 黃標

Huang Sheng-chang 黃勝長

Huang Ta-hsing 黃大興

Huang T'ang-yu 黃唐友

Huang Wen-sheng 黃聞勝

Huang Ya-ch'eng 黃亞威

Huang Ya-sheng 黃亞盛

Hui-chou 惠州

hui-fei 會匪

Hui-lai 惠來

Hung 洪

Hung Ao 洪鰲

Hung-men 洪門

hung-tan yen-ch'uan 紅單鹽船

hung-t'ou 紅頭

huo 夥

huo-chang (petty officer) 火長

huo-chang (gang leader) 夥長

Huo Shao-yüan 霍紹元

(Huo Yung-ch'ing 霍永清,

Huo Jung-chi 霍榮基)

Huo T'ao 霍韜

huyen [hsien] 縣

I A-yu 蟻阿愠

i-chao 恩照

Jao-p'ing 饒平

K'ai-lang ch'uan 開浪船

K'ai-p'ing 開平

Kan-chiao 乾滘

Kan T'ien-ch'iu 甘天球

kang-chiao 港腳

kang-kuei 港規

Kao-chou 高州

Kao Ya-hua 高亞華

Kao-yao 高要

K'e-chia 客家

K'e-ch'uan 客船

Khanh Hoa 慶和
[Ch'ing-ho]

Kou-t'ou-shan 狗頭山

ku 股

k'u 庫

k'uai-ch'uan 快船

k'uai-t'ing 快艇

kuan-hsi 關係

Kuang-chou 廣州

Kuei-shan 歸善

kung-hsiang 公項

Kuo Chiu-shan 郭就善

Kuo Hsüeh-hsien, *see* Kuo P'o-tai

Kuo P'o-tai 郭婆帶
(Kuo Hsüeh-hsien 郭學顯,
A P'o-tai 阿婆帶)

laan (lan) 欄

Lan-shih 瀾石

Lao-Chün-shih 老均十

lao-pan (lao ban) 老板

Lao-tseng ch'uan 撈繒船

Lao-ts'un 勞村

Le [Li] 黎

le-shui 勒稅

Lei-chou 雷州

Lei-lien-ch'iung 雷廉瓊

li 里
Li Ch'ang-keng 李長慶
Li Ch'ang-tzu 李昌仔
Li Ch'ung-yü 李崇玉
li-ho-yüeh 立合約
Li Hsiang-ch'ing, *see* Chin Ku-yang
Li Shang-ch'ing, *see* Chin Ku-yang
Li Sheng-k'o 李生可
Li Ts'ai 李才
   [Ly Tai]
Li Tso-yüan 李作元
Li Tsung-ch'ao 李宗潮
Li T'u-hsing 李土興
Li Wen-pa 黎文巴
Li Ya-ch'i 李亞士
Li Ya-hsing 李亞興
Li-yü-men 鯉魚門
Li-yung 黎涌
Liang Erh-shih 梁二十
Liang K'o 梁科
Liang-kuang 兩廣
Liang Kuang-mou 梁光茂
Liang Kuei-hsing 梁貴興
liang-min 良民
Liang Pao, *see* Tsung-ping Pao
Liang P'o-pao 梁婆保
Liang Wen-keng 梁文庚
Liang Ya-k'ang 梁亞康
Liao-ch'uan 料船
Lien-chou 亷州
Lien-t'ou 練頭
Lin A-chih 林阿芝
Lin A-mu 林阿目
Lin Chang 林暢
Lin Ch'eng-jui, *see* Lin Pan
Lin Fa 林發
Lin Han-chang 林漢彰
Lin Kuo-liang 林國良
Lin Mou-kuang 林茂光
Lin Pan 林泮
   (Lin Cheng-jui 林成瑞)
Lin Shan-k'uei 林善魁
Lin Shuang-wen 林爽文

Lin Sun 林孫
Lin-t'ou 林頭
Lin Tse-hsü 林則徐
Lin Wu 林五
Liu A-chiu 劉阿九
Liu A-t'ing 劉阿聽
liu-lu ch'uan 六櫓船
Liu T'ang-pai, *see* Cheng Lao-tung
Liu Ts'ai-fa 劉財發
liu-tseng ch'uan 劉繒船
Liu Ya-chiu 劉亞九
Liu Yüan-lung 劉源瀧
Lo A-i 羅阿義
Lo Ch'i-ch'ien 羅起潛
Lo-ting 羅定
Lo Ya-san 羅亞三
Lo Yung-hu 羅勇虎
Long Xuyen 隆川
   [Lung-ch'uan]
lu 路
Lu-feng 陸豐
lu-piao 路標
Lu-shui 陸水
Lung-ch'i 龍溪
Lung-hsüeh 龍穴
   [Lung Keio]
Lung-men 龍門
Lung Yüan-teng 龍元篁
Ly Tai [Li Ts'ai] 李才
Ma-ch'i 馬騎
Ma-chou 馬洲
Ma-tzu 媽祖
Mai Ying-pu 馬應步
Mai Yu-chi, *see* Wu-shih San
Mai Yu-chin, *see* Wu-shih Erh
Mai Yu-kuei, *see* Wu-shih Ta
mi-t'ing 米艇
miao 苗
Min-an 民安
ming-sao 命嫂
Minh Hu'ong 明香
   [Ming-hsiang]
Mo Jo-k'uei 莫若魁

Mo Kuan-fu 莫官扶

Mo-tao 磨刀

Mo Ya-kuei 莫亞桂

mou 畝

Mowqua (Lu Wen-wei) 盧文蔚

Mu Kuei-ying 穆桂英

Mu-lan 木欄

Na-yen-ch'eng 那彥成

Nan-ao 南澳

Nan-hai 南海

Nan-yang 南洋

Nao-chou 硇洲

nei 內

nei-hai 內海

nei-ho 內河

nei-yang 內洋

Nghe An 義安
[I-an]

Nguyen 阮

Nguyen Cuu Dat 阮久逸
[Juan Chiu-i]

Nguyen Phuc Anh 阮映安
[Juan Ying-an]

Nguyen Quang Toan 阮光贊
[Juan Kuang-tsan]

Nguyen Van Hue 阮文惠
[Juan Wen-hui]

Nguyen Van Lu 阮文呂
[Juan Wen-lu]

Nguyen Van Ngu 阮文伍
[Juan Wen-wu]

Nguyen Van Nhac 阮文岳
[Juan Wen-yüeh]

Nguyen Van Truong 阮文張
[Juan Wen-chang]

Nhat Le 日麗
[Jih-li]

ni-fei 逆匪

niao-chiang 鳥鎗

Ning-hai fu-chiang-
chün 甯海副將軍
[Ninh hoi phuc tuong quan]

Ning-ming 寧明

O tao tong binh 烏艚總兵
[wu-ts'ao tsung-ping]

pa-tsung 把總

Pai-lien-chiao 白蓮教

Pai Lang 白狼

Pai Ling 白齡

Pai-lung-ch'eng 白龍城

Pai-lung-wei 白龍尾

p'ai 牌

p'ai-t'ou 牌頭

pai-ts'ao ch'uan 白艚船

pai-tzu 白子

pan-chiu 斑鳩

Pan-sha-wei 板沙尾

P'an-yü 畨禺

pang 幫

pao 包

pao-chang 保長

pao-ch'eng 保正

pao-chia 保甲

Pao-t'ang-hsia 寶塘廈

pen-ti 本地

P'eng A-chü 彭阿聚

P'eng Ch'ao-hsiang 彭潮相

P'eng Chao-lin 彭昭麟

P'eng-hu 彭湖

Phuc dai nguyen soai 副大元帥
[fu ta-yüan-shuai]

P'ing-chou 平洲

p'ing-chuan 兵船

P'ing-shan 平山

Phu Yen 富安
[Fu-an]

Po-lo 博羅

Puan Khequa (P'an Yu-tu) 潘有度

Puiqua (P'ei-kuan 沛官, also known
as Wu P'ing-chün 伍秉鈞)

Quan Thu Que Bi Son 管守桂皮山
[Kuan-shou kuei-p'i shan]

Quang Binh 廣平
[Kuang-p'ing]

Quang Nam 廣南
[Kuang-nan]

Quang Ngai　廣義
　[Kuang-i]

Quang Toan　光贊
　[Kuang-tsan]

Quang Trung　光中
　[Kuang-chung]

Quang Yen　廣安
　[Kuang-an]

Qui Nhon　歸仁
　[Kuei-jen]

San-ch'a-k'ou　三汊口

San-chiao (Samcock)　三角

San-ho hui　三合會

San-shan　三善
　(village: 1st reference)

San-shan　三山

San-ta　三達

San-t'iao　三條

San-tien hui　三點會

Sha-ch'i-yung　沙溪涌

Sha-chiao　沙角

Sha-ting　沙亭

Sha-wan　沙灣

Shan-mei　汕美

shang-ch'uan　商船

shao　哨

Shao-chou　韶州

Shen A-szu　沈阿嗣

shen-ch'ih　神香

Shih-ch'eng　石城

Shih Hsiang-ku, *see* Cheng I Sao

Shih Yang, *see* Cheng I Sao

shu-liang　薯莨

shuang-wei ch'uan　雙桅船

shui-chü　稅局

Shui-shih ti-tu　水師提督

Shui-tung　水東

Shun-te　順德

Son Nam　山南
　[Shan-nan]

Su Ch'i-hsiao　蘇其霄

Su Shih-mou　蘇世戊

Su Ya-pao　蘇亞保

Sui-ch'i　遂溪

sui-k'u　隨庫

Sun Ch'üan-mou　孫全謀

Sun Yü-t'ing　孫玉庭

Sung Kuo-hsing　宋國興

Szu-le　思勒

szu-ma　司馬

Ta-chi-mu-ao　大雞母澳

Ta-chi-shan　大雞山

Ta-chou　大洲

Ta-fen　大汾

Ta-huang-pu　大黃浦

Ta-k'ai-po ch'uan　大開波船

ta-ku　大股

Ta-lan　大欖

Ta-lao-pan　大老板

ta-pang　大幫

Ta-pang-tao-shou　大幫盜首

Ta P'ao-fu　大礮艕

Ta-p'eng　大鵬

ta-tan-ch'ien　打單銃

ta-tao-shou　大盜首

Ta-tiao ts'ao-ch'uan　大釣艚船

ta-t'o-feng ch'uan　大拖風船

ta-t'ou-mu　大頭目

T'a Ting-ch'iu　榻定球

Ta-yü-shan (Lantao)　大嶼山

Ta yüan-shuai　大元帥

T'ai-ao (Tai-o)　太澳

T'ai-p'ing　太平

Tan-chou　儋州

T'an A-chao　譚阿招

T'an-chou　潭洲

T'an Ya-jui　譚亞瑞

tang　黨

T'ang Jen-szu　湯人四

T'ang Shih-jui　唐士芮

T'ang Te　唐德

t'ang-ti　堂弟

Tanka (tan-chia)　蛋家

tao　道

Tao-chiao (Tu-chiao)　到滘

tao-shou　盜首

tao-t'ai 道臺

Tay-son (Hsi-shan) 西山

teng-hua 燈花

Thi Nai 施耐

Thien tong 千總
  [Ch'ien-tsung]

Ti 地

Ti Ch'ing 蒂青

t'i-piao 提標

Ti Tsai 笛仔

tiao-lou 碉樓

t'iao-tao 挑刀

T'ien 天

Tien Coc 偄谷
  [Hsien-ku]

T'ien-hou 天后

Tien-mou 電茂

Tien-pai 電白

Tien-pai Ta 電白大

T'ien-ti hui 天地會

T'ien-yün 天運

t'ing 廳

t'o-ch'uan 拖船

t'o-feng (ch'uan) 拖風

to-kung 舵工

Tong binh 總兵
  [Tsung-ping]

Tong Binh Pao Duc
  Hau 總兵保德候
  [Tsung-ping Pao Te-hou]

Tong Phuc Luong 宋福梁
  [Sung Fu-liang]

t'ou-jen 頭人

t'ou-mu 頭目

Tran Ninh 鎮寧
  [Chen-ning]

Trinh 鄭
  [Cheng]

Ts'ai Ch'ien 蔡牽

Ts'ai Shih-chüeh 蔡世爵

ts'ao 槽

ts'ao-chang 艚長

ts'ao-ch'uan 艚船

ts'ao-pai ch'uan 艚白船

Ts'ao Ya-wan 曹亞晚

tsei-shou 賊首

Ts'eng Chih-kuang 曾忘廣

Tso-i-chen 左翼鎮

tsou-che 奏摺

tsu-chia 族家

Tsung Chin 總金

tsung-ping 總兵

Tsung-ping Pao 總兵寶
  (Liang Pao 梁保)

tsung-tao-shou 總盜首

tsung-t'ou-mu 總頭目

t'u 徒

t'u-fei 土匪

tu-piao 督標

tu-szu 都司

t'u-tao 土盜

tu-tu 都督
  [do doc]

t'uan 團

t'uan-lien 團練

t'uan-lien ting-yung 團練丁勇

T'ung Chen-sheng 童鎮塍

T'ung-an 同安

Tung-hai 東海

Tung-hai Pa, Tung-hai Po, *see*
  Wu Chih-ch'ing

Tung-hsing 東興

Tung-kuan 東莞

t'ung-pi-mo 同筆墨

Tung-shan 銅山

t'ung-shan-ts'ao-tao ko-chih
  ta-tsung-tu 統善艚道各支大總督

Tung-ti 東底

Tung-yang 東陽

Tung-yung 東涌

Tzu-ni 紫泥

Van Ninh Chau 萬寧州
  [Wan-ning Chou]

Vo Tanh 武性

Vu Tieu Sanh 武少生
  [Wu Shao-sheng]

wai 外
wai-hai 外海
wai-yang 外洋
wai-wei ch'ien-tsung 外委千總
Wang Chin-hsin 王進馨
Wang Hsin-chang 王信章
Wang Kuo-pao 王國寶
Wang Lun 王倫
wang-ming 王命
Wang Ya-san 王亞三
Wei-chia-men 桅甲門
Wei-chou 潿洲
Wei Ta-pin 魏大斌
Wei-Yüan 魏源
wen 文
Wen A-ku 溫阿鵠
Wen-ch'ang 文昌
Wen Ch'eng-chih 溫承志
Wen Ju-neng 溫汝能
Wu A-fu 吳阿蠹
Wu Ch'eng-ch'üan 吳成全
Wu Chih-ch'ing 吳知青
 (also Tung-hai Pa 東海八,
 Tung-hai Po 東海伯)
Wu-ch'uan 吳川
Wu Hsing-hsin 吳興信
Wu Hsiung-kuang 吳熊光
Wu Lien 吳廉
Wu-p'ing 武平
Wu Shang-te 吳尚德
Wu-shih 烏石
Wu-shih Erh 烏石二
 (Mai Yu-chin 麥有金)
Wu-shih San 烏石三
 (Mai Yu-chi 麥有吉)
Wu-shih Ta 烏石大
 (Mai Yu-kuei 麥有貴)

Wu-ts'ao (ch'uan) 烏艚體
Wu Ya-san 吳亞三
Wu Yao-nan 伍耀南
Ya Hsüan Sao 亞選嫂
Ya-kan 亞甘
Ya-tsung 亞宗
Ya Wu 亞五
Yai-chou 崖洲
Yai-men 崖門
yang 洋
Yang-ch'eng 羊城
Yang-chiang 陽江
yang-ch'uan 洋船
yang-fei 洋匪
Yang Kuang-p'u 楊光普
Yang P'ien-k'e 楊片客
yang-shui 洋稅
yang-tao 洋盜
Yang Tsan-kung 楊咱公
yang-tsei 洋賊
Yang Wei-meng 楊為夢
yao-tao 腰刀
Yeh Ya-wu 葉亞伍
yen-ch'uan 鹽船
Yen Cuong Uc 烟囷澳
 [Yen-kang-ao]
Yen Ju-i 嚴如煜
ying 營
Yü 宇
yüan 圓
Yüan Ya-ming 袁亞明
Yüeh 粵
yüeh-chi 粵妓
Yüeh-nan ta-lao-pan 粵南大老板
Yung-an 永安
Yung-cheng 雍正
Yung-wei-she 涌尾杜

Index

Library of Congress Cataloging-in-Publication Data

Murray, Dian H., 1949–
  Pirates of the South China coast, 1790-1810.

Bibliography: p.
  Includes index.
    1. Pirates—China—Pacific Coast.   I. Title.
G535.M78 1987   951'.2   87-10049
ISBN 0-8047-1376-6 (alk. paper)